RECENT

AMERICAN

PHILOSOPHY

RECENT
AMERICAN
PHILOSOPHY

STUDIES OF
Ten Representative Thinkers

BY

ANDREW · J · RECK

Pantheon Books

A DIVISION OF RANDOM HOUSE

New York

For Rima

PREFACE

AMERICAN PHILOSOPHY has never been fully appreciated for its vitality, diversity, and profundity. Since the end of World War II there has been a growing regard for the contributions of six already "classic" American philosophers of the recent past—Peirce, James, Royce, Santayana, Dewey and Whitehead. However, few have attempted to penetrate beyond the radiance of their work to that of numerous other modern thinkers worthy of esteem. Ten thinkers, generally neglected when recent American philosophers are discussed, are the subjects of the present volume. The philosophies of Ralph Barton Perry, William Ernest Hocking, George Herbert Mead, John Elof Boodin, Wilbur Marshall Urban, DeWitt H. Parker, Roy Wood Sellars, Arthur O. Lovejoy, Elijah Jordan, and Edgar Sheffield Brightman receive here comprehensive, sympathetic, systematic exploration and discussion—in several cases for the first time. Because these philosophers are not as well known as they deserve to be, because in many cases their works are not easily accessible, and because they often found the best words for the expression of their thoughts, I have availed myself of the technique of abundant quotations, to allow them, insofar as possible, to speak for themselves.

In any volume of this sort it is possible to question the selection. Originality of thought and comprehensiveness of philosophic vision have been my primary criteria. I have also been concerned to furnish a fair sample of philosophical thinking for the period from the turn of the century to World War II. By these criteria no one can fault the selection of the ten men included in this book. It is more difficult, perhaps, to justify the omissions. Most of all I regret that it was not possible to present the philosophies of such thinkers as Hartley Burr Alexander and Frederick J. E. Woodbridge. But limitations of space and uncertainty concerning the audience for this volume have persuaded me to offer a smaller book than I might otherwise have preferred. If this volume finds its proper audience soon enough, I promise additional volumes of studies of philosophers who flourished in the period under investigation. Even as this preface is written, a sequel, treating American philosophers who have risen to prominence since World War II, is in the writing.

Questions may also arise concerning the arrangement of chapters. Such arrangement usually follows logical order of topics, temporal sequence of events, or causal influence of ideas. A logical order of topics, however, would have required the segmentation of the philosophies under study, and the re-arrangement of parts without reference to their positions within the individual thought patterns, so that the integrity and wholeness of philosophical outlook offered by each thinker would have been obscured. Similarly, an organization of chapters representing temporal sequence or causal influence could not be employed, since the thinkers under study are contemporaries, and contemporaries do not march before or after each other in any precise fashion. Contemporaries tend to react to an environment which antedates their arrival, which is constant in some respects, and which is punctuated by conspicuous changes in other respects. To a lesser extent, contemporaries act and react with each other. I have therefore arranged the studies in accord with quasi-permanent elements in their intellectual environment, such as the "golden age" at Harvard or the Chicago

School, and with a postulated sequence of significant intellectual events, such as the advent of realism and the
impact of the new physics. Thus I have sought to place
early in the book studies of those individuals whose
thought aids us in understanding the thought of those
that follow, even when there is no temporal line of sequence or causal line of influence. Each study may be
read as a separate and independent essay, although collectively the studies constitute a representative survey of
recent American philosophy. I have never allowed external principles of order to intrude upon and dominate my
explorations of the intrinsic qualities of the philosophies
presented. Another author might have arranged the chapters differently, and the reader is invited to do so at his
pleasure.

It is impossible for me to express my full indebtedness
to others in the composition of this volume. First of all
there are the philosophers whose works I have studied
and from whom I have gained so much of inestimable
value. I have been fortunate in that, in all cases in which
the philosopher under study is alive, he has consented to
read and comment on early drafts of my chapters. Let
me, then, acknowledge my gratitude to William Ernest
Hocking and Roy Wood Sellars. I am also grateful to
Peter A. Bertocci for his helpful comments on my chapter on Edgar Sheffield Brightman and to William K.
Frankena for making available to me papers in his possession when I was preparing the chapter on DeWitt H.
Parker. I am, of course, responsible for all errors and
faults of fact or interpretation in the present volume.

I am indebted also to the writings of the historians and
philosophers who have preceded me in the field of recent
American philosophy: Morris Cohen, Herbert Schneider,
W. H. Werkmeister, and Joseph L. Blau. I regret that
the second edition of Herbert Schneider's *History of
American Philosophy* did not appear in time for me to
make use of it. I owe the idea of a "classic period" or

"golden age" of American philosophy, against which my studies of recent thinkers are projected, to the writings of many, among whom Charles Frankel, Max Fisch, John E. Smith, and Robert C. Whittemore deserve special mention.

I wish to thank the American Council of Learned Societies for a grant which enabled me to study in the Harvard University libraries in the summer of 1961. I wish also to thank the George A. and Eliza Gardner Howard Foundation, administered by Brown University, for the award of a fellowship for the academic year 1962-1963, which, with the supplemental generosity of the Tulane Research Council, furnished me the leisure to complete the volume.

The possibility of a volume of studies devoted to neglected American philosophers first arose as a consequence of the publication of my articles on the philosophy of Andrew P. Ushenko in *The Review of Metaphysics* (1958). With the encouragement of Paul Weiss and James K. Feibleman, my teachers of diverse temperament but of common passionate involvement in the advance of speculative philosophy in America, I embarked upon a series of studies of recent American philosophers. At the suggestion of Vere Chappell I decided to organize the volume by focusing on recent, and excluding current, philosophers. Special thanks are also due the editors of *The Review of Metaphysics*, *The Vanderbilt Law Review*, *Rivista di Filosofia*, *Tulane Studies in Philosophy*, and *The Journal of Religious Thought* for permitting me to incorporate material I previously published in the pages of their journals. That the volume comprises studies of individual thinkers, characteristic of literary rather than of philosophical works, is due, I am sure, to the influence of my wife.

ANDREW J. RECK

New Orleans, Louisiana
April 1964

CONTENTS

THE COSMIC PHILOSOPHY OF
JOHN ELOF BOODIN

THE VALUE-CENTRIC PHILOSOPHY OF
WILBUR MARSHALL URBAN

DEWITT H. PARKER'S METAPHYSICS
OF VALUES

THE CRITICAL REALISM OF
ROY WOOD SELLARS

THE TEMPORALISTIC REALISM OF
ARTHUR O. LOVEJOY

THE CORPORATISM OF ELIJAH JORDAN

THE PERSONALISM OF
EDGAR SHEFFIELD BRIGHTMAN

INTRODUCTION

POETS AND THINKERS appear to be neglected aliens in America. A sprawling company of farmers, engineers, politicians and businessmen, Americans on the whole have entrusted the care of their spiritual life to preachers, lawyers, and soldiers. The very term "culture" arouses mental associations with ladies' clubs, in isolation from the masculine world where work gets done. Because of—or in spite of—neglect, great literature and philosophy are born and flourish in this hostile setting. American literature has won deserved recognition in recent decades. Whitman, Hawthorne, Melville, Pound, Eliot, Faulkner, Hemingway are acknowledged modern classics. Less well known are the achievements of philosophers in America. Yet the period stretching from the end of the Civil War to the eve of the Great Depression has been called "the golden age of American philosophy." During this period pragmatism, an indigenous American philosophical movement born in Cambridge, Massachusetts and baptized at Berkeley, California, invaded the established capitals of old Europe. Charles Peirce, William James, Josiah Royce, John Dewey, George Santayana, and Alfred North Whitehead, thinkers who lived and worked during the golden age, have already become established as "classic American philosophers," and the value of their contributions to our intellectual life is indisputable. Any other nation would be hard pressed to find a half-dozen thinkers in the same period worthy of inclusion in their company.

In addition to this creative and visionary six, many other thinkers have made impressive contributions to recent American philosophy. The ten selected for study in the present volume are Ralph Barton Perry, William Ernest Hocking, George Herbert Mead, John Elof Boodin, Wilbur Marshall Urban, De Witt H. Parker, Roy Wood Sellars, Arthur O. Lovejoy, Elijah Jordan, and Edgar Sheffield Brightman. A proper estimation of the magnitude of their work makes necessary a reassessment of the history of thought.

The established six—Peirce, James, Royce, Santayana, Dewey, and Whitehead—appear in new perspective from the fresh angles of vision furnished by exploration of the work of these thinkers. It is now clear that Royce, whose philosophy has too often been sloughed off as eccentric to the American scene, has exerted as much influence as James on the philosophers who have come after. The systems of Hocking, Boodin, Urban, and, to a lesser extent, Mead and Brightman take up Roycean themes. Although the role of James in shaping American thought is not to be denied, it is evident mainly in the writings of Perry, of Lovejoy, and, to a lesser extent, of Hocking and Boodin. The thought of Peirce, recovered through the publication of his *Collected Works*, came too late in the period under discussion to exert the influence it merited; however, Peirce's influence almost matches that of James, as is evident in the writings of Perry, Mead, and Boodin. Also too late to have much impact on the period was the work of Whitehead, but many writings, such as those by Hocking and Brightman published after World War II, clearly reveal the import and extensiveness of Whitehead's influence. Dewey and Santayana, born four years apart and dying nearly a century later in the same year, came to prominence after James, Peirce, and Royce had

passed from the American scene and before the arrival of
Whitehead. In different ways these two major figures of
the first half of the twentieth century—Dewey so totally
immersed in the problems of American life, Santayana
so wholly alienated and withdrawn from them; the former so poor and imprecise a stylist, the other so polished
and literary—were almost dismissed as serious philosophers. Perhaps Dewey's ideas are most conspicuous in
the writings of Mead, although it may be the other way
around. And if Santayana's ideas dwell anywhere outside his own philosophy, they are found (much modified) in the value theories of Perry and Parker, and in
the writings of such critical realists as Sellars and Lovejoy,
although without the doctrine of essence and indeed in
such a way as to suggest that, far from being a prime
mover in the development of critical realism, Santayana
was a joiner. Actually the influences of Dewey and Santayana, when not too feeble to be discerned, prove to be
more negative than positive. Urban, Parker, Sellars, Lovejoy, and Jordan devote pages to the refutation of Dewey,
and Brightman sets up a metaphysical system sharply con-
tradicting Santayana's.

The history of thought is not a flat plain over which a
few heroes ride to individual conquests. When studied
minutely and thoroughly, it is seen to be a cooperative
social process to which, by means of concurrence and dis-
sent, countless obscure or forgotten thinkers contribute.
No scholar may hope to recover the whole true picture of
the past, but he should attempt to represent its depth
and dimensions. So long as his gaze is fixed upon a few
widely acknowledged thinkers, systems, or movements,
he will never gain a correct perspective. Lovejoy has suggested that the proper method in intellectual history is to
locate and define the dynamic unit-ideas of human
thought, and then, cutting across the major systems and
movements treated in the established histories, to explore
the development of these unit-ideas in the writings of

prominent and obscure philosophers, artists, and scientists. But unless it is assumed that ideas enjoy a kind of Platonic existence independent of the minds of individuals and that somehow on their own they influence the course of thought, it is necessary, before the historiography of ideas can obtain, to represent and reconstruct the thoughts of individual thinkers. Therefore it is an aim of the present volume to explore in depth the thought of representative philosophers who are not usually accorded a rank equal to that of the "classic six." These studies of Perry, Hocking, Mead, Boodin, Urban, Parker, Sellars, Lovejoy, Jordan, and Brightman are offered as the first intensive and comprehensive explorations of their systems of thought. Metaphysical speculation, these studies reveal, is as central to the work of recent American philosophers as practical considerations and moral reconstruction.

Because the thinkers under study reached the peaks of their intellectual activity during the period between the two World Wars, this volume also affords an historical account of recent American philosophy. At the beginning of the period Ralph Barton Perry discriminated four main philosophical tendencies: naturalism, idealism, pragmatism, and realism. Although this classification is useful for organizing the abundant materials of the recent past and although it has been adopted by other historians, to reify the categories into pure and exclusive movements would be misleading. When Perry offered his classification in the years immediately preceding World War I, it seemed that the demise of idealism was imminent. Yet among the ten thinkers here represented, it is usual to regard Hocking, Boodin, Parker, and Brightman as idealists, and possible to add Urban and Jordan. Although pragmatic themes are manifest in the philosophies of many—for example, Hocking, Boodin and Brightman—Mead alone may be designated a pragmatist. As Lovejoy pointed out, pragmatism itself is composed of a sizable variety of philosophical types. The usual view that idealism died at the turn of the century and that pragmatism triumphed to dominate all subsequent thought in the United States proves to be patently false. Nor were naturalism and realism monolithic movements sweeping aside idealism. Naturalism and realism are wedded in the philosophies of Perry, Sellars, and Lovejoy. Yet realism itself soon split, critical realism following upon the heels of new realism—and critical realism, paradoxically, is an epistemological compromise of the strongest points in new realism and idealism. Some thinkers are irenic, either by elaborating a synthesis of idealist, realist, and pragmatist elements or by advancing to a point beyond idealism and realism. Even when philosophers embrace a common position, as do Sellars and Lovejoy as critical realists, their ontological motives differ radically: Sellars, a materialist; Lovejoy, a temporalist. In effect, then, pure types of philosophical activity generating uniform movements are not to be found. The story of recent American philosophy supplies no simple plot but rather a numerous cast of versatile figures who, while maintaining consistency of intellectual character, step in and out of movements.

All but two of the philosophers discussed in this book were born in the United States, and they came from every region except the South. As academic philosophers, they spent their lives in universities. Seven did advanced work in philosophy at Harvard during its "golden age," and four of them earned doctorates from Harvard. Nine, one of whom earned his Ph.D. from a German university, spent periods of study in Europe. Two concluded their teaching careers as professors at Harvard, one at Yale, one at Johns Hopkins, one at Boston University. Four taught most of their lives in the Midwest: two at the University of Michigan, one at the University of Chicago, and one at Butler College. The remaining philosopher, after spending nearly three decades in Midwestern colleges and universities, terminated his career at the University of California in Los Angeles; five of the others were linked, as students, teachers, or lecturers, with the University of California at Berkeley. Despite the conspicuous concentration of philosophers on the Eastern Seaboard of the United States, the present selection conveys a sense of the spread of culture over the geographical expanse of the American continent.

Residing neither on islands nor in ivory towers, the ten American philosophers under study represent, in addition to academic geography and the main movements of philosophical ideas, the broad cultural and social forces of the twentieth century. Their works reflect the confluences and collisions of scientific concepts, religious beliefs, aesthetic and moral values, and social, political, and economic realities.

Science has been the most influential cultural institution of modern times. The theories, methods, and technologies it has proliferated have revolutionized the physical and intellectual worlds. Darwin at the beginning and Einstein toward the middle of the period exerted considerable sway. The impact of the theory of evolution in philosophy is evident in the systems of Boodin, Sellars, Lovejoy, and Mead. And these same thinkers have had to cope with the concepts of relativity physics. Indeed, it is possible to interpret American philosophy of the recent past as reflecting the supersession of Darwin's dominance by that of Einstein. Advances in the natural sciences were matched by achievements in the formal and behavioral sciences. Mathematics has inspired a new conception of logic, giving birth to symbolic logic, with a noticeable tightening of the style of philosophical arguments. The study of human consciousness and conduct became scientific at the turn of the century, with consequent reverberations in the whole of philosophy. To these developments American philosophers made noteworthy contributions, the most significant of which are

Mead's work in social psychology and Perry's in value theory.

No recession of philosophical concern with religion has accompanied the ascendancy of science. Throughout the period naturalism and idealism have proved to be vigorous philosophical tendencies, naturalism being allied with the party of science and idealism with the party of religion. Of dissimilar philosophical persuasions, Hocking, Boodin, Urban, Parker, Sellars, and Brightman have immeasurably and uniquely enriched man's reflections on God and religious experience; and, differing with each other, they have also differed with traditional sectarian doctrines. Through these philosophers novel religious ideas have entered the stream of American thought. If there is any orthodoxy concerning religion among American philosophers, it is heterodoxy.

Although scientific methods were introduced into the investigation of man and society, philosophy did not retreat, but rather, assisted by the sciences, pressed its own investigations. Mead, an early exponent of physiological psychology, revolutionized social psychology through articles and lectures; Hocking drew upon metaphysics as well as empirical psychology to offer a theory of man. The theories of Freud had an unsettling effect upon the way man thought about himself and his behavior, just as, a half century earlier, those of Nietzsche had shaken the foundations. The recent past has been the scene of the birth and growth of a new branch of philosophy—the general theory of value. Through the works of Perry, Urban, and Parker, the whole range of human value experiences and judgments came under examination. Although American philosophers have concentrated more on the moral than on the aesthetic side of man's value experience, noteworthy additions to aesthetics and the philosophy of art, particularly in the writings of Parker, have been made.

The ferment of new ideas concerning science, religion,

and human conduct and values has been quickened by recent social events. Two world wars and a great depression, the dissolution of colonial empires, the upsurge of repressed nationalities, the spread of democratic ideals, the rise and fall of totalitarian regimes, have dramatically punctuated the period. Eighteenth-century political philosophy receded before the onslaught of ideas and movements seared by the doctrines of Hegel, Nietzsche, and Marx. Though treating subjects more lasting than the headlines of the daily press, the works of American philosophers are redolent with the urgencies of the time. At the theoretical level, the general theory of values was in part instigated by the shattering of traditional valuations by World War I. At the practical level, philosophers participated in the turmoil of affairs. Philosophy does not dwell in a vacuum, but is related to the vibrant contexts of life. Perry's tracts on military training and the defense of democracy assisted in the preparation of America for her part in the world wars. Hocking's investigations of the colonial empires, of international politics, and of world religions encouraged America's adherence to the principles of international organization and the self-determination of peoples from underdeveloped countries. These contributions may be multiplied many times by consideration of the efforts of other thinkers. But of them all the most outstanding addition to social philosophy is the corporatism of Jordan. A full-scale critique and metaphysics of modern industrial civilization, Jordan's corporatism is the most penetrating and disturbing theory of society offered by an American, and as the century wears on, it is likely to attract increasing attention.

These studies, centering on these ten thinkers, should deepen appreciation of the originality and the creativity of American thought. All ten were trained professionals, adept in the history of thought, students of all areas of culture. Their scholarship is of the highest order of excellence. Perry, for example, won a Pulitzer prize for biography, and Lovejoy devised the methodology of the history of ideas. Yet all were sensitive to novel ideas and the currents of change. They were creative thinkers of immense stature, and although it is a mistake to suppose that the history of thought is merely a record of the triumphs of great individuals, these ten thinkers, when granted the sort of sympathetic, synoptic, and focal examination accorded the acknowledged giants of the history of thought, appear also to be of giant proportions. The discovery of these new giants is not intended to demote other giants, nor to derogate in any fashion from the rightful merits of any thinker. Rather it indicates that the total picture of American thought should be enlarged to encompass these men whose contributions are undeservedly neglected. Like the American society of which it is a part, American philosophy is pluralistic. Perry, Hocking, Mead, Boodin, Urban, Parker, Sellars, Lovejoy, Jordan, and Brightman are individually brilliant and unique thinkers, and together they form an impressive company. The primary aim of this volume, therefore, is, by concentrated explorations of their philosophies, to heighten awareness of the vastness, profundity, and diversity of American thought.

RECENT

AMERICAN

PHILOSOPHY

———

Chapter 1

THE NEW REALISM OF
RALPH BARTON PERRY

THE PLACE OF PHILOSOPHY IN LIFE

"When I became a college and university teacher instead of a Presbyterian minister," Ralph Barton Perry (1876-1957) once divulged, "I merely substituted the platform for the pulpit, the lecture or public address for the sermon, and the class or audience for the congregation" (1).* While an undergraduate at Princeton, Perry had intended to enter the ministry, but he elected first to study philosophy for a year at Harvard. The result was a radical alteration of personal plans. No description of Harvard as it was in its "golden age" of philosophy equals Perry's in liveliness and in obvious bias: "At Harvard in the late 'nineties it was, for most of us, a choice between James and Royce. Palmer taught us ethics, and by his example taught us how to teach. Santayana was historical and critical, Munsterberg schematic, and Everett learned. These were important elements in the configuration, and they generated both heat and light. But as regards fundamentals, whether of doctrine, method,

* References will be found at the ends of chapters.

or temper of mind, there was the way of Royce and the way of James. Royce was the battleship, heavily armoured, both for defence and offence. James combined the attributes of the light cruiser, the submarine, and the bombing aeroplane. It was natural to suppose that Royce was impregnable and irresistible. To surrender to him was as easy and as unexciting as to be a fundamentalist in Arkansas. James provided the rallying-point for those in whom the youthful spirit of revolt was stronger than tradition and prestige. Royce was the latest and nearest of a mighty race. His philosophy was powerfully reinforced by the texts of Bradley and Green, and by the great cult of Kant. His was the party of law and order, of piety and decency. This was not Royce's fault, nor did it at all adequately express his personal traits; but he suffered, none the less, from the taint of established things. So when James, overcoming his earlier fears, had the audacity to make jokes about the Absolute, there were Athenian youths who laughed with him. Many of us have, since that time, become sadder, and, I hope, wiser. But the spell of absolute idealism was irreparably broken. There arose a generation of younger philosophers who were, as Creighton expressed it (speaking more in sorrow than in anger), 'flippant, like James' " (2, pp. 187-188).

Joining the "flippant" party of James, Perry abandoned the ministry for the career of the teacher and the scholar. "Creeds and dogmas having become impossible," he confessed, "I thought that I had found a way in which I might think freely and still 'do good' " (2, p. 187). For nearly six decades Perry, as professor of philosophy at Harvard and through his abundant writings, has affected the course of American thought. His prodigious contributions as a creative philosopher enriched the new realism and made possible "naturalistic" value-theory. Though he is best known for his technical works in philosophy, his moral fervor to do good expressed itself periodically in numerous tracts on pressing human problems.

On realism and value theory Perry's works include, in addition to abundant articles in various philosophical and psychological journals, such volumes as *The Approach to Philosophy* (3), *The Moral Economy* (4), *The New Realism* (5), *General Theory of Value* (6), and *Realms of Value* (7). They have exerted, first, an immediate impact upon the development of realism in American philosophy during the first quarter of the twentieth century; second, especially in value theory, they have generated a continuing influence on even the most recent publications.

Perry mingled creative work with scholarship. Probably the most widely read of all his books, *Present Philosophical Tendencies* (8), not only contains the most lucid and systematic statement of the new realism, but provides a durable classification of the main philosophical types. As a scholar Perry's most remarkable contributions are his studies of American thought, including his two-volume Pulitzer Prize-winning *Thought and Character of William James* (9) and such other noteworthy books as *In the Spirit of William James* (10), *Puritanism and Democracy* (11) and *Characteristically American* (12).

Besides affording technical and scholarly mastery of abstract philosophical issues, Perry faced up to the practical problems that beset the ordinary man. Evident in such learned volumes as *The Present Conflict of Ideals* (13), published during World War I, and *Puritanism and Democracy* (11), published during World War II, Perry's passionately felt conviction about the role of the philosopher in society pressed him on to examine and to participate in a broad range of concrete concerns: universal military training in *The Free Man and the Soldier* (14) and *The Plattsburg Movement* (15); the struggle between democracy and totalitarianism in *Shall Not Perish from the Earth* (16), *On All Fronts* (17), and *Our Side Is Right* (18); the need of international organization in *One World in the Making* (19); the responsibility of providing for the aged in *Plea for an Age Movement* (20); the alliance of humanism and science in the cause of human progress and enlightenment in *The Humanity of Man* (21); and the responsibilities of the individual voter vis-à-vis the complex issues of the present in *The Citizen Decides* (22). In these books, many of which are little more than tracts and pamphlets, is discernible a theory of liberal democracy, flexible yet firmed by perennial moral principles. Historically rooted in American traditions and perpetually nourished by her philosophers, this theory of democracy is the practical corollary to Perry's realism and value theory.

Throughout a long and productive career, despite continuing adjustments and heightened sophistication, Perry's dominant conception of philosophy, stated in his first book (3), remained essentially unchanged. Whatever originality the book exhibits, Perry claimed, was due to his "great desire that philosophy should appear in its vital relations to more familiar experiences" (3, p. vii). Thus the book in separate chapters examines the relation of philosophy to the practical life of the plain man, to literature, to religion, and to science. Philosophy, Perry held, springs from fundamental human interests. Within men dwells an implicit philosophy which, though initially unarticulated, may be elucidated in conformity with the demands of scholarship and technical precision. Perry's aim in this first book centers on the task of "elucidating the inevitable philosophy" (3, p. viii). Life is the starting-point: for "philosophy, even to its most abstruse technicality, is rooted in life; and . . . it is inseparably bound up with the satisfaction of practical needs, and the solution of practical problems" (3, p. 4). Living is acting, and acting occurs within a situation in which an unrelenting element of compulsion exists. Human life, however, is not simply compelled; for it is accompanied by self-consciousness. As Perry remarked: "As

we live we are all theorists" (3, p. 7). The distinctive
dimension of human life that gives birth to philosophy
is that it is intelligent, purposive activity. "To live the
human life means to pursue ideals" (3, p. 19). As Perry
declared: "life is naturally and organically correlated
with a *thought about the universe in its totality, or in its
deepest and essential character*. Such thought, the activity and its results, is philosophy. Hence he who lives is,
ipso facto, a philosopher" (3, p. 22). Realism tests the
validity of ideals by their consistency with the natural
universe and by their attainability within the objective
framework of nature and society as known by means of
the most exacting methods of observation and science.
Perry's conception of philosophy owes much to the *Le-
bensphilosophie* that flourished at the end of the century (23).

Perry avowed: "I wish that philosophy, for theoretical
purposes, might speak a language of its own, and settle
its disputes in a vernacular that does not arrest the attention of the community" (8, p. 22). But a few pages later
he added: "Philosophy is . . . at once a recondite investigation, and a popular oracle; dispensing logical subtleties to the learned and homely wisdom to the vulgar"
(8, p. 25). The distinctive character of philosophy is disclosed in Perry's discussion of two forms of knowledge:
theory and belief (8, p. 4). Whereas belief, described as
"the old assumptions of life" (8, p. 4), connotes application and is the conservative conviction that guides action (8, p. 7), theory is but "the new word for critical
speculation" (8, p. 4). "Theory does not directly nourish
and sustain life, as belief does; because, unlike belief, it
does not suit the humor of action. To theorize is to
doubt" (8, p. 8). Clearly theory and belief do not exist
in pure forms, but intermingle. On the one hand philosophy is primarily theoretical; on the other it is nourished
upon beliefs.

According to Perry, the division between belief and

theory corresponds roughly to the division between religion and science, both of which serve life. Religion fixes belief in order to guide conduct with reference to the totality of circumstances—the final over-ruling power. Science seeks theory, a dispassionate, critical understanding of things, although it ministers to practice in particular circumstances. Growing out of the interests of life, interests which find overt expression in science and religion, philosophy objectifies the latent opposition between science and religion in life. This opposition is the parent of the two dominant tendencies of modern philosophy—naturalism and idealism. Insofar as the stimulus of philosophy is religion, the offspring is romantic idealism. Insofar as it is science, the offspring is positivism and naturalism (8, pp. 37-38). Reflection upon the relation of philosophy to the interests of life provided Perry's criteria for the discrimination and definition of the main philosophical tendencies: naturalism, idealism, pragmatism, and realism.

Perry defined naturalism as "the philosophical generalization of science—the application of the theories of science to the problems of philosophy" (8, p. 45). Since his conception of science was dominated by the classical Newtonian views on space, time, motion, causality, and matter which prevailed through the nineteenth century, he regarded science and common sense as common proprietors of the same classification, or map, of experience (8, p. 49). Affirming that scientific knowledge exhausts the entirety of knowledge, with no room allowed for extra-scientific knowledge, naturalism assumes two forms: naïve naturalism, or materialism; and critical naturalism, or positivism. Whereas materialism is an explicitly metaphysical endeavor to interpret all reality in terms of energy and motion, positivism is inveterately antimetaphysical, restricted to an analytic understanding of scientific concepts and professing agnosticism about the ultimate constitution of things. Although Perry was convinced that scientific descriptions and scientific categories afforded true knowledge of reality, he nevertheless denied the claim of the naturalists that science and philosophy ought to be one. "Without prejudice to the truth of science or to the validity of its methods, without disparagement of the reality of physical nature, or the reduction of it to dependence on consciousness, it is still open to us to conclude," he insisted, "that *science is not all of truth*, nor *physical nature all of being*" (8, p. 108).

Whereas naturalism originates in science, idealism, in contrast, defends religious belief "against the claim of science to have alienated the world from man" (8, p. 117). Perry defined idealism as "a form of spiritualism in which man, the finite individual, is regarded as a microcosmic representation of God, the Absolute Individual. Man's spiritual nature is a revelation of the *principle* of reality, and his ideals an intimation of the *perfect* and *eternal* reality" (8, p. 113). And he added: "The assertion of the priority of *the cognitive consciousness*, the assertion that *being is dependent on the knowing of it*, may, then, fairly be regarded as the cardinal principle of idealism" (8, p. 114). Not only is idealism wrong when it seeks to discredit the method and categories of science; it also draws upon an erroneous theory of knowledge which cannot, according to Perry, survive the critical objections raised by realism.

Because naturalism and idealism, despite their mistaken foundations and emphases, stem from valid human interests, philosophic reconstruction must take account of these interests. Theory and belief, science and religion, are ubiquitous and indispensable features of human life. Perry imputed the success of pragmatism to the soundness of its revolt in behalf of the interests of life against the division of philosophy into the party of religious belief, the idealists, and the party of scientific theory, the naturalists. "Pragmatism means, in the broadest sense, *the acceptance of the categories of life as fun-*

damental. It is the *bio-centric philosophy*" (8, p. 197).
But for Perry pragmatism fails to accomplish its objective;
it proves, upon examination, to be a halfway house between idealism and naturalism. On the one hand, it
adopts a naturalistic interpretation of mind and life. On
the other hand, it is so concerned to refute monistic
idealism that it construes all topics in terms of human
life, and consequently it is "never far removed from that
dogmatic anthropomorphism, that instinctive or arbitrary
adoption of the standpoint of practical belief, that is so
central a motive in idealism" (8, p. 39).

The task of philosophical reconstruction remains.
Perry, with his associates in the movement of new realism, was convinced that the necessity for, and possibility of, such a philosophical reconstruction defined "the
opportunity of realism" (8, p. 40). Though generated
by the problem of knowledge, "the opportunity of realism" was by no means confined to this abstract issue.
The practical dimension of Perry's "new realism" cannot
be overemphasized. Already in *Approach to Philosophy*
Perry had indicated the intimate connection between
philosophical speculation and the exigencies of life.
Building upon the classification of philosophical types
delineated in *Present Philosophical Tendencies*, Perry
offered *The Present Conflict of Ideals* as a "companion
volume" in which he concentrated on "the moral, emotional, political and religious implications" of rival philosophies (13, p. iii). *The Present Conflict of Ideals* is, as
its subtitle states, "A Study of the Philosophical Background of the World War." The urgency of events had
pressed Perry to seek "to bring to light the deeper conflict of ideas and ideals, of creeds and codes—of philosophies of life, in short—that underlies the conflict of sub-
marines, airplanes, and howitzers" (13, p. 2). As Perry
remarked: "We went to war on a moral issue." And he
added, with firm emphasis: "We went to war deliberately;
in a sense, and I thank God for it, we went *out of our*

way to go to war" (13, p. 5). "The greatest advantage which the Allies enjoy over the Central Powers is a philosophical, a moral advantage" (13, p. 19). In particular Perry joined the chorus of those who indicted absolute idealism for fostering the nationalist and militarist ideology of Imperial Germany, while he described realism as "the unconscious philosophy which underlies individualism, social democracy and humanitarianism" (13, p. 376).

Hence realism furnished the opportunity to think critically and to do good.

THE NEW REALISM

In the first decade of the twentieth century, when new realism was in the air, the problem of knowledge was the crucial problem in philosophy (8, p. 272). New realism, which its adherents described as "primarily a doctrine concerning the relation between the knowing process and the thing known" (5, p. 2), converged on this problem. Philosophical controversy gave the movement its earliest stimulus. "The positive thesis of American realism," Werkmeister has pointed out, "was developed in direct response to a criticism of realism published by Josiah Royce," and he has cited one of Perry's articles, published in 1902, as signaling "for the first time the fundamental position defended by American realists" (24). For Perry had asserted: "The realist believes reality to be a *datum, a somewhat that is given independently of whatever ideas may be formed about it*" (25).

Essays and critical discussions devoted to epistemology filled the pages of the journals, and from the copious mass of writings emerged common points of agreement and disagreement. In 1909, in the pages of the *Journal of Philosophy, Psychology and Scientific Methods,* the philosophers Schmidt, Creighton, and Leighton had argued over the utility and propriety of common platforms and programs in philosophy. Then, in 1910, in the same journal appeared "The Program and First Platform of Six Realists." The brief statements of W. T. Marvin, R. B. Perry, E. G. Spaulding, W. P. Montague, E. B. Holt, and W. B. Pitkin were followed in 1912 by the group's major publication: *The New Realism; Cooperative Studies in Philosophy*. As a cooperative volume representing a movement of many participants, *The New Realism* introduced a style of philosophical publication which has subsequently been adopted on several occasions in recent American philosophy.

But as a philosophical postion new realism remained a tendency and never crystallized into a school. Nevertheless, it had a broad and deep impact upon American philosophical ideas both as a polemic and as an effort at philosophical reconstruction. Moreover, a judicious treatment of the unity of Perry's thought requires consideration of his contributions to new realism.

As a Polemic

As a polemic realism challenged naturalism, idealism, and pragmatism. Since realism proportioned the force of its criticism to its estimation of the eminence of its philosophical alternatives, and since at the turn of the century idealism was dominant, the polemic of realism against idealism is most marked. A technical vocabulary to score the alleged "fallacies" committed by the rivals of realism was developed. To the formation of this vocabulary no one contributed more than Ralph Barton Perry. Six general errors were attributed to the philosophical alternatives to realism: (1) argument from the ego-centric predicament, (2) definition by initial predication, (3) exclusive particularity, (4) pseudo-simplicity, (5) speculative dogma, and (6) verbal suggestion, or equivocation (8, p. 271). A seventh error listed in *The New Realism* is the fallacy of illicit importance (5, pp. 19-21). Each of these errors will be taken up in turn.

(1) Perry has ironically remarked that the term "ego-centric predicament" proved "a successful bit of phrase-making, if one is to judge by the frequency with which it has been misunderstood" (2, p. 192). From its first appearance in the *Journal of Philosophy, Psychology and Scientific Methods* in 1910, the term "ego-centric predicament" became a part of the philosophical vocabulary. The ego-centric predicament consists in the fact that "(*n*)*o thinker to whom one may appeal is able to mention a thing that is not idea,* for the obvious and simple reason that *in mentioning it he makes it an idea*" (8, p. 129). Upon this predicament, Perry surmised, idealism justified its cardinal principle—namely, the thesis that being depends upon the knowing of it. According to Perry's analysis, the argument of idealism is invalid. Of course, thinking of a thing or mentioning it implies having an idea of the thing thought about or mentioned, but this implication is merely a redundancy. "The assertion that an idea is an idea conveys no knowledge even about ideas" (8, p. 131). What the idealist must prove is "that *everything is an idea,* or that *only ideas exist*," and his attempt to prove this from the ego-centric predicament is "simply to take advantage of the confusion of mind by which a redundancy is commonly attended" (8, p. 131).

(2) A second error underscored by Perry's critical polemic is definition by initial predication. From the fact that things are first known as given to consciousness in perception or thinking, the inference is drawn that things are essentially what their predicates reveal. The thing is known first as idea; therefore, the thing is an idea. But, as Perry contended, the initial presentation of a thing as an idea may be quite accidental to it, so that the definition of the thing as an idea requires independent evidence (8, pp. 126, 133).

(3) Closely linked with definition by initial predication is the error of exclusive particularity. "It consists in

regarding some early, familiar, or otherwise accidental characterization of a thing as definitive" (8, p. 128). Because a thing may first be recognized as an idea within the context of consciousness, the idealist wrongly infers that whenever it occurs it occurs as an idea in consciousness. But as Perry insisted, the idealist argument has not demonstrated what it claims; it simply assumes that the classification of things as ideas initially presented within consciousness is important, necessary, and exclusive.

(4) The error of pseudo-simplicity "consists in the failure to recognize the difference between the simplicity that precedes analysis, and the simplicity that is revealed by analysis; between the apparent simplicity of an unanalyzed complex, and the real simplicity of the ultimate terms of analysis; or between the simplicity that is owing to the little that one knows, and that which is owing to the much that one knows" (8, pp. 65-66). In philosophy the error is acute when simplicity is predicated of a complex reality merely because our understanding has not grasped its complexity. This error is by no means confined to idealism.

(5) Speculative dogma consists in "the arbitrary assertion of the ideal of thought" (8, p. 64). It vitiates the arguments of idealism and of materialistic naturalism. As thought inveterately seeks to interpret particulars by reference to general concepts, it generates the quest for an ultimate or final generality in terms of which everything may be construed. "Philosophy is then only an attempt to find the value of x, where x is that something of which everything is a case, and in terms of which every aspect and alteration of everything may be expressed" (8, p. 65). Philosophical monism, whether materialism or idealism, stems from the speculative dogma.

(6) Associated with speculative dogma and the error of pseudo-simplicity is the error of verbal suggestion, or equivocation. By means of this error the philosopher often constructs his position, seemingly amplifying in

univocal terms drawn from ordinary language a comprehensive conceptual scheme. For example: "The fundamental equivocation in idealism is its use of terms that ordinarily refer to characteristic forms of human consciousness—such as 'thought,' 'will,' 'personality,' and 'spirit' " (8, p. 180).

(7) The fallacy of illicit importance "consists in inferring that, because a proposition is self-evident or unchallengeable, therefore it is important" (5, pp. 19-20). The following argument of idealism illustrates the fallacy: it is evident that the awareness of any thing involves subjective experience; therefore, subjective experience is the universal and necessary characteristic of things.

With ponderous deliberateness realism spelled out its charges against its philosophical rivals. In consonance with Perry's conception of the relation of philosophy to life, however, the polemic of realism had a basically practical motivation. As Perry has declared: "As a polemic, realism is principally concerned to discredit romanticism; that is the philosophy which regards reality as *necessarily* ideal, owing to the dependence of things on knowledge. Realism, in other words, rejects the doctrine that things must be good or beautiful or spiritual in order to be at all" (8, p. 329).

As Philosophical Reconstruction

The polemic of realism is preliminary to the formulation of a positive philosophy.

Realism had a program. It advocated: the scrupulous use of words, exact definition of terms, indefatigable analysis of concepts, respect for logical form, accurate division of the philosophical topics under investigation, explicit statements of theses upon which agreement has been reached among different discussants, and, finally, sharp demarcation of philosophy proper from the study of its history (5, pp. 21-31). Realism has had much to do with the rise of an analytical philosophy which employs a technical vocabulary and eschews history for logic. Despite the failure of *The New Realism* to galvanize its adherents into a well-defined school, its program has left an indelible mark upon recent American philosophy, and the promised philosophical reconstruction may be viewed as a significant and fruitful alternative to antecedent idealism and subsequent naturalism in American thought.

As Perry observed: "philosophy is *essentially unitary and systematic*"; then he added: ". . . and thus *superlatively liable to revision*" (3, p. 396). Cognizant that its theses may be revised, realism has offered important theories of mind, knowledge, and life.

Mind. The problem of knowledge "reduces, in the last analysis, to the problem of the relation between a mind and that which is related to mind as its object" (8, p. 273). It is not surprising, then, that Perry should have undertaken to present a theory of mind, a theory which by his own admission (8, p. 305n) owes a considerable debt to the work of E. B. Holt (26).

According to Perry, the study of mind is conducted by two methods: introspection and observation. Introspection explores mind from the inside; observation, from the outside; and an adequate theory must comprehend both aspects of mind (8, p. 274). Introspection, which deals with the internal contents of mind, fails to attain knowledge of mind as action, and so must be supplemented by observation. The difference of methods is correlated with the distinction between *content* and *action*. Mind, or consciousness, reveals, on the one hand, contents given to it, and on the other, the acts of entertaining these contents. As regards the contents, it is Perry's view that they are not exclusively mental. "(N)either peculiarly mental nor peculiarly mine; they are *neutral and interchangeable*" (8, p. 277). The supposition that these contents are mental and private, rather than neutral and interchangeable, is, indeed, an instance of the fallacy of exclusive particularity (8, p. 286). Hence minds are classified "among intersecting rather than exclusive systems" (8, p. 288).

But if contents, apprehended introspectively, are not exclusively mental, what makes them mental at all? To answer this question calls for an examination of mind as action and consequently requires the employment of the method of observation. William James had moved in the right direction when he sought to define mind in terms of bodily feeling, but his strict adherence to the introspective method prevented his discovering the perfect definition of mind. Bodily action, not bodily feeling, Perry insisted, is the essence of mental action. "A sound 'listened to' or 'heard,' is, by virtue of that action, mental content . . . (L)istening and hearing are operations of the living organism, or specific operations of the nervous system, which lie in the field of general observation" (8, p. 285).

New realism assisted in the general movement to transform the philosophical study of mind into a scientific psychology. Although the new realist held the method of introspection in high esteem, he also in revolutionary fashion introduced the method of observation for the understanding of mental action, re-enforcing the development of physiological psychology while, more significantly perhaps, preparing the way for methodological behaviorism. Once and for all, in the study of mind emphasis was placed on the role of bodily activities accessible to empirical observation. Mental actions are the bodily activities of a biological organism when it deals with its environment so as to realize its interests. Mental contents are but parts of the environment upon which mental actions are exerted. Bodily instrumentalities, including sense organs and nervous system, are brought into play in mental action, while the organism interacts with its environment according to its interests. Thus mind is a natural organization "possessing as distinguishable, but complementary, aspects, *interest, nervous system,* and *contents"* (8, p. 304).

Knowledge. The realistic theory of knowledge depends upon two component theories: the theory of immanence and the theory of independence (8, p. 308). As Perry said: "It would not, I think, be far from the truth to say that the cardinal principle of neo-realism is *the independence of the immanent"* (8, p. 313). Understanding this cardinal principle hinges upon understanding its components.

"Epistemological monism" is another term for the theory of immanence; it signifies "that when a given thing, *a,* is known, *a itself* enters into a relation which constitutes it the idea or content of a mind" (8, p. 308). The theory of immanence therefore rejects both the dualism of body and mind and the dualism of thought and thing. In place of the dualism of mental and physical substances is substituted the concept of organizations of content. "Then, instead of conceiving of reality as divided absolutely between two impenetrable spheres, we may conceive it as a field of interpenetrating relationships, among which those described by physics and psychology are the most familiar and typical, and those described by logic the most simple and universal" (8, p. 311). Despite the immanence of things in the mind in immediate knowledge, however, the thing transcends the thought; first, because as content it is wholly distinct from the mental act that apprehends it, and second, because it has its own intrinsic nature whereby it enters into noncognitive (i.e., physical) relations with other things (8, p. 313).

That things are independent of the cognitive contexts into which they enter, Perry argued, is supported by four considerations (8, pp. 317-323). First, there is the failure of idealism to support its case. Second, the argument from external relations shows that, though things may enter into the cognitive relation and be immanent in

mind, they are not affected in their natures by this relation. Third, the sharp distinction between mind and its
content implies that content is mental only when connected with a mental act. Finally, an empirical argument for realism is based upon the science of mind, or
consciousness, which, by defining and describing mind
as "a selective response to a preexisting and independently existing environment" (8, pp. 322-323), requires
that there be something objective to respond to.

In addition to firmly positing an objective natural
world in which dwells mind as a specific sort of action
and organization of contents, new realism advanced a
special theory of truth and error. At first it would seem
easy to dismiss error as subjective, but since subjectivity
itself is constituted by *"perspective,* or *point of view,* in
which a projection defined by the position of the organism is abstracted from the plenum of nature," the appeal to subjectivity explains the possibility of error as itself objective (8, p. 324). To define truth and error as
actualities Perry's version of neorealism borrowed an important page from pragmatism, without, however, interpreting truth merely in terms of subjective estimations of
success or failure of beliefs in action (27). "The truth or
error of the belief is . . . relative to the interest and the
circumstances which determine the success of the action.
. . . In case such action is well taken, it [the belief] is
true; in case it is mistaken, it is false, or illusory" (8, p.
326). The realistic check on the subjectivistic excess of
pragmatism hinges on the recognition that objective *circumstance* is a determining factor in the success or failure of a belief.

PHILOSOPHY OF VALUES

Perry's realistic epistemology and metaphysics may be
viewed as prolegomena to a philosophy of life. Now a
philosophy of life contains "a theory concerning the na-

ture of goodness or value, and a theory concerning the conditions and prospect of its realization" (8, p. 331). Realism inveighed against the romantic conviction that reality and value, being and goodness, are identical. It recognized that the universe, apart from life, is neither good nor bad, and that, with the advent of life, it contains entities that are valuable, others that have negative value, and some that are neither. Realism involved disillusionment, but never despair. The success of life pivots on its awareness of the actual character of its environment. "Well doing is conditioned by clear seeing" (8, p. 329). And realistic disillusionment is tantamount to enlightenment. "(P)hilosophy, like science, shall illuminate things in order that action may be invented that shall make them good" (8, p. 330).

Stripping all illusions away from the world to discover the conditions for the realization of the good life, Perry depicted, in his early and illuminating little book, *The Moral Economy*, the nature of morality in the most realistic terms. "(T)he spring and motive of morality are," he asserted, "absolutely one with those of life," and morality is "only the method of carrying on the affair of life beyond a certain point of complexity" (4, p. 19). In passages which suggest a concept of nature influenced by nineteenth-century physics, Perry described morality as "the forced choice between suicide and abundant life," and emphasized that it is *the massing of interests against a reluctant cosmos*" (4, p. 14). By massing and organizing these interests, morality aids life in "one campaign in which all interests are engaged, and which requires their undivided and aggressive effort. This is the first and last campaign, the war of life upon the routine of the mechanical cosmos and its forces of dissolution" (4, p. 28).

A realistic theory of life, therefore, is preliminary to a theory of values. Inclined at first to simplify, Perry equated value with goodness and identified ethics with the general study of values. He also assigned the study of the conditions necessary to the realization of values to the philosophy of religion (8, p. 331). Later, however, he came to see that ethics, though central to the study of values, is merely a part of a general theory of value, and similarly that the philosophy of religion, though bearing upon the ultimate conditions for man's final achievement of values, is part of a more comprehensive theory of civilization.

In his most famous book, *General Theory of Value,* Perry conceived his task as twofold: (1) to discover the generic character of value present in all the special values of ethics, aesthetics, politics, jurisprudence, economics, and religion; and (2) to provide the rational basis for judgments of comparative value. The general theory of value is prerequisite to grappling with the most prominent problem of the modern world, namely, "that of establishing a principle of selection and a method of reconciliation by which order and harmony shall be brought out of a bewildering chaos and confusion of values" (6, p. 16).

Definition of Value

What is value? To answer this question, Perry first examined the alternative theories of the relation of value to interest: "There are four possible relations of value to interest. In the first place, value may be, in its essential nature, quite irrelevant to interest. . . . In the second place, value may be held to be that character of an object which qualifies it be an end; in other words, that which implies, evokes or regulates interest. . . . In the third place, value may be assigned to objects of certain duly qualified interests, such as the final harmonious, absolute or imperative interest. Finally, there is the simpler and more comprehensive view, that value in the generic sense attaches promiscuously to all objects of all interest" (6, pp. 27-28).

Perry's referral of value to interest for purposes of a general definition was justified, he believed, by the fact that man's affective-motor life, to which the term "interest" properly applies, is operative in all value situations.

After a process of elimination, in which various objections are sustained against alternative theories, Perry's argument led to "the simpler and more comprehensive view" which holds that interest is "the original source and constant feature of all value. That which is an object of interest is *eo ipso* invested with value. Any object, whatever it be, acquires value when any interest, whatever it be, is taken in it" (6, pp. 115-116). "Or, *whatever is object of interest is ipso facto valuable*" (7, p. 3). Perry stated his definition thus: "*x* is valuable = interest is taken in *x*." "(V)alue is thus a specific relation into which things possessing any ontological status whatsoever, whether real or imaginary, may enter with interested subjects" (6, p. 116).

One point should be clear: the definition of value tells what value is, not what things are valuable.

In favor of the interest theory, Perry contended that to imbue objects with value requires nothing more or less than the existence of an interest in them. "The silence of the desert is without value, until some wanderer finds it lonely and terrifying; the cataract, until some human sensibility finds it sublime, or until it is harnessed to satisfy human needs" (6, p. 125). But Perry, the first to demarcate the ego-centric predicament in the cognitive situation and to harp on the alleged idealistic fallacy of arguing from this predicament, must have been peculiarly sensitive to the subjectivistic nuances of this contention. Indeed, in *The Moral Economy* Perry was extremely susceptible to axiological idealism, or subjectivism. There he incautiously designated goodness as the "fulfilment of interest" (4, p. 11), and he generalized that the "*root-value* . . . of which all the higher moral values are compounded, is the fulfilment or satisfaction of the particular interest" (4, p. 82). This passage clearly located value in the subject and equated it with subjective satisfaction and fulfillment. This view is quite close to the kind of theory advocated by DeWitt Parker, who (for one) was severely critical of Perry's definition of value in *The General Theory of Value* (28). But Perry sought to escape subjectivism by means of a relational theory of value. The meaning of the relational theory of value can best be understood by a consideration of the terms entering into the relation: interest and object.

Interest. Perry's theory of value is properly "termed a bio-centric or psycho-centric theory of value, in the sense that values are held to be functions of certain acts of living mind to which we have given the name interest" (6, p. 139). For Perry the term "interest" has a wide range of application. Pointing to the "all-pervasive characteristic of the motor-affective life, this *state, act, attitude or disposition of favor or disfavor,*" Perry called it "interest" (6, p. 115). Thus empiricism and naturalism in value theory were possible without hedonism. In fact, Perry charged hedonism with having committed a fundamental error by "its failure to distinguish between the *concept* of goodness, namely, the desired, and that *object,* namely pleasure, to which this concept is supposed uniquely to apply" (6, p. 607). Interest, therefore, is clearly distinct from its object; the object is that toward which interest is directed. Interest, in any of its modes, resides in a subject, interpreted naturalistically as an organism.

Present within the tendencies of organisms acting in respect to the environment, interest emerges in clear focus when psychological conditions enter. Interested behavior involves more than an organism with certain definite tendencies and an external situation acting upon it and triggering its energies. "Interest is essentially teleological" (6, p. 537). To interpret the situation by reference to some anticipated outcome the organism must possess mind. Purposive, or interested, human behavior displays not mere adaptation to the environment but intelligent planning.

That the object of interest lies in the future is, according to Perry, "one of the fundamental paradoxes in the theory of value" (6, p. 242). For emphasis on the futurity of the object of interest strongly suggests that so long as an object is desired it is valuable, and that once the interest is satisfied, the value ceases. Ironically, common sense lends support to this paradox with its enthusiasm for objects of aspiration over those already attained. "All interest," Perry wrote, "has a forward reference in time; it is a striving after the not-yet-attained" (6, p. 250). To soften the paradox Perry had devised his ingenious conception of recurrent interest. When an object of interest is realized, it remains valuable so long as, while satisfying the original interest, it is an object of a persisting or recurrent interest (6, pp. 244-246).

Although the concept of interest draws its content from the affective-motor characteristics of purposive behavior, it nonetheless involves cognition. Interest is, according to Perry, mediated by cognition (6, pp. 344-346). An interest in an object implicates an interest judgment, for the interested subject recognizes an object or judges that there is one correlative with his interest and capable of satisfying it. The consequent verifications or falsifications of such interest judgments radically affect the systems of values which the organism seeks. Cognition is relevant to values in still another way, since both interest and its objects are facts which may be studied and known empirically. Judgments about interests are empirical judgments within the competence of psychology; judgments about objects of value, not to be confused with interest judgments, are judgments of value and are empirical, too. A judgment of value simply asserts that x is a value, or is valuable; it is true if some interest in x exists. Or it may assert that x is more or less valuable than y; it is then true if it conforms to the empirical tests for comparative value (6, pp. 366 ff). At any rate, by acknowledging the cognitive aspects of interest and value judgments Perry clearly repudiated non-cognitivism and emotivism in recent ethical theory. As history bears witness, he would insist, knowledge affects human desires and responses and, in consequence, governs the systems of values men seek.

Finally, Perry's treatment of interests does not separate or isolate them from one another, but rather conjoins and links them. Interests comprise a *community* when they share a common object (6, p. 370). They enter into a complex relation of *subordination* when the objects of interests are ends in one context, yet serve as means in another context. They even constitute a *mutuality* of interests when interest is taken in interest. Thus interests participate in processes of integration, and rational means effectuate such integration. Persons and societies are integrations of interests, although their modes of integration differ. Direct integration of interests as the acts of one agent is characteristic of persons, whereas indirect integration of interests through their objects is characteristic of societies (6, p. 433). Whether at the personal or the social level, the integration of interests resolves conflicts and produces harmony. Herein consists the paramount purpose of ethics.

Object. Although objects exist independently of the minds that know them, they have value only when interest is taken in them. Value, then, is not the same as the satisfaction of an interest; rather it is a relation between an object and an interest, and it exists so long as the object is the object of interest whether or not this interest is satisfied. A thwarted interest in an object does not deprive the object of its value unless the interest dies, although such frustration may alter interests (6, pp. 569-570). Having repudiated an axiological idealism which reduces value to a subjective state, Perry was none-theless reluctant to embrace an axiological realism which ascribes objectivity to values apart from any relation to interest. He denounced the "persistent unwillingness to accept the palpable fact that values *are* relative in differ-ent senses to different subjects" (6, p. 137). Though he deemed relativism realistic when it recognizes any relation of objects to extant interests as sufficient to con-stitute values, he condemned as vicious that type of rel-ativism which affirms a set of interests belonging exclu-sively to a given subject or group of subjects as "the only centre or point of interest for all values" (6, p. 138).

A realistic theory of the objects of value is evident also in Perry's discrimination of values from the acts of percep-tion, or judgments, by which they are known but of which they are independent. "A value acquires existence when an interest is generated, regardless of any knowl-edge about it" (6, p. 140). This statement clearly ex-presses the causal dependence of value on interest while it affirms the independence of the object of value in re-gard to subjective cognitive states. However, it may tend to obscure the relevance of cognition to interest. As Perry expatiated elsewhere, while the object of cognition is defined as the *"what is expected"* (7, p. 38) and is problematic, "(t)he object of interest is that *in which interest is taken"* (7, p. 40). Nevertheless, the object of interest is "furnished to that subject by cognition. The object of interest, whether presented or represented, is something expected; and possesses the questionable or problematic character of the expected" (7, p. 40).

Thus values are relational, originating when interests are taken in objects, and paradoxically, terminating when interests are satisfied, unless these interests are re-current. An object of interest may be a physical thing, a mental condition, or a possible ideal state of affairs. The failure to realize an object of interest does not detract from its value. Nor are objects of interest equally valuable, as the subjectivist or extreme relativist maintains, since Perry established standards of comparative value.

The Problem of Comparative Value

As the problem of generic value consists in ascertaining the definitions of "good," "evil," or "valuable," instead of discovering cases of them, "the problem of comparative value is to determine the meaning of 'better,' 'best,' 'worse,' 'worst,' or 'more' and 'less' valuable, rather than to discover what, if anything, has these characters" (6, p. 596). For the comparison of values there are three standards of measurement. "These three principles are *intensity, preference* and *inclusiveness,* and they may be summarily stated as follows. An object, wine, is better than an object, water: (1) if the interest in wine is more intense than the interest in water; (2) if the wine is preferred to the water; and (3) if the interest in the wine is more inclusive than the interest in the water" (6, p. 616). These principles are "independent in the sense that they are irreducible one to another, both in their meaning and in their causal variations" (6, p. 619). Widely adopted by philosophy and common sense, they are associated separately with particular schools of thought: intensity with hedonism, preference with humanism, inclusiveness with moral self-realizationism. Perry, however, accepted all three principles.

The desideratum of a theory of comparative value is the establishment of the *summum bonum,* the highest good, whereby, according to time-honored tradition, "all values can be arranged in a single, all-comprehensive and systematic hierarchy, in which every object which is good or bad occupies a unique place determined by its relations of better and worse to all the rest" (6, p. 626). For the determination of the *summum bonum* the three standards of measurement are indispensable. However, since every interest possesses intensity, all interests may have like intensity, from zero to maximum. On the basis of intensity it is possible to compare objects of the same interests, but any discrimination between different objects of different interests of the same intensity can be effectuated only by recourse to the other standards of measurement.

Here preference enters. "That an interest exhibits preference among its eligible objects, or that these objects are more or less eligible, appears to be as fundamental a feature of interest as its having objects at all. Interest not only selects *its* objects from among the objects of the environment, but selects *among* its objects" (6, pp. 634-635).

But often two or more preferences conflict, and if the conflict persists even after cognitive differences have been ironed out, we are "confronted with two undebatable facts both of which have to be accepted by both parties, the facts, namely, that whereas in the last analysis I prefer *b* to *a*, you prefer *a* to *b*. Such a conflict of preference, like conflict of interest, is a datum of value and an instance of its ultimate and irreducible relativity" (6, p. 640). Of course various methods have been devised to regulate preference, but these methods usually presuppose the standard of inclusiveness. The standard of inclusiveness has two corollary formulations: (1) the addition of interests in the same object confers additional value on the object, whereas the withdrawal of interests in the same object subtracts value from it (6, p. 647); (2) the larger the aggregate of objects in which interests are taken, the greater the value of the aggregate, although the aggregate, e.g., James-desiring-pushpin and John-desiring-poetry, while greater than either component of the aggregate, does not constitute "*a* good, any more than a quart of peas constitutes a pea" (6, p. 649).

The standard of inclusiveness is essential to the establishment of a system of values. As Perry has stated: "The first standard, intensity, makes possible the comparison of the several phases of the same interest in the same object; the second, preference, makes possible the comparison of the several objects of the same interest; the third, inclusiveness, makes possible the comparison of the objects of one interest with the objects of another without the introduction of a third interest, and is therefore the only standard by which all interests can be brought into one system having a maximum in all three respects, or on the whole" (6, p. 658).

Moral Value

At first it might seem that the reference to interest in the study of values precludes a fair appreciation of the nature of moral value. The definition of value as the object of any interest suggests that the moral life is determined by the most primitive impulses, or drives. Yet nothing could be farther from Perry's intention. In fact, he scored against what he termed the "Regressive" or "Atavistic Fallacy." This fallacy consists in supposing that the most remote antecedent cause, condition, or complex in a temporal order of causes "functions directly and that it derives additional weight from its remoteness" (7, p. 21). Affirmed Perry: "Human interests can rise above their source. Indeed it might be said to be the very essence of man that both phylogenetically and ontogenetically he *does* rise above his source" (7, p. 28). Nor does Perry's interest theory confer a privileged position upon selfishness, even enlightened selfishness. In *One World in the Making*, Perry stated that selfishness, even when enlightened, does not suffice for a global order, since selfishness collides with morality, and, in the final analysis, the unity of the world must be moral. "The only remedy for selfishness is unselfishness, and the gospel of enlightened selfishness can at best be only a step in that direction" (19, p. 160).

What then is moral value?

In *The Moral Economy*, moral value is defined as *"the fulfillment of an organization of interests"* (4, p. 15). Its essence is the economy it imposes upon interests so that they may be satisfied. Whenever interests conflict the higher interest is the one which effectuates the maximum fulfillment of interests in consonance with the situation. This higher interest, which controls the original interests and is "entitled to do so only because it incorporates them," is what Perry called *"moral purpose"* (4, pp. 53-54). The theme of an economy of interests is reiterated in Perry's treatment of "The Highest Good" at the end of *The General Theory of Value* and of "the norm of harmonious happiness" in *Realms of Value*. As Perry declared: "Morality takes conflict as its point of departure and harmony of interests as its goal" (7, p. 87).

The highest good consists in the most inclusive organization of interests enabling their maximal satisfaction. Within the individual person the effectiveness of an integration of interests seated in one organism is dependent upon inclusive adjustment of interests with each other. Enjoyed by the individual person and enabling him to find maximal satisfactions, this harmony may of course be at odds with interests seated in other organisms. At the social level there is no possibility of fusing these interests into a person of higher order, since a society is merely a collection of individual persons. Morality, then, presents the ideal of the highest good as social, an ideal good which promises to satisfy the interests of all the members of humanity. Following James (29), Perry judged as morally unsatisfactory a situation in which the interests of all members save one are served, precisely because that one is excluded. Not only did he feel pity for the excluded one and disgust for the others, but also he was convinced that the happiness of the many never compensates for the suffering of the one. "As co-exclusive, the claims of the lost soul and of the happy millions are incommensurable" (6, p. 671). The standard of inclusiveness, he contended, demands that somehow the excluded person be brought into the general bliss. Just as at the individual level the personal integration of interests which culminates in maximal, harmonious satisfaction is more desirable than one which is entangled in internal dissension or purchases unity at the cost of frustrating many vital impulses, so at the social level the most inclusive harmony of interests is more desirable than disunity or disharmony. An individual has a moral purpose to the extent that he checks the warfare among his interests and arranges them in an order enhancing their possibilities of mutual satisfaction. Similarly, a society exhibits a moral purpose to the extent that it ministers to the interests of all its members by the efforts of each member to aid the interests of all others.

This ideal situation in which all interests may be satisfied by means of the interests of *all* in the interests of all, foreshadowed in the Christian Golden Rule and the Kantian Categorical Imperative, is the highest good. Perry has, of course, emphasized that this highest good is ideal: "It is the ideal object of an ideal will." And he has added: "The highest good . . . is that definable ideal which, *if* adopted by all as an ideal, *would* be best; and it is the ideal which is by its very nature best qualified to be so adopted. If, then, one asks, 'Does such all-harmonious, all-benevolent and enlightened unanimity exist?' there can, on empirical grounds, be only one answer: 'Alas! no. The outstanding *fact* of life is conflict.' But the whole significance of a theory of value lies in such words as 'Alas!' Why 'Alas!' unless it be true that it were best that such a unanimity *should* exist? The best so defined is a hypothetical and not a historical fact; a hypothesis constructed, however, in accordance with the meaning of the term 'best,' and therefore having the force of truth" (6, p. 687).

In later writings Perry has used the term "norm of harmonious happiness" as synonymous with the term "highest good." Called the first principle of morality, the norm of harmonious happiness is "that organization of interests in which each enjoys the noninterference and support of others, whether within the personal life or the life of society" (7, p. 119). This principle is normative; yet for Perry it is also descriptive: "When an object of interest is taken as a standard with which to compare an achievement, or by which to compare two achievements with one another, it becomes a 'norm'; the judgments which make such comparisons are 'normative judgments.' Since the norm and the achievement are both describable the comparison is a description of the achievement" (7, p. 176). As normative, it is both an ideal for aspiration and a standard of appraisal. It does not, however, prescribe the actual contents of happiness; it rather rules that conflicts of interests must be removed if maximal satisfactions are to be enjoyed. Not to be confused with pleasure or a sum of pleasures, happiness "consists in the sense of positivity of interests . . . (and) is an attribute of the total person. It exists, when it does exist, 'on the whole,' and not in the part" (7, p. 371).

Harmony, then, is an aim of the norm. But here a serious issue arises. On the one hand, Perry insisted that the highest good must be the most inclusive. On the other hand, he has stressed that it must be a harmony. Yet inclusiveness and harmony are distinct and independent of each other. An inclusive whole need not be harmonious, and conversely. However, for Perry such an harmonious and inclusive happiness remained an ideal of aspiration. "Morality," he wrote, "is man's endeavor to harmonize conflicting interests; to prevent conflict when it threatens, to remove conflict when it occurs, and to advance from the negative harmony of non-conflict to the positive harmony of co-operation" (7, p. 90). The norm of harmonious happiness, in effect, is "an ideal future good; a goal the attainment of which is conditioned by plasticity of circumstance, fidelity of purpose, efficiency of control, and growth of enlightenment" (7, p. 92).

How did Perry justify his thesis that the first principle of morality is the "highest good" or "norm of harmonious happiness"? He gave three reasons why the norm of harmonious happiness should be accepted as "the last word in moral matters" in *Puritanism and Democracy*: "First, it is a comparatively clear statement of the standard which, in various guises and verbal formulations, has been most widely in vogue in Western Europe, pagan or Christian, and whether in the social conscience of the average man or in the doctrines of the moral philosophers. . . . Second, this standard plays a unique role in the development of the social arts and institutions. Economy, law, and polity arise out of the conflict of human interests, and serve the purpose of rendering interests compatible and mutually supporting; and they express themselves in the form of enduring institutions because this purpose is a continuing task, which concerns the total community. . . . The third and strongest claim of this standard to be considered the moral standard par excellence lies in the fact that it is commonly presupposed in moral discussion as the principle by which differences of moral opinion can be resolved" (11, pp. 49-50).

Still other arguments for the norm of harmonious happiness are to be found in *Realms of Value*. After dismissing the arguments from intuitionism, authority, and psychology, Perry declared: "the standard of harmonious happiness is *capable* of being agreed on—both theoretically and practically" (7, p. 132). First, it satisfies the demand for objective and universal knowledge. Independent of the personal equation, "it is the same for all knowers who address themselves to the subject" (7, p. 132). Second, it appeals to the practical will of men. "The good of harmonious happiness, since it embraces all interests, is *to some extent* to everybody's interest, and thereby obtains a breadth of support exceeding that of any other good. Every person, including the person to whom the argument is addressed, has some stake in it" (7, pp. 132-133). "The norm of harmonious happiness, furthermore, is the only norm which is capable of appealing to all men not only severally but jointly. It is the only norm which promises benefits to each interest *together with* all other interests" (7, p. 133).

CRITIQUE OF CIVILIZATION

Conclusive proof of Perry's interest theory of values requires a thorough exploration and assessment of "its success in facilitating the solution of all special questions of value" (6, p. 126). If all values fall into place when viewed with interest as the center of reference, then Perry's theory is justified. Already we have noted how moral value is constructed upon the basis of the interest theory. The consideration of moral value was, for Perry, the basic segment of a more comprehensive theory of human civilization. In the concluding paragraph of *The General Theory of Value* Perry looked beyond the definitions of generic value and of standards of comparative value—immensely difficult as these tasks were—and promised "to employ these principles for the rectification of frontiers and the establishment of order among its historically authentic realms" (6, p. 694). This "proper sequel" to *The General Theory of Value*, however, did not appear until 1954, when *Realms of Value*, based on the Gifford Lectures delivered at Glasgow in 1946-47 and 1947-48, was published.

Realms of Value is, as its subtitle states, "A Critique of Human Civilization," conducted in the light of the interest theory of value. At present the need for a critique of civilization is urgent. Theories have conspired with events to challenge objective standards of value. As the world has been caught in a tumult of wars engineered by ruthless ideologies, thinking about values has tended to lapse into relativism and skepticism. In the years prior to the publication of *Realms of Value* by far the most prominent theory of values advanced in the United States was emotivism—a language-oriented theory which treated value terms as expressions of, or inciters of, emotion, devoid of cognitive meaning and objective reference. Emotivism responded to the contemporary predicament in which systems of values contradicted each other without the possibility of recourse to a common principle for the resolution of the conflicts. In contrast, Perry's norm of harmonious happiness is clearly a candidate for the position of ultimate arbiter of conflicts of values. It is also a cognitive principle, and it is supported by arguments. Of course it does not suffice to know and to prove that the norm of harmonious happiness is the first principle of morality. It is necessary to persuade mankind of its validity, since the universal adoption of this norm depends upon nothing less than widespread justice and benevolence. The interests of all men in it must somehow be developed and aroused.

To moral education falls this task. Lamentably neglected in the contemporary world, moral education, which Perry had sometimes equated with propaganda (18, Ch. III, esp. p. 75), is invoked to implant in all a prejudice for, or a disposition toward, justice and benevolence. Moral education, Perry urged, should make two sorts of appeals: (1) an appeal to reason, enabling men to view their interests objectively as worthy of consideration equal to the consideration accorded the interests of others; and (2) an appeal "to that natural sympathy, compassion, or fellow-feeling which moves one individual to adopt another's interest, and be moved to its support" (7, p. 431). Perry has pointed to sympathy as a natural human faculty "by which values are envisaged and multiplied so that a man out of the wealth of goods may be chooser of the best" (21, pp. 31-32). It can be developed by moral education, which, in fact, plays a central role in the development of human conscience. "Conscience as a system of approving and disapproving attitudes, in which sentiment and opinion can be conjoined, can be implanted" (7, p. 200).

Moral education, then, is indispensable to the establishment of the norm of harmonious happiness. Under this norm, the political forms taken by the institutions of ideal human civilization would be democracy and world moral organization.

Democracy

Throughout his life Perry was devoted to the causes of democracy. A militant liberal, he had a fighting faith in democracy. Just as in World War I he advocated American military preparedness, argued the compatibility of freedom and military conscription, and dilated on the moral superiority of the Allied cause over that of the Central Powers, so in World War II he early urged America's entry on the side of the Allies and incessantly attacked and condemned the Nazi and Fascist ideologies. Perry's commitment to democracy, along with his unbending hostility to all anti-democratic ideals, stemmed from his conviction that democracy is identical with morality. "Democracy is the *right* organization of society, or the way in which society *ought* to be organized, or the *good* society; the terms 'right,' 'ought,' and 'good' being given a moral meaning, and 'morality' being taken to mean the organization of interests for the purpose of removing conflict and substituting cooperation" (7, p. 274).

In *Puritanism and Democracy*, a treatise on the historical continuity of democracy with Puritanism in America, Perry declared: "Moralism reduces to democracy for two reasons" (11, p. 412). First, "moralism holds that the justification of the state lies in the good of its members" (11, p. 412). Perry always emphasized that the value of any institution, including the state, consisted in the values that the members who live within the institution enjoy. Consequently, Perry was able to praise the question: "What do I get out of this?" as in major part a fair method for ascertaining the rightfulness of an institution and its policy (11, pp. 443-444). Second, "knowledge of the good is not associated with any hereditary social or personal qualification, but only with the possession of the universal human faculties of reason and conscience" (11, p. 412). Just as every individual can best be depended upon to tell what his interest is, all individuals together can best decide what the public good is.

With emphasis on the good as satisfying the interests of the members and the means for the attainment of the good as being within the control of the moral consciousness of the individual citizens, democracy in the fullest sense, according to Perry, is both social and political. Whereas political democracy focuses on the form of government, in particular upon suffrage and political rights, social democracy has to do with the maximal satisfaction of the interests of the citizenry. On this count Perry considered the laissez-faire economic system inadequate for social democracy; sensitive to its shortcomings in respect to the distribution of wealth, Perry advocated a regulated capitalism (11, pp. 568-575; 7, p. 294). Finally, Perry contended that the public interest did not merely reduce to an aggregate of all individual interests: "The public interest . . . is the will, not of the collectivity as such, but of each and every individual person when these are in agreement in willing the good of all" (11, p. 502).

World Unity

Perry's philosophic defense of democracy was the corollary of a practical readiness to do battle for democracy whenever necessary. In an article published in *The At-*

lantic Monthly before America's involvement in World War I, Perry said: "We must learn to regard war, not as an isolated phenomenon, but as merely the most aggravated and the most impressive instance of the universal moral situation. This fundamental predicament of life, which gives rise to all moral perplexities, is the *conflict of interests*. When war is viewed in this light, we may then see in *justifiable* war a special application of the most general of all ethical principles, namely, the principle of *discipline* or *provident restraint*. Given the natural conflict of interest, this principle defines the only alternative to waste and mutual destruction. It means simply that under actual conditions the greatest abundance of life on the whole is to be secured only by a confining, pruning or uprooting of those special interests which imperil the stability and harmony of the whole" (14, pp. 106-107).

Thus Perry justified offensive as well as defensive war. Whereas defensive war is justified by a double motive: "the narrower motive of national security and the higher motive of general international security" (14, p. 113), offensive war is justified "when undertaken in the interest of an international system or league of humanity" (14, p. 117).

The vision of a league of humanity was Perry's constant preoccupation. Glimpsing its possibility in World War I, he became an untiring proponent of world moral unity during and after World War II. His *One World in the Making* is a noteworthy contribution to the literature on the subject. Although technologically the world has been transformed radically by the increase in contact between and the casual interdependence of its various parts, the upshot has been greater conflicts. As Perry observed: "The crowning unity of the world, by which its existing unity of contact and interaction is made good, is properly described as a *moral* unity" (19, p. 43). Now morality consists in that organization of in-

terests which provides maximal satisfaction. And as Perry
has said: "The moral unity of the world consists of the
extension of this same morality—the same standards,
precepts, and institutions—to the interrelation of nations and of all mankind, so that they may live and let
live, and work together in order that all may live more
abundantly" (19, p. 46). Since, moreover, morality in
politics is identical with democracy according to Perry,
democracy entails international organization: "Democracy is the only form of polity which implies international organization as a phase of its own development"
(19, p. 97). By parity of reasoning, only a democratic international organization is morally justifiable. Democracy, Perry taught, "is the only form of polity which is
fit to be erected on the international scale, because it
gives to nations, and does not take away; or takes away
only in order to give more abundantly, and takes from
one only in order to give to all, that one included. It
is, therefore, the only kind of internationality which is
consistent with the national aspirations of all nations"
(19, pp. 97-98).

The problem of international organization is a specific
application of the problem of morality. Global technol-
ogy affords the opportunity for, but does not guarantee
the existence of, global moral unity. "There must be,"
Perry held, "a widespread and dominant will, which is
for peace and *against* war; *for* happiness and well-being
and *against* misery; *for* the happiness and well-being of
all men and *against* the happiness and well-being of the
few at the expense of the many" (19, p. 223). Once more
the task falls to moral education to engender and foster
human conscience, this time on a global scale.

The problem of global moral unity epitomizes Perry's
conception of the problematic connection of actual fact
and valued ideal. "Morality is the realization of an ideal"
(19, p. 60). It demands a realism about the facts and the
actual interests that require organization and satisfac-

tion. Yet it also requires an idealism in the consideration of goals, both remote and immediate, which promise to satisfy human interests. In this sense Perry was right to declare: "the more realistic, the more idealistic" (19, p. 60).

NOTES TO CHAPTER 1

1. Ralph Barton Perry, "First Personal," *Atlantic Monthly*, Vol. 178 (October 1946), 107.
2. Ralph Barton Perry, "Realism in Retrospect," in *Contemporary American Philosophy: Personal Statements*, Vol. II. George P. Adams and W. P. Montague, eds. (New York: The Macmillan Company, 1930; reprinted by Russell & Russell, Inc., 1962).
3. Ralph Barton Perry, *The Approach to Philosophy* (New York, Chicago, Boston: Charles Scribner's Sons, 1905).
4. Ralph Barton Perry, *The Moral Economy* (New York, Chicago, Boston: Charles Scribner's Sons, 1909).
5. E. B. Holt, *et al.*, *The New Realism: Cooperative Studies in Philosophy* (New York: The Macmillan Company, 1912).
6. Ralph Barton Perry, *General Theory of Value: Its Meaning and Basic Principles Construed in Terms of Interest* (New York: Longmans, Green & Co., 1926).
7. Ralph Barton Perry, *Realms of Value: A Critique of Human Civilization* (Cambridge: Harvard University Press, 1954).
8. Ralph Barton Perry, *Present Philosophical Tendencies, a Critical Survey of Naturalism, Idealism, Pragmatism and Realism Together with a Synopsis of the Philosophy of William James* (New York: Longmans, Green & Co., 1912).
9. Ralph Barton Perry, *The Thought and Character of William James* (Boston: Little, Brown & Co., 1935), two vols. Also *The Thought and Character of William James, Briefer Version* (Cambridge: Harvard University Press, 1948).
10. Ralph Barton Perry, *In the Spirit of William James* (New Haven: Yale University Press, 1938).
11. Ralph Barton Perry, *Puritanism and Democracy* (New York: The Vanguard Press, 1944).
12. Ralph Barton Perry, *Characteristically American; Five Lectures Delivered at the University of Michigan* (New York: Alfred A. Knopf, 1949).
13. Ralph Barton Perry, *The Present Conflict of Ideals; a Study of the Philosophical Background of the World War* (New York: Longmans, Green & Co., 1918).
14. Ralph Barton Perry, *The Free Man and the Soldier; Essays on*

the *Reconciliation of Liberty and Discipline* (New York: Charles Scribner's Sons, 1916).

15. Ralph Barton Perry, *The Plattsburg Movement, a Chapter of America's Participation in the World War* (New York: E. P. Dutton & Co., 1921).

16. Ralph Barton Perry, *Shall Not Perish from the Earth* (New York: The Vanguard Press, 1940).

17. Ralph Barton Perry, *On All Fronts* (New York: The Vanguard Press, 1941).

18. Ralph Barton Perry, *Our Side Is Right* (Cambridge: Harvard University Press, 1942).

19. Ralph Barton Perry, *One World in the Making* (New York: Current Books, Inc., A. A. Wyn, 1945).

20. Ralph Barton Perry, *Plea for an Age Movement* (New York: The Vanguard Press, 1942).

21. Ralph Barton Perry, *The Humanity of Man*, edited by E. A. Masi (New York: G. Braziller, 1956).

22. Ralph Barton Perry, *The Citizen Decides, a Guide to Responsible Thinking* (Bloomington, Ind.: Indiana University Press, 1951).

23. Perry was an accomplished historian of the philosophy of the period. See his *Philosophy of the Recent Past; an Outline of European and American Philosophy since 1860* (New York, Chicago: Charles Scribner's Sons, 1926).

24. W. H. Werkmeister, *A History of Philosophical Ideas in America* (New York: Ronald Press Co., 1949), pp. 372-373.

25. Ralph Barton Perry, "Prof. Royce's Refutation of Realism and Pluralism," *The Monist*, XII (1901-1902), 450.

26. See E. B. Holt, *The Concept of Consciousness* (New York: Henry Holt & Co., 1914).

27. See William James's letter of August 4, 1907, to Perry in reply to the latter's early criticisms of pragmatism, in *Thought and Character of William James*, II, pp. 475-476.

28. See Chapter 6. See also DeWitt Parker, "Value As Any Object of Any Interest," *International Journal of Ethics*, XL (1930), 465-473.

29. William James, "The Moral Philosopher and the Moral Life," *International Journal of Ethics*, I (1891), 330-354.

Chapter 2

THE EMPIRICAL
IDEALISM OF
WILLIAM ERNEST HOCKING

CAREER AS PHILOSOPHER

A "passage beyond modernity" is the phrase of William
Ernest Hocking to describe the general movement of
philosophy in the twentieth century (1, p. vi).

Perhaps no thinker has been more opportunely situated than Hocking to observe and to participate in the
recent movements in philosophy. Born in 1873, Hocking
spent his youth in the Midwest where he worked, studied,
and became, against his will and early faith, an "ardent
disciple" of Herbert Spencer's agnostic naturalism. While
an engineering student at the Iowa State College at
Ames in 1894-95, he read William James's *Principles of
Psychology*, a work which liberated him from the spell
of Spencer, since it contributed to the formation of the
conviction that *"the world as a whole has a meaning"*
(2, Part I, p. 37). Hocking was drawn to Harvard in
1899, when the "golden age of American philosophy"
was in its full glory. With Palmer, Munsterberg, James,

Royce, and Santayana on the Harvard faculty, he became especially attached to Royce. Earning his B.A. from Harvard in 1901, he went to Germany in 1902-03 as a Walker Fellow, and studied briefly under Husserl. He returned to Harvard to complete his dissertation in 1904 (3). After teaching at Andover, at the University of California in Berkeley, and at Yale, he joined the Harvard faculty in 1914. Elected Alford Professor of Philosophy in 1920, Hocking, with Hoernlé, Sheffer, Perry, Lewis, and Whitehead as colleagues, has played a major part in perpetuating the "golden age of American philosophy."

With the publication of *The Meaning of God in Human Experience* (4), Hocking began the impressive authorship which has resulted in a score of volumes. Although *The Meaning of God in Human Experience* is universally recognized to be his most significant contribution to philosophy, other notable works are: *Human Nature and Its Remaking* (5), *Man and the State* (6), *Types of Philosophy*, *The Spirit of World Politics* (7), *The Coming World Civilization* (8), and *The Meaning of Immortality in Human Experience* (9). In appreciation of his work many invitations have been proffered him to deliver prestigious lectures, including the coveted Gifford lectures at Glasgow in 1938-39. He has received numerous high honors, the most recent being the Comte du Nouy award for *The Coming World Civilization*. Now in retirement Hocking manages his farm, nestled at the edge of the White Mountains in Madison, New Hampshire, and continues to write philosophy, concentrating mainly on metaphysics and the philosophy of law.

What is modernity in philosophy? And how has the general movement of thought in the twentieth century passed beyond it? To these questions Hocking's answers are straightforward. "I call modernity," he has written, "the era of thought dominated by the two contrasting aspects of the philosophy of Descartes, the subjective certitude of one's own existence, and the objective certitude of a nature whose process lends itself exhaustively to mathematical expression" (1, p. vi). Seizing upon one side, the ego or nature, to the exclusion of the other, modern philosophers have generated false idealisms and false naturalisms, with far-reaching practical reverberations which, after a long train of sufferings and disasters, have come to confront modern man and modern civilization with total catastrophe. "The disorder of the human world," Hocking has remarked, "is at its root a metaphysical disorder" (10, p. 159). He has cited Nazism's resort to violence as the glaring example of political impatience stemming from metaphysical impatience (10, pp. 159-160). His diagnosis of the failures of modernity in philosophy focuses on two major issues: (1) the inference from the certitude of subjectivity to subjective idealism, or solipsism (8, pp. 25-28); and (2) the inference from the objectivity of nature to a scientific naturalism which excludes God and human values from nature (11). Now solipsism and naturalism are both meaningless —solipsism because it contends that we can know no other with whom the self may communicate, naturalism because it treats as cosmically accidental the meanings which man cherishes. But meaninglessness is precisely what philosophy, regardless of its type, cannot countenance. What philosophy says, above all, is that things have a meaning and that philosophers can, through unflagging intellectual efforts, come to grasp this meaning (12).

Hocking has contributed to the passage beyond modernity by returning to its source—the Cartesian certitude of human experience. Here his procedure has duplicated that of Husserl, with whom he studied. But while Husserl's *Cartesian Meditations* (1928-29) fails to escape solipsism (13), Hocking's own treatment of the Cartesian *cogito* discloses the sociality of subjective experience. Hocking's return to the subjective certitude of

Descartes, originally presented in his doctoral dissertation and later incorporated in *The Meaning of God in Human Experience*, leads to a widened empiricism which places him, for his early recognition of the "I-thou" factors in experience, in the forefront of such "social existentialists" in theology as Martin Buber and Gabriel Marcel (14).

Probing more deeply into and meditating more adequately upon the experience of the human self than Descartes and his successors have done, Hocking has contended that what philosophy needs is a broadened empiricism. He has insisted that metaphysics must make inductions from experience, and that these inductions, since they deal with basic human passions as well as sense data, are akin both to mystical intuitions and to existentialist phenomenological descriptions (15). Equally, Hocking has insisted that philosophy is more than merely descriptive, not only because experience itself contains a concrete *a priori* (4, p. 278), but also because in yet more unsettling ways, experience urges the individual self to speculate, stirring him to glimpse in contemplation the Whole (9, pp. 245 ff.). Within the context of human experience, pervaded by a concrete *a priori* and suggesting at its edges—dimly and enshrouded in mystery—the Whole which embraces the individual self within a community, modernity is overcome, with values established as dimensions of Being, and the solitary self yielding its solitude in a community of selves. Promising to solve the dilemmas of modernity in philosophy, with practical implications for man's contemporary predicament, Hocking's philosophy is an empirical, or inductive, idealism.

In 1912 Hocking criticized idealism on the grounds that the Absolute is not an object worthy of worship. Now he argues that idealism does not do justice to the refractory "obduracy of Fact," leaving Camus and Sartre in possession of the "Absurd." Hocking's metaphysics, presented in his Gifford Lectures, induces three categories from experience and acknowledges Fact as a metaphysical category of equal significance with Field and Destiny (15). This unfinished metaphysics is a widened empiricism which promises not only to complete the passage beyond modernity, but also to accomplish the wedding between idealism and existentialism.

THEORY OF GOD

The Meaning of God in Human Experience opens with Hocking's confession of dissatisfaction with philosophical idealism. The critics of idealism "do not find the Absolute of idealism to be identical with the God of religion; they cannot worship the Absolute" (4, p. vi). To correct idealism it is necessary to discover "what, in terms of experience, its (religion's) God means and has meant to mankind (and) to find the foundations of religion, whether within reason or beyond" (4, p. vii). Influenced by both Royce and James, Hocking set out to convert the categories of idealism into the "hard cash" of experience as demanded by pragmatism. Religion does make differences to human experience, and these differences are the clues to its nature and truth. But the categories of idealism, such as the Absolute, cannot be totally reduced to experience; they persist as immutable universals and not as mere summaries of experiential data. Hocking's method, despite its pragmatic insistence that we ascertain "what religion is by first fixing attention on what it does" (4, p. 4), nevertheless concedes a transcendent aspect to religion which eludes complete translation into experiential phenomena (4, p. 9).

Experience as Method

For Hocking the correct pragmatic method is "negative pragmatism." Instead of equating truth with that which works, negative pragmatism adheres to the formula: *"That which does not work is not true"* (4, p. xiii).

While other methods are employed to find the truth, negative pragmatism discovers whether an hypothesis is false, and so "becomes an element in a type of reasoning which philosophers have called 'dialectic,' the process of self-correction of erroneous ideas in living minds" (11, p. viii). For negative pragmatism, which is a kind of "mental experiment in defective assumptions," functions identically with dialectic, which is utilized to uncover "that effect of experience which is adverse to the assumptions on which we are going, so that we are obliged to revise them" (11, p. 68 n.). Hocking's book, *Science and the Idea of God,* is an extensive application of the method of negative pragmatism to the idea of God. Here the dialectical experiment, insisting upon an "appeal to experience," demands: *"try to get along without God and see what happens"* (11, p. 11). Thus he has admitted: "We might have entitled the book, 'Getting on without God' " (11, p. viii). Of course, the experiment fails.

Efficacious in demonstrating the unacceptability of attempts to do without God, pragmatism, no less than idealism, fails to provide a positive concept of God, although it does direct us to seek such a concept in human experience. But whereas the Absolute of idealism is too remote from human experience to serve as a Person worthy of worship, the God of pragmatism is too much in the making to possess the sort of self-identity and objectivity that inspires worship. The defect of idealism, like that of pragmatism, is that it is unfinished. Although idealism can be completed by including a revised, i.e., negative, pragmatism, the completion of pragmatism entails its supercession, since in the area of religion it demands the recognition of ultimate, unchanging principles, such as the constant self-identity of God, and these principles are in stark contradiction to the tentativeness and short-range practicality of pragmatism. As Hocking has stated, "accepting fully the pragmatic guide to truth, we conclude that the only satisfactory truth must be absolute,—

that is, non-pragmatic. Wherewith, pragmatism ends in consuming itself; appears as a self-refuting theory" (4, p. 206).

Hocking's idealist philosophy of religion contains more than pragmatism with its emphasis on leading up to God from the values and qualities of human experience; it is also realistic, and, beyond this, it is mystical. With realism, Hocking's philosophy asserts that there is an Object for experience; with idealism, it insists that this Object is the Absolute; and with mysticism, it "finds the absolute in immediate experience" (4, p. xix.). In a quandary over the proper label for his position Hocking has confessed: "I know not what name to give to this point of convergence, nor does name much matter: it is realism, it is mysticism, it is idealism also, its identity, I believe, not broken. For in so far as idealism announces the liberty of thought, the spirituality of the world, idealism is another name for philosophy—all philosophy is idealism" (4, p. xx).

Experience is the starting point of philosophy, especially when philosophy undertakes to study religion. "That which chiefly marks the religious soul is a fearless and original valuation of things" (4, p. 31), since the religious man lives "*as if* in presence of attainment, of knowledge, of immortality" (4, p. 32). Thus religion seems to place emphasis on feeling to the exclusion of reasoning (4, p. 33), and accordingly the philosophy of religion has tended to contribute to the growing anti-intellectualism of contemporary culture. In protest against this "retirement of the intellect" Hocking has re-examined the nature of feeling and willing. Feeling does not exist apart from ideas (4, p. 64). Since feeling finds its satisfaction not in further feeling but in an "other-than-feeling," feeling leads to "consciousness of an object" (4, p. 66), so that in a rudimentary fashion knowing is the terminus of feeling (4, p. 68). But the contrast between the finitude of ideas, with their precisely definable boundaries, and the infinitude of the religious object, instigates the disturbing question: "Can we think the Infinite?" Hocking replies: "We think nothing else" (4, p. 94). Knowledge, then, begins with an infinite whole-idea, of which every subsequent idea is a determination. This infinite whole-idea, besides being the original idea with which consciousness begins, is also the "last goal of all idea meanings" (4, p. 119). Whereas the particular ideas by which we understand the whole are constantly undergoing revision, the whole-idea remains unchanged. As Hocking writes: *"deeper than idea is Idea"* (4, p. 108). The primacy of the whole-idea in experience, moreover, is borne out in valuation. "(A)ll valuing (and so all feeling) is a way of knowing objects with one's whole idea" (4, p. 129). "(W)hatever object becomes before the mind of any man must inevitably be judged at last by that man's sense of the nature of the reality with which he has, in the end, to do" (4, p. 136). The whole-idea permeates feeling, both as the "passion for objectivity, for reality, for Substance, quite prior to other passions" (4, p. 123), and as "the chief determinant of the value level in any consciousness" (4, p. 136).

Idea of God

But is the whole-idea the same as the idea of God? On this question at first it would seem that reason is silent. "The world would be consistent without God; it would also be consistent with God: whichever hypothesis a man adopts will fit experience equally well; neither one, so far as accounting for visible facts is concerned, works better than the other" (4, p. 143). Here resort to voluntarism and pragmatic idealism is tempting: By willing to believe in the divinity of the whole-idea we make it so. Explicity Hocking rejects the grounding of religious truth upon the will to believe rather than upon "that which independently Is" (4, p. 150). Religious truth, identifying the whole-idea with the idea of God, is "founded *upon experience"* (4, p. 154). This appeal to human experience does distinguish the Absolute of idealism from the God of religion. As Hocking has said: "I do not say that the Absolute is equivalent to God; I say that God, whatever else he may be, must needs also be the Absolute" (4, p. 206). Though the Absolute is an essential aspect of God, God is more in that he ministers to human needs, specifically the needs of man facing pain and evil in the world. Now for Hocking the consideration that evil will pass and the world become better is insufficient consolation; no prospective set of occurrences, but only a condition or being which explains evil now will suffice. Only God, a being other than ourselves and so not implicated as a guilty agent in the situations of evil, satisfies the human needs. And the idea of God best suited for this purpose is not the idea of a supreme power lording it over all the other powers in the world, nor the miracle-worker bursting into the regularity of nature without warning, nor even the aloof judge who dispenses cosmic justice; rather it is "God as intimate, infallible associate, present in all experience as that by which I too may firmly conceive that experience from the outside" (4, p. 224).

Hocking's argument for God as man's associate in facing evil is supplemented by his thesis in *Science and the Idea of God,* in which he maintains that the efforts of the special sciences to abandon the idea of God entail theoretical and practical meaninglessness. "Without God, meaning is simply a human specialty, the vast universe devoid of meaning. With God, the world has sense, perhaps direction" (11, p. 19). Each of the main sciences is cited. In psychology the essentially metaphysical character of feeling reveals a restlessness within the psychical life of man tantamount to the quest for God. "May we not say that *God is the law of the normal mental life?*" asks Hocking (11, p. 49). Similarly, social science, which attempts to discard God and ground all norms on man in society, proves inadequate, succumbing to value relativism and political totalitarianism. Since the standards of value whereby men and societies are evaluated stem from a source beyond men and beyond society—namely, God—it follows that "God is the law of a normal social life" (11, p. 83). Finally, physics and astronomy, the sciences which at the beginning of the modern epoch originally abandoned God, have become the arena of new developments which tend to reinstate him. Hence, "the experiment of getting on without God has led to a new perception of his presence" (11, p. 115).

The idea of God and the truth of this idea, therefore, are founded upon experience: "God is to be known in experience if at all" (4, p. 229). And since "whatever is matter of experience must also become, in time, matter for reason" (4, p. 155), metaphysics as intellectual meditation upon experience assumes paramount importance for discovering and understanding God. Affirming that "men have no rights to the satisfactions which their religion affords them except as they earn the right by successful metaphysical thought" (4, p. 214), Hocking has added that experience is metaphysical, "being the region of our continuous contact with metaphysical reality" (4, p. 215). Although the Absolute is the constant factor in experience, the Changeless Ultimate or Eternal Fact, which constitutes a permanent frame for human efforts (4, pp. 186-187), the Absolute alone engenders no implications for human experience. Conjoined with the Self as minor premise, however, the Absolute as major premise contributes to a metaphysical syllogism from which flows the world of concrete actions and process (4, pp. 189-190). "What Is makes no difference; that which produces difference is Consciousness of What Is" (4, p. 203). "*Sein* and *Bewusstsein* together give *Werden*" (4, p. 204).

With Hocking's conception of the metaphysical structure of experience as an encounter of the Self with the

Absolute, the Cartesian *cogito,* from which stems modernity in philosophy, is reinstated at the center of contemporary philosophical inquiry. At the same time interpretation of the *cogito,* which fosters an unsatisfactory
"retreat into subjectivity" by guaranteeing only the existence of the subject, is corrected. The reflective meditation by the Self on its own experience reveals "always
the Absolute within *in conjunction with the Absolute
without.* The whole tale of Descartes' discovery is not
told in the proposition, I exist, knowing. It is rather told
in the proposition, *I exist, knowing the Absolute;* or, *I
exist, knowing God"* (4, p. 202). Clearly, then, experience is not a heap of private psychological states locked
up within isolated, monadic subjects. The argument is
pressed by means of the dilemma: "Experience is always
and necessarily social, or never—these are our alternatives" (4, p. 282). The universal and necessary sociality
of experience is evident in the fact that men live in a
common world and communicate with each other. Here-
with Hocking's philosophy enters the borders of realism,
since like realism it posits the objectivity of nature. However, "the objectivity of Nature is its community, not two
facts but one" (4, pp. 288-289). Hocking's realism is,
consequently, a *"realism of social experience"*; it is "a
super-natural Realism, or a Social Realism, or more truly
a Realism of the Absolute—not far removed from Absolute Idealism" (4, p. 290).

J. A. Martin, Jr., has severely criticized Hocking for inconsistencies between his professed empirical method
and his metaphysics of experience (16, p. 16). Indeed,
the concept of experience is so broadened that "the idea
of Other Mind is at the same time an experience of Other
Mind" (4, p. 278). The idea of Other Mind is therefore
"a fundamental and constant experience, bound up with
my equally permanent experiences of Self and Nature,"
and while "not *prior* to experience," it "is indeed prior
to all *further* social experience, to all such as is intermit-

tent and subject to error. This fundamental experience, and its idea, deserve, from their position in knowledge, to be called a *concrete a priori* knowledge" (4, p. 278).

Existence of God

Upon this fundamental experience Hocking has based his discussion of the existence of God. Knowledge of the world of nature presupposes that it is a common world; and, moreover, the world of nature is never known except as common—that is to say, is known by another mind. Hence "a knowledge of Other Knower is an integral part of the simplest knowledge of Nature itself" (4, pp. 268-269). Indeed, the natural objects encountered in experience, the objects whose reality is the exclusive preoccupation of philosophical realism, turn out to be given not by a physical world but by an Other Mind, or, as Hocking has expressed it in a later book, "by an active will, which intends to communicate that experience" (1, p. 246). Thus "the 'objectivity' of this object-world is something more and other than alien stuff. . . . (T)he 'It' discloses itself as a 'Thou' " (1, p. 309).

Just as knowledge of nature leads to Other Mind and thence to God, so knowledge of other human minds depends fundamentally upon knowledge of God. "My current social experience, the finding of any fellow finite mind, is *an application* of my prior idea of an Other; in a sense, an application of my idea of God. It is through the knowledge of God that I am able to know men" (4, p. 298). From such grounds did Hocking draw his idealistic conclusion that "the world is a self," adding immediately, "in explanation, that the self, so far from being a wholly evident and graspable being, as Descartes and Berkeley seemed to assume, is infinite in its depth and mystery" (1, p. 315).

Since for Hocking the original source of our knowledge of God is "an experience of not being alone in knowing the world" (4, p. 236), he has undertaken to demonstrate the existence of God by means of a form of the ontological argument, proceeding not as a strict deductive proof but as a clarification of the initial experience. "The ontological argument, in its true form, is a report of experience" (4, p. 312). The argument starts from the recognition that the experience of the Self and Nature is less than reality. Although other arguments for God "reason that *because the World is, God is,*" Hocking has contended, "The ontological argument reasons that *because the world is not, God is*" (4, p. 312). Incapable of functioning as a stable premise from which the existence of God is deduced as the conclusion, the world "appears as a conclusion from something more substantial, . . . God" (4, p. 312). The argument is thoroughly rooted in experience. Thus Hocking has preferred to state it ". . . not thus: I have an idea of God, therefore God exists. But rather thus: I have an idea of God, therefore I have an experience of God" (4, p. 314). In a separate essay, appearing two decades after the publication of *The Meaning of God in Human Experience*, Hocking restated his ontological argument, stressing that "the essence of God must be real, because it is in essence inseparable from my continuous consciousness or experience of reality" (17, p. 65).

Although Hocking's analysis of experience as a relation between the Self and God involves metaphysical concepts which, despite their utility in the construction of a theology, demand an intellectual discipline remote perhaps from the concerns of the religious man, it is intrinsically a form of mysticism. In this respect Hocking's discussion evinces a wide appreciation of the varieties of religious experience and worship. As "the practice of union with God in a special act of worship" (4, p. 352), mysticism is a deed, not a doctrine or escape (4, p. 355). As a deed, moreover, it is not a retreat into the inaccessible, inarticulate recesses of the subject, but "a redemption of solitude" (4, p. 404). It encourages no negative metaphysics which enervates moral action and rejects the world. On the contrary, it is a way of belonging to the world as the world is in its most essential substance—in Hocking's phrase, "an unlimited attachment with an unlimited detachment" (4, p. 493). Mysticism, therefore, is realistic. "I believe," Hocking has said, "in the 'concrete universal' as a metaphysical doctrine: God and the world belong together—neither is anything without the other. . . . God and the world, I maintain, must be worked in with one another forever; forever they must be pursued in alternation" (4, p. 407).

THEORY OF MAN

Distressed by the decline of religious values in the face of rising philosophies of moral realism and by the moral decay erupting into and issuing from world war, Hocking described the contemporary situation as "a drastic judgment of *non-reality* upon the pieties of Christendom" (5, p. viii). He has argued that the scientific exclusion of value from the objective world of nature has led to the mental and moral inconsistencies that betray the meaninglessness of modern man. "(E)veryone today knows, not by rumor but by introspection, that modern man is tired of himself" (18, pp. 6-7). Of course the "healing fact" for the disease of modernism is man's acceptance of the "the truth of the existence of God" (18, p. 59). Since the passage beyond modernity must not undo the gains of science, the problem of philosophy with respect to a theory of man becomes: How is it possible to retain and extend the essence of religious value without suppressing the new knowledge, achieved by science, of man and his institutions and without obscuring the unsettling insights into the nature of man afforded by the turmoil of recent times?

Original Human Nature

In *Human Nature and Its Remaking* Hocking has sought to define the original material of human nature and to ascertain "the broader principles which govern the process . . . of remaking, of educating, of civilizing, of converting or of saving the human being" (5, p. vii). Man uniquely is "for himself an object of artful reconstruction." Philosophy's task is to evaluate the various standards which are presented as models for the remaking of human nature. This task can be divided into three intimately connected questions: "What is original human nature? What do we wish to make of it? How far is it possible to make of it what we wish?" (5, p. 11). Although the failures encountered by religion and politics in prescribing what men ought to become testify to the causative presence of an original human nature, men have "an immediate consciousness of freedom, that is to say, of wide margins of possibility" (5, p. 15). The success or failure of an ideal is as much a function of its desirability as it is of the fixity of man's essence. Human desires are directed toward objects, goals, and meanings which lie beyond nature for their fulfilment, and which serve as standards for the criticism and remodelling of human nature and conduct. Thus "what guides our wishes and instigates all the remaking is a spark not lighted in 'nature'" (5, p. 45). And so the theory of man leads logically to the consideration of a reality beyond nature.

The Self as Will-to-Power

With naturalism Hocking views human nature, like animal nature in general, to consist of instincts, patterns of behavior which, though untaught, exhibit a more or less complex series of operations requiring the use of specific organs, responding to particular stimuli, and leading to ends favorable to the survival of the individual or the species. The purposiveness of instincts indicates the presence of rudimentary consciousness, since it involves *a priori* expectations as to the ends that will be realized by responses to given stimuli. For man this signifies that prior to experience there exists an internal knowledge of *"what good is,"* although experience alone teaches "what *things* are good" (5, p. 91). "(T)he ideal is a joint product of experience and the latent idea of good" (5, p. 92). Human instincts, moreover, "have a region of coalescence, being related as the fingers of a hand rather than as the separate twigs in a bundle" (5, p. 87). Hence man is not reduced to a bundle of instincts, for the instincts are properly offshoots of a more fundamental motive, or interest, which functions as "a permanent principle of selection" (5, p. 90). This permanent principle is what Hocking calls the "will," for "to have a stable policy is to have, in the specific sense of the word, a *will*" (5, p. 92). The instinctive center of the human being is the *will-to-power*. Not a desire merely to survive or exist, the will-to-power is, more radically, the "active and creative quality" of man (5, p. 96). Not physical but spiritual energy, this will-to-power is the self.

Mind and Body

Hocking's idealistic conception of human nature is conspicuous in his statement that the body is "the symbol of the mind, not the mind of the body" (5, p. 108). Equating the essence of man with the will-to-power, conceived as spiritual energy, Hocking's theory of the relations of the self to its body repudiates materialism and its corollary in psychology, behaviorism, as well as "delusive dualism" and "points in the direction of some sort of spiritual monism" (19, p. 96). However refined the concept of matter offered by contemporary physics may be, mind cannot be reduced to matter nor deduced from it. For mind, unlike matter, is not restricted to space or to time (19, pp. 31-32); besides, it is the source of meaning and value (19, pp. 35, 43). The extant natural sciences study not the mind itself, but "substitutes for mind, —systems of objects which are equivalent to mind only for certain restricted purposes,—Near-minds, we may call them." To consider mind as an object in nature with a specific spatiotemporal situation and dominated by inexorable sequences of causality is to neglect, on one side, the "boundless depth of selfhood," and, on the other, the direction of the mind beyond existence "toward the non-existent essence—the good" (20).

Despite emphasis upon the primacy of the mind, Hocking has acknowledged the necessity of the body. He has defined the self as "a system of *purposive behavior emerging from a persistent hope*" (19, p. 46). The core of the self is its hope, its will to do and be some value which, at present merely a possibility, may be realized through directed action and behavior. As hope, the self is mind, unrestricted to present time and place and imbued with future meaning and value. As a system of behavior, the self is embodied; it has need of a body. Here immediate experience, upon which Hocking's idealism joins hands with common sense, justifies the distinction between the self and its body, while it underscores their close relationship. Not only does the self have a sense of intimate being with a body that belongs to it, but also its abilities and desires, though springing perhaps from the mind, refer to a body as indispensable aspect of their source (19, pp. 78-80). Even the distinction between thought and deed, upon which the existence of the self as a moral agent depends, demands that the self have a body (19, p. 81). "A self without a body would be a self without a will" (19, p. 84). And character, consisting largely in habits, requires the body as the storehouse in which the deeds of the self "shall leave *an accumulation of power* behind them" (19, p. 85). Finally, only through the body can the self "*give and take* with the world beyond" (19, p. 94). Hence, "the self cannot be without its body," although the body is not an appendage or tool but an organ of the self (19, p. 95).

Though necessary to the self, the body is dependent upon the self, and not the converse. Indeed, the body is a part of the self. Nevertheless, the self has nature over against it, being but half of all it perceives, and the body is a part of nature. "As a Mind, man does not see himself as part of nature, but *nature is over against him,* as a field of objects, *his* objects. As a Body, he is a part of nature" (19, p. 8). As a part of the self and also a part of nature, the body must serve two masters. As a part of nature, the body must conform in its behavior to the objective sequences of physical causality. Although nature is objective—its otherness indicated by the "given quality of sense data," its "relentless order," and its "publicity" (19, p. 126)—this objective otherness of nature depends upon other minds, in particular, upon a community of minds. Nature belongs "to a community of selves: it is not within any one of them, but it might be an identical part of all of them" (19, p. 135). All the wills of different selves converge in the will to live together, establishing the lawfulness and the publicity of nature. For Hocking, nature is an other, over against him and before him, and as such it is that which is to be used. In this sense nature, like the body, is an organ of the self (19, p. 141).

Freedom

Human freedom comes into clear focus. Whereas the body is always situated in a particular space and a particular time, the mind is capable of thinking all-space and even a plurality of spaces, and it enjoys a time-span inclusive of the past and future. The mind, or self, then, may inhabit simultaneously a plurality of spaces and of times, and so is *"space-free* as the body is not" (19, p. 31) and *"time-free* as the body is not time-free" (19, p. 35). "As a vinculum between a plurality of space-time

orders" (19, p. 177), the human self is free. Just as a man
who is informed that he is a factor in a causal series
wholly determining his actions may find freedom in reflection on or self-awareness of his position, since it reveals to him new alternatives (19, pp. 155-156), so a
man discovers when he reflects upon the laws of nature
that, despite their status in nature, they are instances of
the law of meaning. As Hocking has said: "Things hap-
pen because of what they mean to us; and as our meanings grow, things take different courses. Nature is a realm
of common and steadfast ingredients of will: its relia-
bleness is implied in the law of meaning" (19, p. 161).

By reflection, then, the self faces not a single spatiotemporal course but a plurality of spaces and times. By
reflection, too, it is confined to no single causal order
but finds alternative systems of meaning enabling it to
reconstruct the laws of nature. Reflection, therefore, is
the key to human freedom; and as there are degrees of
reflection, there are degrees of freedom, corresponding
to "the liveliness" of hope that is the kernel of the self
(19, p. 169) and "the degrees of our own reality" (19,
p. 170). "Our ultimate freedom," Hocking has asserted,
"lies in the fact that we are free to control the degree of
our freedom" (19, p. 169).

Conscience

Though the themes of freedom and the will-to-power
have been the cues for modernists to strike down the re-
straints of morality, they become for Hocking indispensable elements in the development of man into a moral
agent. Resident in the will-to-power is conscience, which
"is at once, in some sort of germ, deposited in man's
original nature, and at the same time one of the chief
instruments of his remaking" (5, p. 114). Now conscience is not an outgrowth of social pressure, since social imperatives are meaningful only if they address and
arouse internally felt senses of obligation: "In brief, the

'You ought' addresses itself to the answering 'I ought' within; and unless the 'I ought' responds, it has missed its target" (5, p. 118). Nor is conscience a separate moral faculty wholly independent of, or opposed to, the life of man. Rather it "stands outside the instinctive life of man, not as something separate, but as an awareness of the success or failure of that life in maintaining its status and its growth" (5, p. 123). Whereas conscience is the intellectual ally of the will-to-power, sin is the intervening and obstructing factor in the realization of the will-to-power.

Remaking Man

Remaking human nature is part of original human nature, since the will itself transforms its fragmentary and particular impulses, and each transformation, tantamount to an alteration of desire, requires the will in conjunction with outer occasions which furnish the materials and incentives for self-judgment. Experience is just this "co-operation of inner with outer factors" (5, p. 172). Furthermore, experience translates general instincts into particular habits by means of the principle of pleasure and pain, and by means of an intellectual factor, an after-image which accompanies any action. The recall of this after-image prior to any action controls the continuance or cessation of the action. In this sense, "the transformation of instinct, under experience, consists essentially in the series of hypotheses which a given mind adopts,— hypotheses about the ways in which impulses are to be followed in order to satisfy the complete will" (5, p. 187). For example, the general instinct of pugnacity is first manifested as undirected destructiveness, but as the agent who has suffered injury further specifies this instinct, it assumes the form of revenge. When the agent discerns that revenge falls short of the whole aim, pugnacity emerges as punishment. Hence, "the work of experience is the dialectic of the will" (5, p. 187).

Hocking's theory of the remaking of human nature accentuates the role of the individual human being. Whatever advance society makes in the direction of higher moral values is achieved as a continuation of a moral development begun within the dialectic of individual experience. "The will has a way of its own, through and athwart custom" (5, p. 195); and "man is to be found in his *Sehnsucht*, his longing or yearning, rather than in his accomplished ends" (5, p. 242). As "man, if not by nature good, has a natural bent to goodness" (5, p. 195), his subjection to social modelling, at its best, continues this "inward righting-tendency" and, at its worst, is nothing but an "elaborate social meddling" (5, p. 199). Here Hocking has located what he earlier described as "the valid basis of an individualistic theory of society" (5, p. xi). "The individual life, with its natural dialectic, (is) . . . the standard to which social pressures must conform" (5, p. 209). Not only must the society adhere to the postulate of identical ideals, according to which "(w)hat others wish must be identical with what I myself wish to be" (5, p. 213), it must also, in the institution of the State, transform every competitive interest into a "non-competitive, or an ingredient in a non-competitive interest" (5, p. 227).

When institutions excessively deform human nature, the resultant dissatisfaction recoils upon the institutions and causes them to be changed (5, p. 248). Against the pressures of society stands the conscience of the individual, and while the individual may attack an existing order when it fails to measure up to his moral demand, the society in turn may put down the individual as criminal or rebel. "Here lies the perpetual and unavoidable opening for tragedy in history," Hocking has remarked. "The last relations of individuals and societies are found in the darkness of solitary judgment" (5, p. 282).

In transforming human nature, society leaves some essential part of man out of its scheme. The will-to-power divides into the major instincts of ambition and love, the former giving rise to the public order and the latter generating the private order, e.g., the family. Man alternates between these two orders, but since "neither order is capable of including the other" (5, p. 308), this life of alternation is incomplete. The values of the private human being, while appreciated within the family, never find satisfactory expression within the public order, although the public order possesses a scope and objective stability which the private order lacks. If man's instinctive nature is to be satisfied in its totality, "there must be an objective arena of unlimited scope . . . in which a veritable and unqualified success of some sort is possible. . . . There must be, in brief, an *adequate and attainable object* for the human will to power" (5, p. 314). Art and Religion are two such arenas, and, though regarded as social institutions, they "appeal primarily and originally to the exploring and originating self" (5, p. 315).

Art constitutes a world created by the will-to-power, and so affords a measure of absolute success to the instinctive nature of man. Nonetheless, it falls short of the complete satisfaction and transformation of human desires. Its objects, created symbols of beauty, prove unstable except insofar as they refer to a reality with which Religion properly deals. This is not to minimize the significant role that Art plays in transforming the instincts of man, but it is to recognize that it does not touch much of what is essential and profound in man.

The Special Role of Religion

Only Religion can save this surplus in man neglected by the other agencies affecting and remaking human nature. More than this, Religion bears upon the whole man, subordinating all agencies to its own all-encompassing operations. Despite the contrast Religion, with its emphasis upon the power of the supernatural, offers to Life, it remains nonetheless the moral substance of Life and its institutions, the objective arena of the will-to-power. "There is a 'spirit of the laws,' something which one might call a moral substance, which shows itself in a spontaneous faith in current institutions and ideals and fellow citizens, a willingness to serve them and work with them, a spirit which society can neither give nor take away, and yet without which there is no society" (5. p. 301). This moral substance is religious in origin, so that, in a fundamental sense, the will of God underlies the will-to-power which is central to instinctive human nature.

In remaking original human nature, no religion, according to Hocking, is more radical and effective than Christianity. Christianity does not attend solely to external human conduct; rather, it addresses its injunctions to the inner emotions and volitions of men. What it commands is love, not merely neighborly conduct. Thus Christianity requires nothing less than a "complete transformation" of human instincts (5, p. 367). Its effectiveness is evident in the transformation of such basic general instincts as pugnacity, sex, love, and ambition. Transformation is not repression; it is simply more adequate satisfaction; and satisfaction under Christianity continues to flow from the socially acceptable transformations: "the absolute which Christianity prescribes . . . intends to live with the relative, not displace it" (5, p. 394).

Ambition illustrates the point. For Hocking, "ambition is the essence of religion" (5, p. 398), just as it is the ground of institutions in the public order. In the early stages of the dialectic of experience the will-to-power as ambition is satisfied with power *over* objects and persons, which economic and political institutions afford. In time it comes to revise its aims. "(T)he pursuit of power-over becomes the pursuit of power-for. As power must have its object, it is so far dependent upon the existence of the object, and must seek its welfare. . . . Christianity places itself at this point and defines, as the goal of the transformation of ambition, *the conferring of spiritual life*" (5, p. 398). Transforming ambition into missionary zeal, Christianity simultaneously imparts by transformation the highest satisfactions the other basic instincts seek, love becoming the passion for souls and pugnacity the passion of converting souls from evil to good (21). The missionary intention of Christianity, therefore, "is the same form of the will as that which gave the final meaning to human love, the will to confer immortal life. . . . It is, in truth, *the point in which the meanings of all instincts converge.* It is the positive meaning given by Christianity to the human will as a whole" (5, pp. 399-400).

Presumption is the crux of Christianity, because Christianity professes to be the only Way for the salvation of souls. Attaching to all Christians, this presumption gives rise to a grave dilemma: "To be disposed to save others, we must first be saved ourselves; yet to be saved ourselves we must be disposed to save others" (5, pp. 408-409). The Christian is required to act like God yet be humble; the paradox is rectified only if somehow he participates in the will of God. Thus Christianity claims that the individual derives his power from the outside: "the power is conferred upon him by way of a loan. It is nothing inherent in us that is to do the work, but something in which we participate" (5, p. 409). "The salvation of a soul requires a divine intervention" (5, p. 418). The Christian conception of God as a restless pursuer of souls becomes Hocking's doctrine of "the Divine Aggression" (5, pp. 416-425). This Divine Aggression effectuates ultimate transformation of instinctive human nature. Because God is an aggressive lover able to invade the wills of men, individual wills to power are transmitted into love of God and of man.

The Divine Aggression is joined by the dynamism of the human will-to-power to press man to engage in unending creative endeavors. Despite his finite status man seeks a meaning to his life which reaches beyond its natural frame. In its deepest expression the will-to-power is "*the will to overcome death*" (5, p. 167). Within man emerges the *soul*—i.e., the self as capable "of feeling the natural bent of desire as invested with the omen of finitude" and yet "aware of, and seeking to control, its metaphysical status. It is original man in his full stature" (5, p. 168). By virtue of the will-to-power, man is "a self-changing being," and his moral quality is "simply the self-conscious will taking a broad cosmic responsibility for the work of self-being, making itself present partner with man's remoter destiny" (5, p. 171).

Man and the Metaphysical Categories

In this context Hocking's later discussion of the metaphysical categories is illuminating. (22, pp. 529-545). These categories are all empirical inductions from human experience. First comes the category of Fact, of simply what is, the immediately felt datum, so obvious, yet so problematic, endured as the conflict between a man's sense of freedom and the arbitrariness of his situation. The category of Fact is descriptive of the plurality of facts, although it is not competent to apply to all reality, but must be supplemented by the background to relate the plural facts. This background of relatedness is the empirical category of the Field, exemplified originally by Space and Time. Since pluralism is ruled out by Hocking in that every plurality of facts is embraced by a field, there must be a Field that embraces all Fields embracing the facts. Now such a Field of Fields is not identical with the conservative system of nature, because the conservative, being uncreative, cannot be its own source. Only the creative can be the ultimate Field, and since only the self is creative "the Self here functions as the Field of Fields" (22, p. 542). At this point a third category, Destiny, enters. Though empirical, the category of Destiny is "a speculative and distant future—the reverse of anything that could be immediately felt" (22, p. 545).

These three metaphysical categories are intimately linked with the topic of human immortality, or to adhere strictly to Hocking's terminology, "immortability, the conditional possibility of survival" (9, p. 74). According to fundamental human feelings and conviction man ought to survive natural death (9, pp. 76, 218), but the question remains: How is immortality possible? (9, p. 189) Hocking's answer is double-pronged.

First, the self is dual. Man is at once (1) "the excursive self, which is (relatively) actual, finite, time-limited, time-discontinuous, created," and (2) "the reflective self, which is (relatively) potential, infinite, time-inclusive, time-continuous, creative" (9, p. 59). While the excursive self is dated and vanishes at death, "the reflective self, having attained a measure of reality in that creative deed, is ready for another stage, not excluding the first, in knowing and embodying the depth of being" (9, p. 152).

Second, and here Hocking's argument is amplified in connection with the physics of space and time, the single space-time system, enclosing the human self within its particular arbitrary situation, need not be its permanent prison, especially insofar as the self is regarded as "a way of linkage—may we say *vinculum*—holding plural spaces within a brace of simultaneous awareness" (9, p. 229). Although the self, in its excursive function, is bound up in the space-time world of physical nature, it yet reflects upon alternative systems of events from which distinctive space-time fields are derived, as, indeed, its freedom hinges upon this confrontation by the self of the alternative possible events with their alternative spatial fields (9, p. 229). There is no single whole of space, integrating plural spaces, apart from the self. In this sense the self is a "field of fields" (9, p. 234). At every moment in its experience the self may be aware of another spatial field different from the spatial field of natural events.

This distinctive spatial field is the other world (9, pp. 233-235).

Is this other world imaginary or real? "The criterion of reality is creativity, both for the world and the individual" (9, p. 243). Confronting the other world in the concrete exercise of his creative freedom, man's reflective self does not perish at the hand of death, but passes on into the other world where, with God, he continues to create. The Destiny of the human self is, as Hocking has said, "a Destiny for free souls, not a Fate—a Destiny without predestination. It is a call to the finite creator, not to carry out a set of statutes, preordained, nor to realize an ideal type, but to fill a need which is a world need, that meaning be realized in his unique and factual situation, a contribution to the life of God, as the hidden meaning of creation *ex nihilo*" (22, p. 547).

THEORY OF POLITICS

In the Preface to *Man and the State*, his major work in political philosophy, Hocking has said that "politics needs a science of human nature, that is, a psychology; a science of right, that is, an ethics; and a view of man's place in the world, that is, a metaphysics" (6, pp. ix-x). Despite the temptation to treat political philosophy as a logical extension of psychological, ethical, and metaphysical concepts, however, Hocking has constructed his theory of the state and its relations to other states in a world society by constant reference to hard facts and current problems. Hocking's empirical method is obscured mainly by his style in such works as *Man and the State, Present Status of the Philosophy of Law and of Rights* (23), and *The Lasting Elements of Individualism* (24). However, it is quite clear in such other books as *Morale and Its Enemies* (25), *The Spirit of World Politics, Freedom of the Press* (26), *Experiment in Education,* and *Strength of Men and Nations* (27).

Since political groupings have their psychological origin in the instinctive nature of man, Hocking has defined politics as an art founded upon human impulses
but practiced by means of conscious purposes. Though
common interests unite men, they also divide them—as
men, for example, join in the hunt but clash over the
apportionment of the bag. The first important task of
politics is to resolve the conflicts provoked by common
interests. With attention focused on arbitration, the
politician appears in the guise of the judge. The other
great task of politics pertains to what Hocking has
called "the commotive process." This process is "group-
forming" rather than "term-making," and consists "in
bringing the scattered intentions of several minds into
the current of common action" (6, p. 14). Here the emphasis is on doing things, i.e., making history, and the
politician assumes the guise of a leader. Yet, as Hocking
has remarked, "It must be recognized that the judicial
process and the commotive process are abstract aspects
of a single art" (6, p. 20).

The State

Tracing the rise of states back to the instinctive nature of man, Hocking initially defined the state as a
"stable or partly stable" arrangement of arbitrational
and commotive processes, an arrangement realized when
human impulses, which are the springs of political actions and concerns, are surveyed by conscious purposes.
"The state is a relatively stable artificial social environment, subject to slow change as the political art adds to
its cumulative store of generalizations, legal concepts,
principles of settlement, and so perfects its own work"
(6, p. 33).

As a stable environment established by the conscious
will of man, the state, in spite of its artificiality, is rooted
in the nature of man. And the essence of man is the
will-to-power, but this will-to-power is rational, not brut-

ish. "The will to live, in man, takes the form of the will to power, i.e., the will to be in conscious knowing control of such energies as the universe has, and to work with them in reshaping that universe" (6, p. 309). Prerequisite for the satisfaction of the human will-to-power are such conditions beyond individual control as "a permanent order, an available storehouse of acquired wisdom, the conquest of disorder by peace, and of chance by impersonal reason and justice" (6, p. 323). Briefly, Hocking's hypothesis is that the state exists to establish these objective conditions (6, p. 325).

The state, further, is the confluence of the wills of its members into a common environment which, while conditioning each member's activities, yet affords him opportunities for the satisfactions of his own interests. Consequently, the state approximates an extension of the personalities of its individual members, although it is *not* a person in its own right. Hocking's theory is summed up in the term "will-circuit," representing an idea which is reminiscent of Rousseau's conception of the general will, provided this conception is interpreted strictly in individualist terms. Thus "the state is the circuit required by the will to power of each member, coincident for all the people of a defined territory, and including them" (6, p. 371).

Individualism and the Co-Agent State

Hocking's political philosophy is individualistic but not liberal. As early as *Human Nature and Its Remaking* Hocking had expressed the hope of sketching "the valid basis of an individualistic theory of society" (5, p. xi); and in *The Lasting Elements of Individualism* this hope is fully realized. Individualism is defined as "simply the belief in the human individual as the ultimate unit of social structure" (24, pp. 3-4), and liberalism is interpreted to be "a faith that the welfare of any society may be trusted to the individuals who compose it" (24, p. 5).

Convinced that "(l)iberalism . . . has been the most successful conscious political hypothesis of human history" (24, p. 38), Hocking has contended that it "has done its work" (24, p. 40). Because of three main defects: the incapacity to achieve social unity, the separation of rights from duties, and the loss of emotional force (24, pp. 40 ff), liberalism must be superseded.

But what sociopolitical ideal is to replace liberalism? Hocking's conception of the future ideal society underscores two basic elements: the commotive function and the incompressible individual. "The commotive function is that function which enables, and leads, a group of men to move together in the achievement of a common purpose" (24, pp. 106-107). This commotive function cannot "ever be built on a purely economic motive, which is essentially competitive" (24, p. 114), but must well up "from unacknowledged springs of human feeling and from a passion for justice" (24, p. 114). Ethical passion is its substance. Lacking purpose and emotional force to weld men together into a cohesive whole, liberal societies have met their worst failure. The ideal society, therefore, must possess the commotive function, its existence translated into purposive action. And the second prerequisite for the ideal society is the acknowledgment of the "incompressible individual." The confluence of individual wills into the will-circuit of the state occurs rightly only on condition that "public purposes are prolongations of individual purposes, and derive their life therefrom. The individual thus remains mentally prior to the state; and the principle of every future state must be this: *that every man shall be a whole man*" (24, p. 133). Thus individuals and not collectivities are the sole creative agents responsible for cultural advance. Herein resides the "immortal soul" of liberalism, its emphatic defense of "the right (of individual men) to generate ideas and get them worked into the social fabric" (24, pp. 137-138).

The ideal state, then, is one which is an extension of

the individuals who compose it, or, to use Hocking's term, "the Co-agent State." "The co-agent state is the state for which this coincidence (of individual wills), now occasionally realized, is the normal state of things. The co-agent state is based on the unanimous action of free individuals" (24, p. 150). "The co-agent state is the state whose primary function is the commotive function issuing in action, which is at once particular, history-making action, and unanimous action, an extension of every citizen's will" (24, p. 151).

As Hocking has retained for his conception of the state the basic elements of individualism while adding the commotive function most conspicuously exercised in contemporary totalitarian societies, he also has adopted, with radical modification and adjustment, facets of political idealism and political realism, despite initial rejection of both. On the one hand, political idealism conceives the state as externalized reason, and consequently errs insofar as the state omits much that is rational and includes much that is irrational in its members (6, p. 49). On the other hand, political realism equates the state with force, and consequently errs to the extent that right attaches to the laws of a state even when they are violated by superior force (6, p. 70). Whereas the idealist is wrong in supposing that what ought to be really is, the realist, who recommends the study of facts exclusively and the disregard of values in political science, is wrong in taking the facts as the standards, in thereby tacitly accepting what is for what ought to be. "No fact," Hocking has stressed, "can evade the question of its justification, least of all a fact of human will" (6, p. 76). The political realist is essentially right, however, when he directs our attention to the role of power or force in the life of the state. Against anarchists who would destroy the power of the state and pluralists who would divide it among several lesser institutions, Hocking has defended the sovereign power of the state as the capacity to get things done and to make the final decisions. But he has never held the thesis of political realism that facts alone are significant and that ideals are trivial and impotent in political affairs. Granted that facts of sociability or of economics are causative in the structure of the state, they are not the sole causative principles, for sociability presupposes the prior existence of human individuals and economics requires the prior union of these individuals by social bonds. Even the emphasis of political realism upon power or force introduces the topic of will, and will, if it is anything, is purposive. This, Hocking remarks, obliges us "not to give up the search for a conception of the state's purpose which will explain . . . why the state does what it does, and why it refrains from doing what it does not do" (6, p. 107). This search is inductive, but it is "induction from the functions which the state *ought to have,* and from exclusion of functions it *ought not to have"* (6, p. 107). Here enters the political idealist, but his idealism is based not upon reason alone but upon rationalized will, or better, idealized force. What is the purpose of the state as rationalized will? Hocking's answer is that "the form of the state's aim is the making of history; its substance is the making of men" (6, p. 173).

Laws and Rights

Now to regard the state as maker of history and of men is to move strikingly near totalitarian statolatry. However, Hocking's political philosophy is an individualist theory not only because it considers individuals the sole sources of creativity within the state, but also because it respects individual rights as essential components of justice. In the *Present Status of the Philosophy of Law and of Rights* Hocking has established as a fundamental principle of law the maxim "that no known injustice may be done" (23, p. 49). The justification of law by reference to its utility to culture, therefore, is subordinate to the demands of justice, demands which are known independently of law and social utility (23, p. 50). Law must serve the culture of a nation, since what does injury to a culture is never known to be just (23, pp. 50-51), and what serves a culture is never known to be unjust (23, p. 52). But law may be evaluated and criticized—in fact, must be—by appeal to justice. And although it would be easy to define this ideal of justice by adoption of the traditional doctrine of natural rights, Hocking has explicitly introduced two departures from the natural rights doctrine: (1) a reduction of the list of rights, and (2) a specification that rights are conditional. Concerning the conditionality of rights, Hocking has stated: ". . . it seems to us that one of the conditions under which any man ought to hold his rights is *his own good-will* toward his fellow citizens and the public welfare" (23, p. 55). Because a moral condition is indispensable to an individual's claim to and exercise of a "right," legal rights prove to be "presumptive" rights, and are therefore changeable whenever, by virtue of new evidence or altered social conditions, the presumptions change.

Well, then, are all rights relative? No, says Hocking. "It is right, or absolutely right, that an individual should develop the powers that are in him. He may be said to have a 'natural right' to become what he is capable of becoming. This is his only natural right" (23, p. 74).

The relativity and conditionality of all rights except this one natural right in no way signal the attenuation of specific cherished rights, as Hocking makes clear by his strong defense of such rights in *Freedom of the Press*. The rights pertaining to speech, press, worship, etc., must be preserved not only against the encroachments of the state but also against their abuse by private institutions and persons. Rights impose obligations upon their users as well as restrictions upon the state. The "most important freedom" is a duty and a right; it is "the freedom to perfect one's freedom" (26, p. 70). Freedom and rights, grounded within the individual, moreover, are rooted in his will-to-power. Nature and society may mould the forms the will-to-power assumes and even influence its directions, but they cannot touch it in its inviolable privacy. For Hocking the will-to-power emerges in its most intimate expression as the will-to-power through ideas. Self-perfection of this will is a duty which is tantamount to a moral obligation to seek out and adhere to the perception of the truth, and political institutions are morally bound to respect this inner freedom by specific guarantees.

International Politics and World Civilization

To the study of international relations Hocking has brought the same convictions about the primacy of metaphysics and of universal ethical principles that operate in his theories of man and of the state. In *Spirit of World Politics*, a book which is reminiscent of Montesquieu's *Spirit of the Laws* not solely because of its title, but also for its consideration of all the factors— economic, geographical, climatic, religious, philosophical —that converge to shape the constitutions of nations, Hocking says: "The philosophy of unlimited relativity is the negation of all international politics, both in thought and in practice. The only philosophy which can sustain any international understanding or undertaking or law is a philosophy which can recognize the common, universal, necessary element in our human standards of judgment. We must declare open war on the frivolities of our current pragmatisms, instrumentalisms, relativisms, agnosticisms and other modes of abandoning the necessary basis for all hopeful international life. Men enjoy and live in an identical reason." (7, pp. 21-22).

Formulated with specific reference to British and French Mandates in Africa and the Middle East after World War I, Hocking's philosophy of international

politics repudiates the prevailing tendency to divorce
ethics from politics, and it departs from the dominant
temper of the times by an avowed "(h)ostility . . . to
any kind of determinism, economic or other, which re-
signs the affairs of the world to the contest of interest
and Powers" (7, p. viii). Many of Hocking's charges
against British and French imperialism in Africa and
the Near East are now commonplaces, although they
were not so when they were written. But if the brunt of
criticism falls upon Britain and France, it could have
been directed elsewhere, had time and travel permitted
—at the United States for her treatment of Latin American nations (7, p. xi) and because of her refusal to
join the League of Nations (28). Even Zionism is held
culpable (7, pp. 363-392) for pressing its political ambi-
tions at the expense of the Arabs (29).

Hocking's theory of international politics, though
presented with specific problems in mind and containing particular recommendations, has not been superseded with the passage of the mandates, because it ex-
pounds political and moral propositions which claim
universal validity. At the level of specifics, Hocking's
insistence that the capacity of a nation to learn from its
mistakes, rather than a demonstrated efficiency to man-
age its affairs on a par with that of the most advanced
states, be taken as the criterion for granting it independence, and that this capacity be judged by an international body, such as the League of Nations, is pertinent today. And Hocking's conception of the nation as
an experiment in living which enriches the world of
man justifies a pluralism of nation states. This view, on
the one hand, provides theoretical support for the pressing practical problems of co-existence between the United
States and the Soviet Union, and, on the other hand,
sustains the aspirations of other nations to remain neutral and to express themselves culturally in freedom and

independence without being strait-jacketed by the models the Great Powers aim to impose.

Recently Hocking's internationalism has found expression in books dealing with the relations between the United States and Germany and the Soviet Union. In *Experiment in Education* Hocking, having employed to good advantage a visiting professorship at the University of Leiden in 1946-1947 to gather first-hand experience of the American military government in Germany after World War II, examines, in the words of the subtitle, "What We Can Learn from Teaching Germany." What we can learn is (1) that Germany's rejection of Nazism is due not to the "knight errantry" of American educational programs but to her own political experience and ethical awareness, and, more important, (2) America would do well to adopt for her own system of education German standards for intellectual excellence and creativeness.

Hocking's latest book, *Strength of Men and Nations,* is emphatically "in spirit a pamphlet, a tract for the times" (27, p. 7). The urgency of this "Message to the USA *vis-a-vis* the USSR" stems from the ominous menace of thermonuclear war. "It has become the fate of this moment of world history to confront the Worst, the blank end of things. To see the Worst as actual possibility, to see it steadily and not retreat—this is our particular call to adequacy, perhaps to greatness" (27, p. 124). Contending that capitalism and communism cannot be a real issue between the United States and the Soviet Union, since advanced societies incorporate elements of both economic systems, and that basically the United States and the Soviet Union are diverse but converging and complementary experiments in living and hence are capable of coexistence, Hocking urges Americans to accept the "call of greatness" and engage in a diplomacy of "creative risk" with the Russians. In this way the vicious circle of distrust, in which each nation girds for war against the other, may be broken, and a way let open for peace with justice.

With civilization tottering on the brink of thermonuclear disaster Hocking is confident that a peaceful resolution of the conflict will result from an act of creative trust by one power bloc in the other. And though the plurality of nation states persists as fertile ground for hostilities, this plurality, testifying to a multiplicity of experiments in living, is desirable. Such a plurality of nation states, each presumably the depository of sovereign power within its territory, constitutes an opportunity for prophecy about the coming world civilization. At present, notes Hocking, the all-powerful state is found impotent in such fundamental areas as crime, education, family relations, economy, and recreation, and this impotence he ascribes to the separation of the modern state from religion (8, pp. 1-20). Religion alone can supply the moral motivation upon which the state depends. Consider, for example, the punishment of the criminal. The overt penalty lacks moral force unless the criminal apprehends that justice is being done, and this recognition requires that he possess a sense of moral obligation, a sense which in the last analysis has a religious origin. Of course the impotence of the state is, at first thought, an ostensible obstruction to an emerging civilization. Upon further reflection it can be seen to mark a gain, since it betrays the inadequacy of a modernity which, by isolating each man in a solitary solipsism claiming rights without corresponding duties and by positing a valueless objective nature, has emasculated the state through secularization and so has brought man to his present impasse. It is therefore practically necessary to pass beyond modernity if we are to attain the coming world civilization, although this passage must be accomplished without discarding the gains of modernity—individual rights and scientific method, which Hocking calls the "unlosables" in history (8, pp. 49 f).

At the theoretical level philosophy provides the conceptual instruments for a passage beyond modernity; at the practical level the task falls to Christianity to effectuate the coming of the world civilization. For Christianity, although the origin of modernity, contains the resources to pass beyond it, since it is addressed to the instinctive nature of men, remaking human passions and desires in behalf of higher aspirations. However, the effectiveness of Christianity as the agent for the coming of the world civilization depends upon its reconception. Here Hocking's thesis in the recent *Coming World Civilization* (1956) iterates a line of argument he expounded earlier in *Living Religions and a World Faith* (1940).

Instead of rudely displacing one religion by another or of crudely synthesizing the various elements of different religions, the method of reconception intuitively grasps, i.e., induces, the essence of a religion, and discovers its capacity for concrete universality, its inclusiveness of the values of alternative religions without sacrificing its own fundamental historicity (30, pp. 190-208). The reconception of Christianity unleashes its essence, and this essence, Hocking says, is threefold: (1) faith that the core of being is a suffering, active, creative, loving mind; (2) the code that demands the rebirth of human desire and instinct, its remaking to love; and (3) the deed that hinges on the identification of the essence of Christianity with an existent historical force seeking realization in time (8, p. 108). Essential Christianity is, then, not restricted to the West: *"it was in making 'the West' that Christianity became 'Western'"* (8, p. 127). Hence the passage beyond modernity in philosophy and the reconception of Christianity in religion, tasks to which Hocking has unstintingly contributed, are both advances in theory and preparations in the making of a world civilization.

NOTES TO CHAPTER 2

1. William Ernest Hocking, *Types of Philosophy*, 3d ed. (New York: Charles Scribner's Sons, 1959). The first and second editions of this book appeared in 1929 and 1939, respectively. Quotes in the text are from the third edition, which Hocking prepared in collaboration with his son, Richard, professor of philosophy at Emory University.

2. William Ernest Hocking, *Varieties of Educational Experience* (*Being fragments of a conceivable educational autobiography, serving as connective tissue, and to some extent as interpretation, for papers on education to be placed in Harvard College Library*) (Madison, New Hampshire, 1952). This mimeographed work, deposited in Archives, Widener Library, Harvard University, is divided into two parts: Part I (1952, pp. 1-44) covers Hocking's experience with elementary education. Part II (1954, pp. 1-83) deals with secondary and higher education, including discussions of his and Mrs. Hocking's part in the founding of Shady Hill School.

3. William Ernest Hocking, "The Elementary Experience of Other Conscious Being in its Relations to the Elementary Experience of Physical and Reflexive Objects" (Cambridge, Mass.: Harvard, 1904). This typewritten thesis is deposited in Archives, Harvard's Widener Library. Of it Richard C. Gilman has written: "The main thesis of the work, which might be restated as 'How We Know Other Minds' is the original statement of Chapters XVII to XX of *The Meaning of God in Human Experience.*" *The Bibliography of William Ernest Hocking from 1898 to 1951* (Waterville, Maine: Colby College, 1951), p. 4.

4. William Ernest Hocking, *The Meaning of God in Human Experience: A Philosophic Study of Religion* (New Haven: Yale University Press, 1912). Since a few verbal changes were made in its second printing in 1913, all citations will be made to the second printing.

5. William Ernest Hocking, *Human Nature and Its Remaking* (New Haven: Yale University Press, 1918). A new, revised edition appeared in 1923 and a printing of the revised edition with additions occurred in 1929. References here are to the 1929 printing.

6. William Ernest Hocking, *Man and the State* (New Haven: Yale University, 1926).

7. William Ernest Hocking, *The Spirit of World Politics with Special Studies of the Near East* (New York: The Macmillan Co., 1932).

8. William Ernest Hocking, *The Coming World Civilization* (New York: Harper & Brothers, 1956).

9. William Ernest Hocking, *The Meaning of Immortality in Human Experience Including Thoughts on Death and Life* (New York: Harper & Brothers, 1957). *Thoughts on Death and Life* originally was published in 1937. All references will be made to the 1957 edition.

10. William Ernest Hocking, *Experiment in Education; What We Can Learn from Teaching Germany* (Chicago: Henry Regnery Co., 1954).

11. William Ernest Hocking, *Science and the Idea of God* (Chapel Hill: University of North Carolina Press, 1944). See also William Ernest Hocking, "Science in Its Relation to Value and Religion," in *Rice Institute Pamphlet*, XXIX (1942).

12. William Ernest Hocking, "What Does Philosophy Say?" *Philosophical Review*, XXXVII (1928), 133-153. This was Hocking's presidential address to the Eastern Division of the American Philosophical Association, delivered December 1927 in Chicago, Ill.

13. William Ernest Hocking, "From the Early Days of the 'Logische Untersuchungen,'" *Edmund Husserl 1859-1959; Recueil commemoratif publié à l'occasion du centenaire de la naissance du philosophe* (Hague: Martinus Nijhoff, 1959). Citing Husserl as one of the prophets of the widened empiricism, Hocking adds: "To this technical *Wesensschau*, I have come to see, we must add for the furtherwidened empiricism of our opening era, a just recognition of the presence in experience of *three aspects of metaphysical reality*—the Self, the Other, and the Thou" (p. 7).

14. Marcel dedicated his *Journal Metaphysique* (1927) to Bergson and Hocking. See Hocking, "Marcel and the Ground Issues of Metaphysics," *Philosophy and Phenomenological Research*, XIV (1954), 439-469.

15. See the following articles by William Ernest Hocking: "Outline Sketch of a System of Metaphysics," *Philosophical Essays in Memory of Edmund Husserl*, Marvin Farber, ed. (Cambridge: Harvard University Press, 1940), pp. 251-261; "Metaphysics: Its Function, Consequences, and Criteria," *Journal of Philosophy*, XLIII (1946), 365-378; "Fact and Destiny" (I), *Review of Metaphysics*, IV (1950), 1-12; "Fact and Destiny" (II), *Review of Metaphysics*, IV (1951), 319-342.

16. J. A. Martin, Jr., *Empirical Philosophies of Religion* (New York: King's Crown Press, 1945).

17. William Ernest Hocking, "The Ontological Argument in Royce and Others," *Contemporary Idealism in America*, Clifford Barrett, ed. (New York: The Macmillan Co., 1932).

18. William Ernest Hocking, *What Man Can Make of Man* (New York and London: Harper & Brothers, 1942).

19. William Ernest Hocking, *The Self: Its Body and Freedom* (New Haven: Yale University Press, 1928).

20. William Ernest Hocking, "Mind and Near Mind," *Proceedings of the Sixth International Congress of Philosophy*, Edgar Sheffield Brightman, ed. (New York & London: Longmans, Green and Co., 1927), pp. 210, 212.

21. Hocking's conviction that missionary work is centrally significant in the spiritual life of man and in the transformation of human instinctive life into its highest spiritual forms is borne out by the time and effort he has devoted to the problems of missions. In 1931-1932 he served as Chairman of the Commission of Appraisal appointed by the Laymen's Foreign Missions Inquiry to study missions in the Far East and to make recommendations concerning their future activities. Hocking edited the report of the Commission and authored Part I, Chapters 1-4, entitled "General Principles." See *Re-Thinking Missions: A Laymen's Inquiry after One Hundred Years* (New York: Harper & Brothers, 1932). Perhaps it should be emphasized that Hocking did not view Christianity as the missionary religion with a monopoly on spiritual values. In fact, he recommended that Christian missionaries come to appreciate positively the spiritual values of the religions indigenous to the Orient.

22. William Ernest Hocking, "Fact, Field, and Destiny: Inductive Elements of Metaphysics," *Review of Metaphysics*, XI (1958).

23. William Ernest Hocking, *Present Status of the Philosophy of Law and of Rights* (New Haven: Yale University Press, 1926).

24. William Ernest Hocking, *The Lasting Elements of Individualism* (New Haven: Yale University Press, 1937).

25. William Ernest Hocking, *Morale and Its Enemies* (New Haven: Yale University Press, 1918).

26. William Ernest Hocking, *Freedom of the Press: A Framework of Principle* (Chicago: University of Chicago Press, 1947).

27. William Ernest Hocking, *Strength of Men and Nations; A Message to the USA vis-a-vis the USSR* (New York: Harper & Brothers, 1959).

28. See Hocking's letter to the *New York Times*, 70, October 25, 1920, p. 14, in which he stated his opposition to the election of Harding since it threatened America's entry into the League and argued that "the habitual Republican voters (as he identified himself) who want a prompt and honest entry into the League can do no other than vote for Cox."

29. For a recent statement of Hocking's stand on Zionism see his *Peace by Persuasion in the Middle East; an Analysis with Pro-*

posals for Solution of the Arab-Israeli Problem, with editorial commentary by V. C. Gildersleeve (New York: n. p., 1958).
30. William Ernest Hocking, *Living Religions and a World Faith* (New York: The Macmillan Co., 1940).

THE CONSTRUCTIVE PRAGMATISM OF GEORGE HERBERT MEAD

THE MEANING OF PRAGMATISM

Among the group of thinkers who gathered at the University of Chicago at the turn of the century and who soon came to be known as the "Chicago School," George Herbert Mead (1863-1931) after John Dewey was most prominent. Mead's achievement is evident in all its scope and depth not only in those scanty writings published during his life (1), but also in the four posthumously published books based upon his lectures and papers: his Carus lectures published as *The Philosophy of the Present* (2), notes from his lectures in his course in social psychology published as *Mind, Self and Society* (3), notes from his lectures in his course on "Movements of Thought in the Nineteenth Century" published under the same title (4), and unpublished papers, supplemented by notes from lectures, published as *The Philosophy of the Act* (5). In 1931 Dewey, describing Mead as "the most original mind in philosophy in America of the last generation," said, "I dislike to think what my own thinking might have been were it not for the seminal ideas which I derived from him" (6). Overshadowed by Dewey, whose ascendancy he acknowledged, Mead was never unappreciated. As Charles Morris has remarked, "If Dewey gives range and vision, Mead gave analytical depth and scientific precision. If Dewey is at once the rolling rim and many of the radiating spokes of the contemporary pragmatist wheel, Mead is the hub" (3, p. xi).

In rendering pragmatism scientifically precise and in imparting to it philosophical depth, Mead was concerned with what Arthur Murphy has called "constructive pragmatism" (2, p. xiii). Instead of dissipating itself in polemics against traditional doctrines, "constructive pragmatism," buoyed by its "enthusiasm for experience," has succeeded in detailed elucidation of the processes of knowing and of the structures of its objects.

Mead grasped the meaning of pragmatism within its historical setting and social milieu. Noting that "what philosophy has been doing, especially since the time of the Renaissance, is to interpret the results of science" (4, p. 343), he considered pragmatism a product of the conjunction of two scientific developments: behavioristic psychology and scientific methodology (4, p. 351). The behavioristic foundation of pragmatism stems from Darwin's theory of biological evolution. Viewing the living organism as engaged in an endless struggle for control over its environment, Darwin's theory entails a naturalistic conception of mind which radically redefines thinking or intelligence. "Thinking is an elaborate process of selecting, an elaborate process of presenting the world so that it will be favorable for conduct. . . . (T)he test of intelligence is found in action" (4, p. 345). The methodological foundation of pragmatism is rooted in research science, which is "only the evolutionary process grown self-conscious" (4, p. 364). For it, too, is essentially a problem-solving activity. And the problematic situations with which scientific method copes are similar to the obstacles with which animals struggle; both sets of problems obstruct activity, whether it be the activity of intelligence or the muscular-motor activities of organisms. The aim of the scientist in his laboratory, like that of the beast in the jungle, is to control facts, to cope with the environment so as to further activity. As Mead said: "The animal is doing the same thing the scientist is doing" (4, p. 346).

Springing from the peculiar confluence of two scientific developments, the behavioristic and the methodological, pragmatism concentrates both upon behavior, or conduct, and upon the verification of ideas by means of experience. This concern with conduct implies a theory of action, but except for Dewey's suggestions (including his paper on the reflex arc concept), no one before Mead had attempted to advance a philosophy of action on a large scale based on pragmatic principles. In regard to the empirical demand of pragmatism that ideas be subjected to the tests of experience, it is important to note that the pragmatic conception of experience, in Peirce, Dewey, and Mead, excludes the subjectivism usually associated with traditional empiricism. Not only is experience conceived in terms of verbs—in terms of doing rather than of passively receiving—but also it is understood to be a social process.

Mead's "constructive pragmatism" is based upon a theory of the act and of social experience. It includes a social theory of the mind and of the self. This theory, called "social behaviorism," has influenced the field of social psychology considerably. Here Mead's basic ideas go back to the early days of the Chicago School, to the earliest articles he published, and to the course in social psychology which he introduced at the University of Chicago in 1900. In that milieu, as Charles Morris reported, "the heavily charged psychological air precipitated itself into functional and behavioristic forms" (3, p. xii). Recently Mead's ideas have been revived in phenomenological and existential contexts. In the past decade his philosophy has confronted Husserlian phenomenology through the writings of Maurice Natanson (7), Buber's social anthropology through the works of Paul Pfuetze (8), and Zen Buddhism and Sartre's existentialism through the articles of Van Meter Ames (9). A Frenchman, David Victoroff, in the most sensitive and balanced study of Mead's philosophy to appear so far, has contended that Mead's thought spreads out from social psychology to general philosophical principles—that, in effect, his cosmology is built in the image of his sociology (10).

Although his work in social psychology gave Mead a lasting reputation, he sought to expand his philosophy into a cosmology and a metaphysics. More often than not, of course, the terms "metaphysics" and "metaphysical" in Mead's writings bear pejorative connotations because, like Dewey, he was critical of traditional metaphysics for stressing static values which transcend experience, for bifurcating mind from nature, and for seeking a finality alien to the scientist's method of "continued reconstruction in the face of events emerging in ceaseless novelty" (2, p. 102). However, Mead recognized another, more positive, significance of the term. In a posthumously published fragment he asked: "Is there a type of metaphysical thought that may be in some sense descriptive of the world so far as it comes within the range of our thought? Can we find out the essential characters of the world as they enter into our experience without attempting to present the universe as a whole?" (5, p. 626). His answer seems to have been affirmative. By first discovering the essential natures of the objects about us, we could, he wrote, "try to bring them into our actual conduct, our actual life, thus presenting a less transcendental view. That is, our philosophy has ceased to be other worldly in character; it is something that can be found in experience" (5, p. 627).

But how is a metaphysics based upon the principles of pragmatism possible? Does not metaphysics, except as a neo-Kantian critique of categories, always lead to transcendental leaps beyond experience, beyond this world? Mead never put the question quite so bluntly; however, his writings reveal at least the direction of an answer. Philosophy, he said, is "at home in the world in which we live and move and have our being" only so far as it "enables us, who are parts of this evolving universe, to capture the meaning which it has for us because its evolutionary process appears in us as intelligence" (5, p. 515). Thus Mead sought a cosmological philosophy, a metaphysics "concerned . . . with the import of the appearance and presence in the universe of human reflective intelligence—that intelligence which transforms causes and effects into means and consequences, reactions into responses, and termini of natural processes into ends-in-view" (5, p. 517).

According to pragmatism, scientific methodology is a problem-solving activity; its problems are specific, restricted to partial regions of a world which the scientist takes for granted; and its purpose is to find solutions that continue the activity. On the whole it would appear that knowledge is too self-interested and too narrow to allow room for the kind of investigations required by a cosmological philosophy. Mead's "constructive pragmatism," although operating within the framework of the pragmatic conception of inquiry as a problem-solving activity, nevertheless found a place for metaphysics, the concern with the most general conceptions of the world and the pursuit of knowledge for its own sake. As Mead has written: "Knowledge for its own sake is the slogan of freedom, for it alone makes possible the continual reconstruction and enlargement of the ends of conduct" (11, p. 225).

As problem-solving but disinterested, metaphysics deals with problems of heightened generality—problems, for example, which stem from the discrepancy between the world views fostered by scientific conceptual systems and common experience, between scientific objects and the perceptual objects of ordinary experience, or from the theory of causal determinism postulated by scientific investigation and the doctrine of emergence favored by the scientific theory of evolution. In his first article published in a philosophical journal Mead, setting out from Dewey's concept of the reflex arc, attempted to outline a theory of the philosophical disciplines based upon a dialectic of the act. He identified metaphysics as the discipline which makes "the statement of the problem." In his view a "metaphysical situation" involves a persistent problem that cannot be ignored, such as the affirmation of the reality of one type of experience at the price of allegation of the unreality of another equally valid type. Examples are the theological claim for a teleological interpretation of nature at the expense of the mechanical interpretation required by science, and the Platonic insistence on the idea at the cost of sensuous experience. Mead defined metaphysics as "a statement of an essential problem in permanent form, in terms of the reality of an idea or system of ideas and the unreality of that which conflicts with it." "The solution of the problem," he continued, "carries with it the disappearance of the problem and the metaphysical system at the same time" (12).

Mead's "constructive pragmatism," with metaphysics as a reconstructive activity addressed to those problems of greatest generality, faced up to the revolutions in physics wrought by relativity theory and quantum mechanics. Because Mead was the only pragmatist who did so, his thought belongs, as Arthur Murphy has observed, to that *genre* of the philosophy of nature which flourished in the 1920's and which culminated in Whitehead's *Proc-*

ess and Reality (2, p. xv). Whereas the other philosophers of nature were interested simply to describe reality and the stages of its genesis and to propose categorial schemes of explanation, Mead as a pragmatist philosopher was motivated always by the need to find solutions to problems, and consequently, his philosophical efforts are scattered in essays, lectures, and incomplete fragments. Because the main problems with which he dealt and the solutions he offered sketch the outlines of a major unfinished system of philosophy, it is our aim in this chapter to place these problems and their solutions in focus.

THEORY OF THE ACT

The concept of the act is the key to Mead's "constructive pragmatism." This concept owes much to the functionalist psychology of James and Dewey, and in his appreciation of the metaphysical potentialities of this dynamic conception, Mead went beyond them. "Act" is Mead's term for the relation between organism and environment. He wrote: "Our primary adjustment to an environment lies in an act which determines the relation between the individual and the environment. An act is an ongoing event that consists of stimulation and response and the results of the response" (5, p. 364).

Since acts comprise situations whereby the characteristics of the environmental stimuli and the organic responses are co-determined, Mead's philosophy of the act is an instance of what A. E. Murphy has aptly called "objective relativism" (13). Consider Mead's discussion of food. "There was, to be sure, no such thing as food where there were no organisms capable of ingesting, digesting, and assimilating it. It is equally true that there is no food when in the presence of such organisms there is no nutriment present. Food as an object exists in a certain biological situation, in which are found both the organic forms and the environment in adaptation to each other" (5, p. 71). This transaction between organism and environment, at first restricted to stimuli and responses having to do with the life of the organism and the qualities of that life, is generalized to bear upon all the categories of reality. In this respect Mead was profoundly affected by Whitehead's "philosophy of organism." Prior to Whitehead it was possible to regard the environment, at least in its categorial features of space, time, and causality, as independent of the organism. It was not possible to do so after Whitehead, who assumed that the organism and the environment are inseparable, neither having the same quality and structure it has without the other (5, p. 542). And like Whitehead's "philosophy of the organism," Mead's "philosophy of the act" is an essay in metaphysics, but the essay is clearly grounded upon pragmatic principles. Stephen Pepper has properly named this type of metaphysics "contextualism" (14).

The Stages of the Act

According to Mead, an act unfolds in three general stages: perception, manipulation, and consummation.

Perception. Perception is defined as a "relation between a highly developed physiological organism and an object, or an environment in which selection emphasizes certain elements" (5, p. 8). Perception is a temporal process pervaded by activity. There is the action through the media which stimulates the senses; there is the action of the organism selecting this stimulus; and there is the total perceptual response to this interaction. Thus the first phase of the act has "all the elements of an act—the stimulation, the response represented by the attitude, and the ultimate experience which follows upon the reaction, represented by the imagery arising out of past reactions" (5, p. 3). Besides "an immediate sensuous stimulation," there is present in perception what Mead called "an attitude toward this stimulation" (5, p. 3). The term "attitude" refers to "the beginnings of acts" which lie within the organism (3, p. 5); it designates "those processes in the upper reaches of the central nervous system in which the coordinations take place which make complex reactions possible" (5, p. 130). Accompanying the response to the stimulation, a response determined by attitudes, is imagery taken from past experience of similar stimulations, with their responses and their outcomes. In this sense, the first stage of the "act" is itself a process, involving stimulus, attitude, and response (15).

The process of perceiving is subjectively experienced as sensing. Sensing is no passive presentation of content; rather it is an activity, or a complex of processes and activities. Each type of sensing requires specific bodily acts on the part of the organism, e.g., the focusing of eyes. The activity of sensing, furthermore, proceeds according to the sensitivity and the selectivity of the organism. For example, without eyes capable of perceiving colors, there are no colors.

Before the perceiving organism stands the perceptual object. This object, in part originating in the world independent of this particular organism, is also in part a product of the physiological structure, responsiveness, and selectivity of the organism. It is perceived to be colored, to emit sounds and odors, etc. Furthermore, it is perceived to be out there, at a distance from the perceiving organism. "The object in perception is a distant object" (5, p. 12). As a distant object, it invites not only action, but questions as to whether or not it actually possesses the properties it is perceived to have. Such questions, of course, arise "only when the conduct which the characters of the object call out does or does not reach a successful conclusion" (5, p. 11).

Perception, then, leads directly to the next stage of the act. "Sense perception is an outgrowth of the behavior by which organisms relate themselves to what is spatio-temporally away from them. This relation is a form of conduct that leads the organism toward or farther away from the object according as the act predicates contact or the absence of contact" (5, p. 141).

Manipulation. As the second stage of the act, manipulation involves contact with the object. Inasmuch as the organism is a physical thing, describable in terms of physical mechanisms that condition its act—the muscular contractions, the nervous irritations connected with these contractions, the nervous centers affected thereby, the motor paths traversed (5, p. 451)—the manipulatory stage of act involves the organism in conduct which brings it in contact with the object or which avoids such contact. "Contact is the test of the success of the act" and also the test of the reality of the object of perception (5, p. 141).

Consummation. As perception presents an object at a distance which stimulates the organism, and as manipulation is a mediate activity which brings the exterior of the organism into contact with the object, consummation is final; it completes the act. Although Mead described the perceptual and manipulatory phases of the act behavioristically and physiologically, he employed the language of values to depict the consummatory stage. Of course, the physical thing performs a role in consummation, but only an instrumental one. As Mead said: "Every act . . . is moving on from its physical objects to some consummation. Within the field of consummation all the adjectives of value obtain immediately. There objects are possessed, are good, bad, and indifferent, beautiful or ugly, and lovely or noxious. In the physical things these characters are only mediately present" (5, p. 25). The values of consummation "are all ultimates in the different parts of the whole act. They are want, effort, and satisfaction. They are all values" (5, p. 451).

Temporality of the Act

The act has duration and is temporal. "The unit of existence is the act, not the moment. And the act stretches beyond the stimulus to the response" (5, p. 65). The act is an event going on in a present but it has a past reference and a future reference. The past is in the act, in the sense that familiarity with the perceptual object evinced in recognition and the facility with which the organism manipulates the contact object are "products of past reactions" (5, p. 25). Similarly "the future is already in the act" (5, p. 25). The perceptual object at a distance lies in the future of the organism which moves forward to manipulate it, just as consummation is future for the organism engaged in its perception and manipulation. Both the past and the future qualify the present in which the act is.

Sociality of the Act

The act is a transaction between organism and environment. The organism's course of action, i.e., its conduct, gives the framework within which objects of perception arise. Different kinds of conduct give rise to different fields with different objects. Among the genus of acts, there is a class of social acts. A social act is one "in which the occasion or stimulus which sets free an impulse is found in the character or conduct of a living form that belongs to the proper environment of the living form whose impulse it is" (2, p. 180). Mead tended to restrict the term "social act" to acts which involved cooperation among different individuals and to characterize it by reference to a "social object" (2, p. 180).

Reflection

Frustrated action is the cause of thought. "Reflective thinking arises in testing the means which are presented for carrying out some hypothetical way of continuing action which has been checked" (5, p. 79). At one with the other pragmatists and heavily influenced by Dewey (16), Mead has outlined the experimental method of inquiry in five steps: (1) the presence of a problem, (2) the statement of the problem in terms of the conditions of its possible solutions, (3) the getting of ideas, or the forming of hypotheses, (4) the mental testing of the hypothesis, and (5) the experimental test of the hypothesis (5, p. 82). "Truth is . . . synonymous with the solution of the problem" (17, p. 73). Such solution involves reconstruction of the situation to allow action to go on. Into the problematic situation in which action has been checked, "the judgment comes with healing in its wings" (17, p. 82).

THEORY OF MIND

In social psychology Mead sought to solve two problems. Both problems testify to the failure of idealism and to the impact of the theory of biological evolution upon psychology. The first problem has to do with "finding such a place for mind in nature that nature could appear in experience" (2, p. 161); the second problem is concerned with the existence and the development of the personal self. Because Mead regarded the act as the ultimate unit of existence, of experience, he approached these problems from the standpoint of acts, or conduct. His method is, therefore, a kind of behaviorism.

The Method of Social Behaviorism

Mead has said: "Our behaviorism is a social behaviorism" (3, p. 6). By "social behaviorism" he meant "an approach to the study of the experience of the individual from the point of view of his conduct, particularly, but not exclusively, the conduct as it is observable by others" (3, p. 2). He expounded his method of social behaviorism explicitly by means of expanded criticisms of Watsonian behaviorism. Watson, Mead held, was essentially right when he sought to make psychology the science of overt behavior; he was wrong, however, when he confined psychology to the study of the behavior of indi-

viduals and when he denied the existence of consciousness on the grounds that it could be detected only by
means of the dubious method of introspection. Against
the individualistic behaviorism of Watson: "Social psychology studies the activity or behavior of the individual
as it lies within the social process; the behavior of an
individual can be understood only in terms of the behavior of the whole social group of which he is a member,
since his individual acts are involved in larger, social acts
which go beyond himself and which implicate the other
members of that group" (3, pp. 6-7). Mead was too much
of a functionalist in psychology to embrace the identity
materialism implicit in Watsonian behaviorism. According to functionalism, mind, or consciousness, emerging
at the late stage in the history of biological evolution,
performs a distinctive function in the life of the organism
(18). Although mental behavior can be explained in
terms of nonmental behavior, it "is not reducible to nonmental behavior" (3, p. 11). There is, then, a private irreducible side to mind.

This individual subjectivity, however, does not for
Mead establish another world apart from the physical
organism. Rather it is a function of this organism, integral
to this natural world. Mead long acknowledged its role
in knowledge. "The experience of the individual in its
exceptional character," he wrote, "is the growing-point
of science, first of all in the recognition of data upon
which the older theories break, and second in the hypothesis which arises in the individual and is tested by
the experiment which reconstructs the world" (11, p. 221).
Subjectivity, moreover, is the inner counterpart and, indeed, the source of overt behavior (3, p. 5). Unlike
Watson's behaviorism, which neglects the inner side of
behavior, that "part of the act" which "lies within the
organism and only comes to expression later" (3, p. 6),
Mead's social behaviorism acknowledges the existence of
the inside, the inner, the private. "It simply works from

the outside to the inside instead of from the inside to the outside, so to speak, in its endeavor to determine how such experience does arise within the process. The act, then, and not the tract, is the fundamental datum in both social and individual psychology when behavioristically conceived, and it has both an inner and an outer phase, an internal and an external aspect" (3, p. 8).

Mind

Mead traced the genesis of mind back to a primitive situation constituted by social acts. Indebted to Wundt (19), Mead seized upon and exploited the concept of the gesture as the key to the evolution of mind (20).

Gesture. Gesture is effectively illustrated by the example of the dog fight, wherein "the act of each dog becomes the stimulus to the other dog for his response" (3, p. 42). And it is defined as "that part of the act which is responsible for its influence upon other forms" (3, p. 53). Of all gestures the vocal gesture is singled out, since the agent organism can be aware of and respond to his own vocal gesture and so can more easily control it. "One hears himself when he is irritated using a tone that is of an irritable quality, and so catches himself" (3, p. 65). Among vocal gestures some constitute what Mead called "the significant symbol." "Gestures become significant symbols when they implicitly arouse in an individual making them the same responses which they explicitly arouse, or are supposed to arouse, in other individuals, the individuals to whom they are addressed" (3, p. 47).

Meaning. Meaning has its logical foundation in the significant symbol. In the definition of meaning Mead utilized the triadic relational theory. Although he probably derived this theory from his teacher, Josiah Royce, he restated it within the context of experimental naturalism, thereby putting it in closer accord with the theory of its original author, C. S. Peirce (21). Consider Mead's statements: "A gesture by one organism, the resultant of the social act in which the gesture is an early phase, and the response of another organism to the gesture, are the relata in a triple or threefold relationship of gesture to first organism, of gesture to second organism, and of gesture to subsequent phases of the given social act; and this threefold relationship constitutes the matrix within which meaning arises, or which develops into the field of meaning (3, p. 76). . . . (T)he existence of meaning depends upon the fact that the adjustive response of the second organism is directed toward the resultant of the given social act as initiated and indicated by the gesture of the first organism. The basis of meaning is thus objectively there in social conduct, or in nature in its relation to such conduct" (3, p. 80).

This behavioristic conception of meaning fixes meaning in the social conduct of organisms within nature. "(T)he meanings of things, our ideas of them, answer to the structure of the organism in its conduct with reference to things" (3, p. 117). There is a reciprocal relation between language and the evolution of mind, since meaning is dependent upon capacities within the individual. As Mead said: "It is through the ability to be the other at the same time that he is himself that the symbol becomes significant." Universal meaning arises "through the individual generalizing himself in his attitude of the other" (22). This capacity is rooted in the organic structure of the central nervous system (3, p. 117). Thus the meaning of an object is dependent on the organism's responsiveness toward it, mediated by his capacity to adopt the standpoint of others. "The meaning of a chair is sitting down in it, the meaning of the hammer is to drive a nail—and these responses can be innervated even though not carried out" (3, p. 104).

Language. Defining language as a set of symbolically significant gestures, Mead joined Watson in regarding mind as linguistic behavior, differing, however, in his emphasis upon the social process. Mead ascribed the origin of mind to language: "Out of language emerges the field of mind" (3, p. 133), and again "Mind arises through communication by a conversation of gestures in a social process or context of experience—not communication through mind" (3, p. 50).

Social Process. Although Mead held that linguistic behavior accounts in large part for the genesis of mind, he nevertheless refrained from reducing mind to a language process going on within the brain of the isolated individual. "Consciousness," he said, "is functional, not substantive; and in either of the main senses of the term it must be located in the objective world rather than in the brain—it belongs to, or is a characteristic of, the environment in which we find ourselves" (3, p. 112). Mind and its natural environment are grounded in the social process. "The whole content of mind and of nature, in so far as it takes on the character of meaning, is dependent upon this triadic relation within the social process and among the component phases of the social act, which the existence of meaning presupposes" (3, p. 112).

Reflexiveness. In addition to linguistic behavior, an "essential condition for the development of mind" within the social process is reflexiveness. By "reflexiveness" Mead meant "the turning-back of the experience of the individual upon himself" (3, p. 134). Through reflexiveness, "the whole social process is thus brought into the experience of the individuals involved in it; it is by such means, which enable the individual to take the attitude of the other toward himself, that the individual is able consciously to adjust himself to that process, and to modify the resultant of that process in any given social act in terms of his adjustment to it" (3, p. 134).

Self

Minds evolve in a social process. Yet, as Mead held, "only selves have minds" (2, p. 178). What, then, is a self? It is, Mead taught, an organization of social experience (3, p. 91). Furthermore, it is not to be confused with either the body or consciousness. Indispensable to the self, the body is not the self, although it is the locus of consciousness. Nor is consciousness, which Mead at one point described as "the private or subjective thereness of the characters of objects" (3, p. 169), the same as the self. The essence of the self consists in the capacity to be an object to itself. "This characteristic is represented in the word 'self,' which is reflexive, and indicates that which can be both subject and object" (3, p. 136).

The Genesis of the Self. Despite the distinction of the self from the physical organism, Mead never minimized the biological foundation of the self. As he put it, the "essential psychological problem of selfhood" is to explain how an object, a physical organism, can become an object to itself. The solution of the problem resides, of course, in social experience. "The individual experiences himself as such, not directly, but only indirectly, from the particular standpoints of other individual members of the same social group, or from the generalized standpoint of the social group as a whole to which he belongs" (3, p. 138). Three social activities especially promote the genesis of the self. Most fundamental of all is language, since in the use of language one responds in the same way to his vocal gestures as he expects others to respond. But alongside linguistic behavior stand play and organized game behavior as causal factors in the emergence of selves. In play one assumes various roles and so organizes his conduct from the standpoint of others. In the organized game the individual acts according to rules which require him to regard his conduct and that of each other participant from the standpoint of all others. Mead has termed his new standpoint that of "the generalized other." He wrote: "The organized community or social group which gives to the individual his unity of self may be called 'the generalized other.' The attitude of the generalized other is the attitude of the whole community. Thus, for example, in the case of such a social group as a ball team, the team is the generalized other in so far as it enters—as an organized process or social activity—into the experience of any one of the individual members of it" (3, p. 154).

Thus there are two stages in the evolution of the self: (1) the constitution of the individual self "simply by an organization of the particular attitudes of other individuals toward himself and toward one another in the specific social acts in which he participates with them," and (2) at a higher level of development, the constitution of the self "by an organization of the social attitudes of the generalized other or the social group as a whole to which he belongs" (3, p. 158).

The primacy of the social process in the genesis of selfhood should be underscored. "The process out of which the self arises is a social process which implies interaction of individuals in the group, implies the pre-existence of the group" (3, p. 164). This pre-existence of the group vis-à-vis the self is both logical and temporal (3, p. 186). "A person is a personality because he belongs to a community, because he takes over the institutions of that community into his own conduct" (3, p. 162).

The Structure of the Self: The "I" and the "Me". The self is a social structure that emerges from the social process; yet, it is individual. Its individuality is paradoxically implicated in its sociality (23). The individual self is individual only because of its relation to others. The essence to the self is reflexiveness: its ability to take itself as an object from the standpoint of others. This reflexiveness, moreover, is essentially cognitive. Hence, the self "is cognitive; it (the self's essence) lies in the internalized conversation of gestures which constitutes thinking, or in terms of which thought or reflection proceeds" (3, p. 173).

By viewing the self as essentially cognitive Mead placed himself on the side of Kant against such empirical theories of the self as that of William James. In 1903 Mead distinguished two aspects of the self: the "I" and the "me," and commented on "the loss of dignity" suffered by the "I" in modern positivistic psychology (18, p. 104). And in his paper on "The Social Self" (24) Mead approached the task of defining the self by means of introspection. The self, he reported, cannot appear in consciousness as an "I." What appears in consciousness is always an object, i.e., a "me." The "me," however, is inconceivable without an "I," a subject for which it can be an object. But since this "I" cannot be a presentation of consciousness, it must be a presupposition.

Despite noticeable alterations of phraseology in later years, Mead's distinction between the "I" and the "me" crops up in all of his subsequent discussions of the self. Recently it has spurred considerable comment, these conceptions of the "I" and the "me" being compared with Bergson's conceptions of the dynamic self and the static self, or with Sartre's conceptions of the self and the situation. Mead himself wished to avoid a metaphysical explanation of the distinction and to elucidate its significance strictly "from the point of view of conduct itself" (3, p. 173).

Inasmuch as Mead's distinction between "I" and "me" is meant to be functional rather than metaphysical, memory illustrates the interchangeable roles of these two phases of the self. For "in memory . . . the 'I' is constantly present in experience" (3, p. 174). The "I" remembers, but the self it remembers is always a "me." Consequently, the "I" that is remembered is drained off into the "me" that another "I" remembers now. This fact alone affords the present "I" with a measure of free responsiveness toward the "me" and hence toward its past. In like manner the "I" is free as regards the social situation of the self, although it is the "me" which internalizes that situation within the self (3, p. 182). As Mead said: "The 'I' is the response of the organism to the attitudes of the others which one himself assumes. The attitudes of the others constitute the organized 'me,' and then one reacts toward that as an 'I' " (3, p. 175). Hence the "me" is both the past and the social situation to which the "I" responds, and its response may be an action which is more than an adjustment to the passive "me," since the "I" is often motivated by the recognition of ends which lie in the future. Thus it is the "me" that is conservative: "The 'me' is a conventional, habitual individual" (3, p. 197). And while this conservatism is invaluable to the social self and to society, guaranteeing integration and stability; its equally invaluable complement is novelty and progress. This the "I" supplies.

THEORY OF TIME

The problem Mead undertook to solve by means of his theory of time is so grave that he called it "the task of philosophy today," namely, "to bring into congruence with each other this universality of determination which is the text of modern science, and the emergence of the novel which belongs not only to the experience of human social organisms, but is found also in a nature which science and the philosophy that has followed it have separated from human nature" (2, p. 14). On the one hand, science posits emergence, the occurrence in the evolutionary process of novel elements. On the other hand, the rationalistic procedure of scientific method is deterministic, postulating that every event can be causally explained by its antecedent conditions. Hence a serious antinomy arises between the principle of emergence and the principle of causation, both espoused by science and scientific philosophy. This antinomy illustrates the nature of a metaphysical problem, since the assertion of the reality of one side seems to entail the allegation of the unreality of the other. Its solution, Mead held, rests upon an adequate theory of time, which, by reconciling emergent novelty with casual conditioning, eliminates the problem and the types of metaphysics entailed therein.

The key to Mead's construction of a theory of time, as in the case of his theory of mind, is his theory of the act, and it is within the context of the philosophy of the act that Mead incorporated those insights into the nature of time which he borrowed from the process philosophy of Bergson and Whitehead and upon which he heavily leaned. Time is linked to change (5, p. 638). But since time consists in a whole of past, present, and future, and change does not, time is not identified with change. "(T)he continual slipping of one present into another, which is always taking place in experience, does not itself involve a temporal order, though it does involve change" (5, p. 638). In addition to change, human intelligence is necessary to produce time (5, p. 263). The ultimate source of time, like that of space, resides in the structure of the act on the part of intelligent organisms. As Mead wrote: "Time and space . . . appear in the situations of organic forms" (5, p. 262).

Present

Mead's theory of time is a "philosophy of the present," for, as the opening sentence of his Carus lectures declared, "reality exists in a present" (2, p. 1), or, as this statement is later modified somewhat, "a reality that transcends the present must exhibit itself in the present" (2, p. 11). As the locus of reality, a present is an occurrence of existence, an act, or an emergent event. Yet no present is a totally isolated existent; it refers beyond itself. "The present," said Mead, "implies a past and a future," but he immediately added: "to these both we deny existence. . . . Existence involves non-existence; it does take place" (2, p. 1).

What is the meaning of the concept of the present? As Mead said, "that which marks a present is its becoming and its disappearing. While the flash of a meteor is passing in our own specious presents it is all there if only for a fraction of a minute" (2, p. 1). A present therefore is an event, an act, however long it may take. When Mead rejected Bergsonian duration because of its psychological limitations, he praised that "correction of the Bergsonian philosophy which," it seemed to him, "Mr. Whitehead has most effectively made, up to the present at least" (4, p. 325). Unfortunately Mead did not live to see Whitehead's last works, such as *Process and Reality* and *Adventures of Ideas*. Undoubtedly he would have found in them suggestions and principles in closer agreement with his own thinking than in those earlier writings of Whitehead, *The Concept of Nature* and *The Principle of Relativity*, from which he drew so much, but not without pointed criticism.

In making the present the locus of reality and in describing it as a becoming and a disappearing, Mead was in his own way formulating a concept akin to Whitehead's actual entity, or actual occasion. For according to Mead, what is seated in the present—the content essentially identical with the present—is the emergent event. He said: "A present, then, as contrasted with the abstraction of mere passage, is not a piece cut out anywhere from the temporal dimension of uniformly passing reality. Its chief reference is to the emergent event, that is, to the occurrence of something which is more than the processes that have led up to it and which by its change, continuance, or disappearance, adds to later passages a content they would not otherwise have possessed" (2, p. 23).

It is this emergent event, moreover, which is the basis of the temporal structure of present, past, and future. "Past, present and future belong to a passage which attains temporal structure through the event, and they may be considered long or short as they are compared with other such passages. But as existing in nature, so far as such a statement has existence, the past and the future are the boundaries of what we term the present, and are determined by the conditioning relationships of the event to its situation" (2, p. 24).

Past

In quest of a solution to the antinomy between the universal conditioning of the present by the past in consonance with the causal principle of science and the emergence of novelty in the present as posited by the theory of evolution, Mead proceeded to define the past. Although he began *The Philosophy of the Present* with a denial of existence to the past, he went on to credit the past with "producing all the reality that there is" (2, p. 26). "The past is there," he claimed, "conditioning the present and its passage into the future" (2, p. 17). The line of argument seems to lead inescapably to an absolute causal determinism, disallowing any possibility of novelty: "Everything that is taking place takes place under necessary conditions" (2, p. 16). Furthermore, Mead ascribed utter irrevocability to the past; "That which has happened is gone beyond recall. . . . There is a finality that goes with the passing of every event" (2, p. 3). Now if the past is irrevocable and if it absolutely conditions what is present, it would seem logical to conclude that there is no room whatever for an emergent event characterized by novelty. In Mead's theory, however, this conclusion turns out to be unwarranted.

While expounding his own conception of the past, Mead took care to repudiate a conception that crops up in the metaphysics of the Minkowski space-time continuum and in certain uncritical methodological assumptions of research in history and science, although he conceded that it is "perhaps the common background of thinking" (2, p. 9). According to this rejected conception, the past exists in itself, independent of and unaffected by what is going on in a present. It supposes "that there is behind us a scroll of elapsed presents, to which our constructions of the past refer, though without the possibility of ever reaching it, and without the anticipation that our continual reconstructions will approach it with increasing exactness" (2, p. 30). To this scroll concept of the past Mead's fundamental objection is not that it contradicts by implication the possibility of novel emergent events, but rather that it does not meet the methodological requirements of the past in historical or scientific research. "Such a scroll, if attained, is not the account that our pasts desiderate. If we could bring back the present that has elapsed in the reality which belonged to it, it would not serve us. It would be that present and would lack just that character which we demand in the past, that is, that construction of the conditioning nature of now present passage which enables us to interpret what is arising in the future that belongs to this present. . . . A string of presents conceivably existing as presents would never constitute a past" (2, p. 30).

Mead's conception of the past, clearly distinguished from a pre-existent scroll, is nevertheless the conception of a reality that is real in the sense that anything is real; it is somehow in the present, which is the locus of all reality. Otherwise it could not condition the present. As Mead said: "(I)n passage the conditioning of that which is taking place by that which has taken place, of the present by the past, is *there*. The past in that sense is in the present" (2, p. 17). It "lies with all its characters within that present" (2, p. 26). Such a past refers also to "that conditioning phase of the passing present which enables us to determine conduct with reference to the future which is also arising in the present" (2, pp. 28-29). Thus past and future are somehow both in the present; they qualify it. This does not mean that the present, as Bergson suggested, accumulates all the past, for Mead argued: "The present does not carry any such burden with it" (25). It does mean a continuity of the past with the present. As the condition of the present the past lies within the present and hence is not an external fixity. "The actual passage of reality is in the passage of one present into another, where alone is reality, and a present which has merged in another is not a past. Its reality is always that of a present" (25, p. 235).

The appearance of the past in the present assumes the form of memory images and historical records. Here the past is conceived as the meaning of what has transpired for the present. In this connection Mead has alluded to two different senses of the past discernible upon consideration of the methods of historical research. First, there is the past "when we are at grips with a problem and are seeking its solution. . . . (I)t takes on now one sense and now another. We analyze it into one set of factors and then into another; we are seeking its meaning, endeavoring to find in it the course we should follow" (5, p. 507). But once we have formed a solution to the problem, "the whole falls into a single story that we read in terms of a causal series. . . . (W)e build up a hypothesis which we test and perhaps act successfully upon, and then the problem takes the interpretation which our hypothesis places upon it" (5, p. 507). Here what we touch upon is not the mere occurrences that have been, but the meaning of the past for what is now. Because with every present the meaning is revisable, it follows that the past, though real as the conditioning within the present, is fundamentally hypothetical. As Mead said: "Our reconstructions of the past vary in their extensiveness, but they never contemplate the finality of their findings. They are always subject to conceivable reformulations, on the discovery of later evidence" (2, p. 29).

Now this account of the past, consistent with scientific methodology, supports emergence. For the past as the meaning of the condition of the present is subject to change as the present changes. Just as an absolute determinism of the past over the present excluding emergent novelty is ruled out, similarly the irrevocable character of the past is attenuated. "We speak of the past as final and irrevocable. There is nothing that is less so, if we take it as the pictured extension which each generation has spread behind itself. One past displaces and abrogates another as inexorably as the rising generation buries the old. How many different Caesars have crossed the Rubicon since 1800?" (5, p. 95).

The Emergent Event

An emergent event is an event containing novel features not wholly derived from antecedent presents; at the same time it exists in a present and is conditioned by the past. In Mead's words: "The emergent when it appears is always found to follow from the past, but before it appears it does not, by definition, follow from the past" (2, p. 2). As the source of novelty in life and in nature (2, p. 35), the emergent event is not a deduction from what took place prior to its appearance; nevertheless, it is conditioned by the past, but only according to that sense of the past which, as real, is located in the present. Although every emergent event is produced by the past, since production, or causation, is "the relation of any event to the conditions under which it occurs," and since this relation is established by the emergent event itself in the present, no emergent event can be reduced to what preceded it (2, p. 33). The past of every emergent event is, in one sense, a past of its own making or choosing. Thus the novelty of the emergent event in the present is matched by the novelty of the past that it reconstructs.

The emergent event is, then, an act which both adds novelty to the world and also socially establishes a relation to this world through adjustment and reconstruction. As unique and novel, the emergent event appears under the guise of discreteness, and seemingly disrupts the social process with discontinuity. As produced by the past, the emergent event appears as a member of the social process, augmenting its continuity. The present, the emergent event, the act is social. "Sociality," Mead wrote, "is the capacity of being several things at once" (2, p. 49). Since the "novel event is in both the old order and the new which its advent heralds," it exemplifies sociality par excellence.

THEORY OF REALITY

The discrepancy between objects as they are presented in experience (perceptual objects) and objects as they are conceived by science (scientific objects) led Mead to work on a theory of objects, with metaphysical suggestions for a general theory of reality based upon the philosophy of the act. This discrepancy, like the antinomy between emergent novelty and causal conditioning, is properly a metaphysical problem, since the assertion of the reality of one type of objects seems to entail the allegation of the unreality of the other. If perceptual objects alone are real, then scientific objects are merely mental constructs. If scientific objects alone are real, then perceptual objects are merely appearances. The classic form of this problem has to do with the distinction between objects composed merely of primary qualities as required by science and objects enriched with secondary qualities as they appear in ordinary experience. The most recent form of the problem, and perhaps the gravest, has to do with the nature of objects as conceived by relativity physics and quantum mechanics, the ultimate wave-like packets of energy in relative space-time, and the ordinary objects of common experience. Mead faced both forms of the problem and offered solutions based upon his theory of the act.

The Perceptual Object and the Act

The perceptual object is for Mead the object of ordinary experience. It is an object that emerges within the social process, its qualities and contours determined by the act. In other words, objects are reified, i.e., become real, within a process involving the interaction of organism and environment. In spite of multiple usages of the term "object," the primary meaning of this term in Mead's writings is "an expression of a peculiar relation between itself and the individual," the relation itself being "objective" (5, p. 7). So awkward a formulation serves to underscore the reciprocity of object and organism. The situation which consists in the interaction of organism and environment exhibits elements which are denotable as "objects." These elements depend, of course, upon the biological constitution of the organism and its particular selectivity, and the organism within the situation is also an object when it is so regarded. Requisite to the existence and the nature of objects are the acts of organisms.

Now the act has three stages, with which the properties of the object of the act may be correlated. The object of the perceptual phase of the act is the object at a distance; it is made up of secondary qualities—color, sound, odor, and so on. The object of the manipulatory phase is the contact object; it is comprised of the primary qualities of mass, solidity, figure, motion. The object of the consummatory phase is the value; it is constituted by the satisfactions and dissatisfactions registered in immediate experience. According to Mead, to assign to some of the properties of the object a subjective status and to other properties an objective status is an error which, in fact, the traditional doctrine of primary and secondary qualities conspicuously instantiates.

No set of properties is exclusively subjective. All properties are functions of their contexts. "As grass is food in the situation constituted by its relation to the ox and is not food in the situation constituted by the tiger, so the distant object is colored in the perceptual situation constituted by its relation to an individual with our visual apparatus but is not colored over against an angleworm" (5, pp. 76-77). For support Mead appealed to experimental science, since it "recognizes objects as existing, and arising in situation. . . . When a new situation arises, new objects arise" (5, p. 77). And he added: "If plesiosauri and rhododendra can arise in the organic situation, surely all the colors of the spectrum may arise, and all the odors of Araby" (5, p. 78).

Since the perceptual object, i.e., the object of ordinary experience, evolves along with the human organism, its properties, even its so-called primary qualities, exist within a context determined in part by the organism. The primary qualities, including the physical causality of the thing, arise primarily when resistance is offered to the organism by the contact object in the manipulatory phase of the act (5, p. 143). As it appears in the manipulatory stage of the act, the perceptual object is identical with the physical thing. The explanation of the genesis of the physical thing in contact experience consists in the transference of the pressures of bodily surfaces against each other, primarily of one hand against the other, to the object (2, p. 121). By virtue of this transference, which is facilitated by the principle of sociality enabling the organism to adopt the role of the other and to assume the attitude of the other, the thing acquires an inside (2, p. 122). Thus what the thing is, its essence or matter, the inside of the thing, the cluster of primary qualities, is equated with the resistance which the organism has transferred to the thing.

The resistance of the thing is, however, not a passive event; it is an action on the part of the thing (5, p. 144). Though "the resistance is there only over against effort or the action of other things, . . . (t)he resistance is in the thing as much as the effort is in the organism" (2, pp. 123-124). Indeed, our perception of the physical thing within experience is causally grounded in its action over against the organism's effort. "This action of things," Mead remarked, "gets into our experience, into our perspective, as the inside of perceptual things, and these perceptual things in the perceptual environment serve to define the organism as a perceptual thing" (5, p. 144). Yet instead of isolating the thing from the organism, resistance actually establishes their relatedness, since, as an activity, it "is a fundamental character which is common to all physical objects, including the organism" (5, p. 145). Furthermore, when the organism encounters the resistance of the thing, it is engaged in a cooperative process with the thing. As Mead said: "We are seeking the sort of resistance that we ourselves offer in grasping and manipulating things. We seek support, leverage, and assistance. The mediate act is completed in the resistance of the thing. It is the sort of resistance which one hand offers to the other. The inside of the thing is the same stuff as the inside of the organism" (5, pp. 143-144).

The object of the act, then, has its primary and its secondary qualities as objective but relative to the perceptual and manipulatory phases of the act. What remains is to ascertain whether it also has values, which occur only in the consummatory stage of the act. Although the physical thing has only instrumental value, its intrinsic value being restricted to the context of immediate experiences of enjoyment (such as eating), values are no more subjective than the other properties of the object. They are objective as relative to consummation. "The values of the world . . . are there in the world" (5, p. 316).

Mead's analysis of the perceptual, physical, and value properties of the object of ordinary experience carefully avoids any ontological discrimination among these properties. Each set of properties has its reality in relation to a specifiable phase of the act. If the question is raised: How is the unity of the object possible? the answer can only be: The unity of the object is guaranteed by the unity of the act in all stages toward it.

The Scientific Object and the Metaphysics of Relativity

The philosophy of the act saves the properties of the perceptual object from the erroneous ontological discrimination instigated by the doctrine of primary and secondary qualities. However, the metaphysics of relativity, the congeries of philosophical conceptions such as the Minkowski space-time continuum inspired by the scientific theories of relativity, offers a still more critical challenge to this object. The philosophies of classical Newtonian physics, with their distinction between primary and secondary qualities, provided an object which, insofar as it was composed of primary qualities, resembled the object of ordinary experience in the manipulatory stage of the act. The metaphysics of relativity, however, posits objects wholly different from the objects of ordinary experience. These scientific objects have, apparently, nothing in common with perceptual objects. Commenting on the profound change relativity introduced in the scientific conceptions of objects, Mead noted the disappearance of motion in Minkowski geometry, the abandonment of ether, the substitution of events for physical things, the fusion of space and time, the curvature of space and time, the concept of perspectives and shifting frames of reference. "The result is to carry the whole world of perception and perceptual imagination into perspectives that exhibit only a logical correlation between patterns affected with transformation formulae and events in a four dimensional space-time and intervals between them. By definition both events and intervals here lie outside of any experience. . . . This hypostatized structure of logical entities satisfies our desires for an absolute reality to which our confessedly relative experience shall refer" (2, pp. 153-154).

In addition to the postulation of scientific objects wholly beyond experience by the metaphysics of relativity, the science of relativity theory, when applied to perceptual objects, impugns the integrity of these objects. Whatever perceptual objects may be, at least it would seem that they have fixed characteristics of volume, mass, weight, length, and so on, determinable by standard units of measurement. However, relativity gives "different values to the fundamental units of measurement, spatial, temporal, and energetic, if they are regarded from the standpoint of the time system within which they are at rest, or if they are regarded from the standpoint of other systems. . . . The result of this is that objects have different natures in so far as they exist in different environments. The question then arises: By what right are they considered the same objects when they have this different nature in the different environments or time systems?" (5, p. 543). Now this is a serious question which philosophers of relativity must face in due time, for it cuts at the heart of physical thinghood. Lack of an answer jeopardizes the whole physical world of objects, the proper domain of the science of physics, of which one part is the theory of relativity.

Mead met the challenge of relativity by maintaining the methodological indispensability of the perceptual object and by proposing a philosophical interpretation of relativity which would organize perspectives and preserve the integrity of perceptual objects.

Scientific Method and the Perceptual Object

In the "Introduction" the editors of *The Philosophy of the Act* clearly delineated Mead's defense of the perceptual object in terms of the requirements of scientific method. This defense, as they rightly point out, is based upon wholly practical considerations. As they state, "when reason acts as a problem-solving procedure (as in scientific method), our total behavior, reflective and overt, unquestionably accepts as real the contact things of the laboratory" (5, p. xxxvii). They have helpfully marshalled Mead's reasons for contending that the practice of scientific reasoning posits the reality of perceptual objects.

First, science as reflective behavior, at its outset accepts the reality of perceptual things (2, p. 140). Second, the scientist returns to the perceptual world of perceptual things, a world he never questions, for verification of his hypotheses (2, p. 140). Third, the scientific method of measurement, although its results are not statable in terms of physical things, nonetheless makes use of physical things, i.e., the instruments of measurement, and so presupposes their reality (2, p. 150).

Fourth, the "exception" which instigates the scientific investigation depends upon the acceptance of the reality of perceptual things in the manipulatory area of the act (2, p. 149). Despite the discrepancy between perceptual and scientific objects, scientific methodology assumes the function of reality of the former. The research scientist, moreover, abstains from the dogmatic metaphysics of relativity. His goal in the pursuit of knowledge, Mead insisted, "is not a final world but the solution of his problem in the world that is there" (5, p. 60). The conclusions of experimental science, the scientific objects, instead of enjoying final metaphysical reality, are socially developed symbols referring to characteristics of the world that the problematic situation has rendered

prominent and which science has abstracted (5, p. 61).
The analyzed elements of science cannot be more real
than experience: "whatever breath of reality these elements possess has been breathed into them by some unanalyzed experience." "(T)he ultimate touchstone of
reality" in scientific investigation is, Mead said, "a piece
of experience found in an unanalyzed world" (5, p. 32).

Relativity and the Reality of Perspectives

Defending the reality of the perceptual object on
methodological grounds, Mead interpreted relativity
from the standpoint of the philosophy of the act. Abjuring the metaphysical interpretations of relativity, Mead
vigorously upheld the scientific achievement of relativity.
Aware that as a scientific achievement relativity presents
philosophical problems which rival those the theory of
biological evolution raised in the last century, he undertook to frame an acceptable interpretation. Unfortunately, he never lived to complete this work, but it is
possible to discern the outlines of a perspectival theory
of reality grounded upon the principle of sociality and
upon the theory of the act as an emergent event in the
present.

Mead regarded the concepts of perspective and emergence as equally significant points of orientation for contemporary philosophy (5, p. 640). Having considered
Mead's concept of emergence, we may properly turn
here to the concept of perspective. The rising importance
of this concept, no doubt, is due to the coincidence of
the advocacy of realistic epistemologies and the advance
of relativity physics. Etymologically linked to the perceptual situation, "perspective" denotes that basic situation of which Mead declared: "The perceptual object is
there over against the organism as a physical object"
(5, p. 151). Its "most unambiguous instance" is the
relation between organism and environment. "The perspective is the world in its relationship to the individual

and the individual in his relationship to the world" (5, p. 115). Perspectives, moreover, are objective. "The perspective emerges out of the relation of the percipient and the perceived and is as objectively there as anything can be" (5, p. 281). A perspective is rooted in the constitution of the organism and its relation to its environment. "The conception of a world that is independent of any organism is one that is without perspectives. There would be no environments" (5, p. 165).

Whereas classical Newtonian physics interpreted perspectives as loci in absolute space, relativity physics with its spatiotemporal continuum construes perspectives as spatiotemporal. Further, for relativity, since spatiotemporal characteristics vary with the events to which they pertain, the world of events divides into an indefinite multiplicity of perspectives. Unless the world is to be shattered into a plurality of perspectives without unity or community, the philosopher of relativity is confronted with the necessity of finding some principles for their organization. In quest of such principles Mead emphatically rejected the solution of absolute idealism. Readily admitting that "there are an infinite number of perspectives," he denied that any one of these perspectives is "the right one metaphysically," and he unstintingly condemned the idealistic procedure of "mystical engulfing of all the perspectives and ourselves with them in the Absolute." And he added: "the Absolute answers no queries. It provides emotional aspirations at the price of intellectual immolation" (5, p. 99). For reasons already outlined Mead also rejected the solutions offered by the Minkowski space-time continuum and by Whitehead, although, of course, he credited Whitehead with having contributed the conception of nature as an organization of objective perspectives (2, p. 163).

The task, according to Mead, was not merely to assert the organization of perspectives within nature, but primarily to explain the mechanism of such an organization.

In a fragment Mead recognized three systems of organizing perspectives: "The first is that of mechanical causality, which lies, however, within a system, such as is indicated by the principle of action and reaction, or the principle of least action. The second is that of life, or of living organisms, which also lies within a system, that of form and environment. The third is that of human intelligence, usually called that of consciousness" (5, p. 606). Despite the fact that this fragment was never amply elucidated, we can, with the support of other passages in Mead's writings, detect the direction of his thought and ascertain the form of his principle for the organization of perspectives. Each system, it should be clear, assists in the performance of the task, but in its severe form, having to do with "the perspectives in relativity (which) are mutually exclusive" (5, p. 698), only the third system of human intelligence, interpreted as social acts, will work.

Mead cited Whitehead's filiation with Leibnizian monadology as a recent philosophical expression of the severity of the problem of perspectives bequeathed to philosophy by relativity, and he accepted Whitehead's formulation of the problem without adopting his solution. Instead, Mead appealed to the principle of sociality as this principle was elucidated in his theory of mind. Accordingly, human individuals are able to view objects with themselves as stationary points of reference—or, for that matter, they can project themselves into objects, i.e., assume the attitudes of these objects, converting them into stationary points of reference. So he asked: "Is this capacity for placing ourselves in the plane when we are on the earth, or on the earth when we are in the plane . . . due to some power that belongs to thought as such, or is this power of thought due to the capacity to place ourselves in the attitude of the object which presents itself in experience?" (5, p. 545). Mead's answer was, of course, the latter, namely, "that meaning as such, i.e., the object of thought, arises in experience through the individual stimulating himself to take the attitude of the other in his reaction toward the object" (5, p. 545).

The thinking individual is the key to the organization of perspectives because the very structure of meaning enables him to occupy the perspectives of others as well as his own. Mead has referred to this character of meaning as a "perspective which is the organization of different perspectives"; he has concluded that "(i)t must . . . be a universal, at least in the identity which belongs to the different perspectives which are organized in the single perspective." Further, he has described this universality as one which "may logically be indefinitely extended" (5, pp. 545-546).

In the social acts of intelligent organisms Mead located the principle for the organization of perspectives in nature. Founded upon acts, the principle of sociality undergirds the structure of the cosmos. The counterpart of this image of a social cosmos in the making is a cosmic society in the making. Nature and human society both witness a process which socializes as it individuates. Here, indeed, is the inspiration of Mead's naturalization of Royce's "blessed community." "(T)he human social ideal—the ideal or ultimate goal of human social progress . . . is the attainment of a universal human society in which all human individuals would possess a perfected social intelligence, such that all social meanings would each be similarly reflected in their respective individual consciousnesses" (3, p. 310).

NOTES TO CHAPTER 3

1. See my forthcoming edition of Mead's *Selected Writings* (New York and Indianapolis: Bobbs-Merrill Co., Inc., 1964).
2. George Herbert Mead, *The Philosophy of the Present*, edited, with introduction, by Arthur E. Murphy with prefatory remarks by John Dewey (La Salle: Open Court Publishing Company, 1932).

3. George Herbert Mead, *Mind, Self and Society from the Standpoint of a Social Behaviorist*, edited, with introduction, by Charles W. Morris (Chicago: University of Chicago Press, 1934).

4. George Herbert Mead, *Movements of Thought in the Nineteenth Century*, edited, with introduction, by Merritt H. Moore (Chicago: University of Chicago Press, 1936).

5. George Herbert Mead, *The Philosophy of the Act*, edited, with introduction, by Charles W. Morris in collaboration with John M. Brewster, Albert M. Dunham, and David L. Miller (Chicago: University of Chicago Press, 1938).

6. John Dewey, "George Herbert Mead," *Journal of Philosophy*, XX (1931), 310-311.

7. Maurice Natanson, *The Social Dynamics of George H. Mead* (Washington, D.C.: Public Affairs Press, 1956).

8. Paul E. Pfuetze, *The Social Self* (New York: Bookman Associates, 1954). Reprinted in 1961 as a Harper Torchbook entitled *Self, Society, Existence*.

9. Van Meter Ames, "Mead and Sartre on Man," *Journal of Philosophy*, LIII (1956), 205-219, and "Zen to Mead," *Proceedings and Addresses of the American Philosophical Association*, XXXIII (1959-1960), pp. 27-42.

10. David Victoroff, *G. H. Mead: Sociologue et Philosophe* (Paris: *Presses universitaires de France*, 1953), p. 6.

11. George Herbert Mead, "Scientific Method and Individual Thinker," *Creative Intelligence: Essays in the Pragmatic Attitude* (New York: Henry Holt & Co., 1917).

12. George Herbert Mead, "Suggestions toward a Theory of the Philosophical Disciplines," *Philosophical Review*, IX (1900), 2-4.

13. A. E. Murphy, "Objective Relativism in Dewey and Whitehead," *Philosophical Review*, XXXVI (1927), 121-144.

14. Stephen C. Pepper, *World Hypotheses, A Study in Evidence* (Berkeley and Los Angeles: University of California Press, 1942).

15. So conspicuous is activity in the perceptual process that Mead's editors of *The Philosophy of the Act* divide the act into four stages, introducing the term "impulse" to denote the first stage. If by "impulse" is meant the predisposition of the organism to respond to a given stimulus, rooted in its physiological structure, then strictly speaking, impulse is anterior to the act of perception.

16. See John Dewey, *How We Think* (Boston: D.C. Heath & Co., 1910), pp. 70-78.

17. George Herbert Mead, "A Pragmatic Theory of Truth," in *Studies in the Nature of Truth*, University of California Publications in Philosophy, XI (1929).

18. See George Herbert Mead, "The Definition of the Psychical," *The Decennial Publications of the University of Chicago*, First Series, III (1903), 77-112.

19. See George Herbert Mead, "The Relations of Psychology and Philology," *Psychological Bulletin*, I (1904), 375-391, and "The Imagination in Wundt's Treatment of Myth and Religion," *ibid.*, III (1906), 393-399.

20. See George Herbert Mead, "Social Psychology as Counterpart to Physiological Psychology," *Psychological Bulletin*, VI (1909), 401-408.

21. For Mead's acknowledgment of indebtedness to Royce as regards theory of meaning, see "Social Consciousness and the Consciousness of Meaning," *Psychological Bulletin*, VII (1910), 399. Charles Morris has explored the Peirce-Mead relation on theory of signs. See Charles Morris, "Peirce, Mead, and Pragmatism," *Philosophical Review*, XLVII (1938), 109-127. See also Charles Morris, *Signs, Language and Behavior.* (Englewood Cliffs, N.J.: Prentice-Hall, 1946), pp. 39-49.

22. George Herbert Mead, "A Behavioristic Account of the Significant Symbol," *Journal of Philosophy*, XIX (1922), 161.

23. See Grace Chin Lee, *George Herbert Mead: Philosopher of the Social Individual* (New York: King's Crown Press, 1945), pp. 35, 50, 77. For an excellent discussion of Mead's conception of the self see also Paul E. Pfuetze, *The Social Self* (N.Y.: Bookman Associates, 1954), esp. pp. 89-96.

24. George Herbert Mead, "The Social Self," *Journal of Philosophy*, X (1913), 374-380.

25. George Herbert Mead, "The Nature of the Past," *Essays in Honor of John Dewey* (New York: Henry Holt & Co., 1929), p. 238.

Chapter 4

THE COSMIC
PHILOSOPHY OF
JOHN ELOF BOODIN

THE CONCEPTION OF PHILOSOPHY

"Philosophy is the love of the wholeness of things both human and divine." In this quotation from Plato, cited in the opening sentence of *The Posthumous Papers* (1), John Elof Boodin (1869-1950) expressed his conception of philosophy, a conception which guided him in a series of important works, including *Time and Reality* (2), *Truth and Reality* (3), *A Realistic Universe* (4), *Cosmic Evolution* (5), *God and Creation* (two volumes), *Three Interpretations of the Universe* (6), *God* (7), *The Social Mind* (8), and *The Religion of Tomorrow* (9). This list of philosophical works testifies to the intellectual scope of the author.

Boodin was born on a farm in southern Sweden in 1869 and emigrated to America in 1887. Settling in an Illinois mining town, he worked in a blacksmith's shop and obtained, on the side, what schooling he could. A graduate of Swedish secondary schools and of an Illinois Normal school he briefly attended the universities of Colorado and Minnesota, eventually finding his way to Brown University where he studied philosophy under James Seth. In 1897, a decade after his arrival in America, he realized his dream to enter Harvard, whose department of philosophy was then in full glory. Of the Harvard luminaries Boodin later named James and Royce as his prime mentors, and singled out Royce as "the master with whom I wrestled for the salvation of my soul from 1898 to 1900" (10). Indeed, his first major publication, *Time and Reality*, took off from his doctoral dissertation which had been based on a paper presented before Royce's seminary as early as 1898. This work not only manifests the metaphysical talent characteristic of Boodin by presenting a strikingly imaginative "creeping in" theory of time as dynamic nonbeing, but also, by taking time seriously as a negative factor in the cosmos, it erected a counterpoint to the Absolute of Royce's idealism.

With his Harvard Ph.D. Boodin embarked in 1899 on a teaching career—first at Grinnel in Iowa, then at the University of Kansas, next at Carleton in Minnesota, and finally, in 1928, at the new University of California in Los Angeles, remaining there until his death in 1950. Boodin has said: "My philosophy has thus taken form on the prairies of the great Middle West—the heart of old America—with its strong common sense and conservative social philosophy. The expansiveness of nature, with its unimpeded vistas and yet its sense of homely friendliness, must, it would seem, in the course of years get into a man's spiritual outlook" (10, p. 138).

Despite an obvious propensity for speculative daring, Boodin was sensitive to the epistemological and methodological strictures by which the pragmatists and the new realists sought to chasten metaphysics at the beginning of the century. From a consideration of the problems of methods and knowledge came Boodin's epistemology of pragmatic realism in *Truth and Reality*. Although *Truth and Reality* began with a plea for the toleration of different metaphysical interpretations, on the ground that each system is the result of the peculiar perspective afforded by the temperament of the particular philosopher, Boodin nevertheless promised in the "Preface" to publish a metaphysics, entitled *A Realistic Universe* (3, p. viii). A bold philosophical adventure, *A Realistic Universe* claimed nothing less than the application of pragmatic method to the task of constructing a metaphysical system. By this Boodin meant "that we must judge the nature of reality, in its various grades and complexities, by the consequences to the realization of human purposes, instead of by *a priori* assumptions" (4, p. vii). "The only key we have to reality is what reality must be taken as in the progressive realization of the purposes of human nature" (4, p. 73). The synoptic vision afforded by metaphysics, inextricably linked to a conception of reality as that with which human purposes must cope, is moreover grounded in the procedures and results of the empirical sciences. "Whenever philosophy has been vital," Boodin wrote in the "Introduction" to the first edition of *A Realistic Universe*, "it has always followed close upon the heels of science and human interest."

A Realistic Universe appeared in 1916, with Europe caught in the noisy orgy of World War I and unlikely to note the metaphysics of an American professor whose work had "grown up for the most part on the western prairies" and reflected, he hoped, "the homely sanity of the great West" (4, p. x). But the book constituted, according to its author in the "Preface" to the second edition fifteen years later, "the first systematic effort in the English language to create a metaphysics in the intellectual climate of the twentieth century" (4, p. xi). What Boodin had sought to accomplish was the synthesis of pragmatic methods in theory of knowledge with empirical scientific results and procedures, in order to produce a systematic, synoptic metaphysics in which human life is both understood and idealized. As he remarked: "We build philosophies and air castles for the spirit, as we build houses for the body, to keep out the blast and cold of an unfriendly cosmic weather" (4, pp. xx-xxi). Such a philosophical structure, moreover, must agree with empirical science. "The philosopher must be a poet who makes use, in so far as he is able, of the material of science" (4, p. xxxv). Thus his numerous writings take account of what the sciences teach. As the second edition of A *Realistic Universe* reveals, Boodin was ever alert to update his philosophical hypotheses to keep abreast of scientific advances, although he felt that these advances left the major outlines of his system undisturbed.

Boodin's metaphysics is shot through with references to developments in the sciences. His conception of reality was shaped by the reduction of matter to energy in contemporary physics. Similarly, his approach to the theory of mind was affected by the new discoveries in physiology and psychology which claimed to overcome the traditional Cartesian dualism. Other important areas of his thought, such as his theory of evolution and his conception of social institutions, owe their substance and color to the results and procedures of the sciences. It might seem, then, that Boodin's philosophy merely copied science. But if this were true, his philosophy would be only the handmaiden of science and any scientific change would subject it to dismissal or radical overhauling. However, in spite of a profound concern with science and what it tells about reality, Boodin never wanted to exaggerate its role. As he remarked: "Why should we suppose that science alone can capture reality? Art gives us reality, love gives us reality, worship gives us reality. We need all the various openings of human experience to capture the meaning of nature. To do so is man's momentous adventure. It is a far off goal, but we are on the way and we have time in store" (1, p. 83).

Boodin's conception of philosophy as a whole that draws upon all the aspects of man's experience in order to forge an understanding of the world and man's place in it, consistent with the findings of the sciences, fostered the quest for *Gestalten*, or wholes, within the subject matters investigated. Thus Boodin's key to the cosmos is the concept of form, an illuminating structure which, progressing in inclusiveness, embraces and interlaces all parts in a synoptic whole. It is no wonder, then, that Boodin, with breadth of vision and a keen interest in the sciences, concentrated on formulating a theory of evolution, inasmuch as many suspect that evolution can explain not only the forms of life but even the genesis of the laws of nature and nature itself. But in Boodin's case, there was, in addition to the scientific interest, a metaphysical motive, traceable to *Time and Reality* where he had conferred upon time a pre-eminent position in the galaxy of basic concepts. The first sentence of the first chapter of one of Boodin's books reads: "All reality is history and all history is a process of evolution" (6, p. 13). Boodin's examination of evolution resulted in his book *Cosmic Evolution*. Although at first he thought he had originated the special interpretation of evolution this work offered, he was delighted later to discover that he had been anticipated by Plato in the *Timaeus*.

Striving to articulate the most comprehensive whole suggested by science, art, religion, and all other areas of human experience, Boodin's holistic philosophy logically could not halt with a theory of evolution. By the necessary dynamism of its own conception this philosophy had to pursue the theological and sociological implications of its epistemological, metaphysical, and cosmological theses. The two volumes of *God and Creation*, supplemented nearly a decade later by *The Religion of*

Tomorrow, map out the theological and religious dimension of Boodin's thinking, and *The Social Mind* amplifies his approach to social theory and practice. Thus, Boodin furnished a general philosophical system with universal scope.

THEORY OF KNOWLEDGE

Published in 1911, a year before the appearance of *The New Realism*, Boodin's *Truth and Reality* presents his theory of knowledge, a theory which he named pragmatic realism. By "realism" he meant not a "brand of metaphysics" but an "epistemological attitude" (3, p. 252). "What realism insists," Boodin wrote, "is that objects can also exist and must exist in a context of their own, whether past or present—independent of the cognitive subject; that they can make differences within non-cognitive contexts, independent of the cognitive experience" (3, p. 253). Within epistemology Boodin did not wish to decide between the metaphysical interpretations of idealism and materialism, although he acknowledged that both positions contribute concepts useful in inquiry and explanation (3, p. 256). As a method pragmatic realism, he contended, remains primarily critical. He defined pragmatism as "simply the application of the ordinary method of the scientific testing of an hypothesis to philosophic hypotheses as well" (3, p. 186). Explicitly crediting his pragmatism to C. S. Peirce (3, p. 184; 4, p. vii), Boodin abjured James's equation of the true with the useful and Schiller's identification of pragmatism with humanism. What verifies hypotheses, Boodin held, is not human nature, but "their tallying with the constitution of the object aimed at, as it appears in further experience" (3, p. 192). Thus pragmatic realism is realistic: "It means the willingness to acknowledge reality for what it is; what it is always meaning for us, what difference it makes to our reflective purposes" (3, p. 260). Despite the disavowal of metaphysics, this epistemology of pragmatic realism, it should be clear, involves a metaphysics of mind and its objects.

Mind, according to Boodin, is instinct. Instinctive response, moreover, is "response that is called off as a result of organic structure, given the proper stimulus" (3, p. 35). Initially universal, instincts become more restrictive with increased development in the organism. "(A)ll our fundamental adjustments or categories are instinctive or organic adjustments; (and) . . . the stimuli, which constitute the environment, are simply the occasion for calling into play the structural tendencies of the organic growth series" (3, p. 15). Since the efficacy of the environment in stimulating the organism depends upon the prior development in the organism of the appropriate structural tendencies, intellectual reflection, like sexual love, is biologically dependent upon the evolution and maturation of the organic structure (3, p. 31). Three stages of mind, each with its appropriate instincts, are delineated: (1) physiological or sensitive reaction, with egoistic-preservative instincts: (2) associative memory, with social instincts; and (3) reflection, with ideal instincts (3, p. 34). The instinctive tendencies, inherent in the structure of the organism, operate, therefore, as *a priori*, innate categories which, though dependent upon the biological evolution of the organism, shape and articulate its experience.

Like Kant, Boodin acknowledged the *a priori*; but, anticipating the later work of C. I. Lewis, Boodin's *a priori* is pragmatic. Undertaking a deduction of categories in terms of the structure of the knowing organism, he provided a table of categories justified by their survival through processes of trial and elimination. Categories are certain inherited "tendencies to reaction which are brought into play by the stimuli of the organism; and by continuous trials and the elimination of unsuccessful movements, these reactions become definite" (3, p. 44).

There are fifteen categories, tendencies, or laws which are part of our mental constitution and are not learned by experience:

A. Categories of Perception
   1. Space
   2. Time
   3. Habit
   4. Imitation
B. Categories of Reproductive Imagination
   5. Contiguity
   6. Similarity
   7. Set
C. Categories of Empirical Generalization
   8. Quantity
   9. Quality
   10. Causality
   11. Individual interpenetration
D. Categories of Idealization
   12. Ego
   13. Nature
   14. History
   15. Absolute (3, pp. 45-46; cf. 1, pp. 37-61)

Boodin's equation of the categories of intelligence with organic instincts did not rule out the constructive role of thought in experience and knowledge. His description of the cognitive activity is cast in the language of idealistic voluntarism. Thinking, as the adaptation of one's self to a novel situation, "is a form of volitional conduct, which asks the why and whither" (3, pp. 69-70). Hence "conative leading . . . constitutes the core of thought" (3, p. 81). As Boodin wrote: "Thought is a living, moving will, a will which has set itself a definite conscious goal—the realization of its intent with reference to the nature of the environment. It is will, awake as to its direction. Instinct bequeaths to thought certain tendencies or demands, among them the theoretical demands. . . . Thought bequeaths to instinct the definiteness of articulate and self-conscious purpose, instead of vague groping impulse" (3, p. 83). Hence Boodin's theory of truth, treating the process, form, content, and test of truth, is developed within a framework which conceives thought as voluntaristic.

Now "the process of truth is the process of judging" (3, p. 98). And judgment "involves, on the one side of the will, a specific attitude or set . . . (and), on the side of the content, certain relations which the judging process must imitate. . . . Judgment is a certain set toward certain content relations" (3, p. 106). The morphology of the truth process conforms to the type of judgment. Negative judgment initiates thought, the consciousness of non-being preceding the consciousness of being. "Our first consciousness, in the breakdown of the old habits or the customary forms of judgment, is consciousness of *no*" (3, p. 89). Next, thought advances to the hypothetical judgment. Thought "proceeds through the trial stage of ideal construction and verification, which flows out in advanced knowledge into the disjunctive schematization of alternatives." Here thought adopts "a provisional scheme for conduct." Finally, thought concludes in a categorical judgment. "The end of thought is a consciously adopted type of conduct. The judging process terminates in a method of control or plan of procedure, physical or logical" (3, p. 94). In the last phase, the categorical judgment becomes "thought stereo-typed into social habit" (3, p. 96). Thought, therefore, is teleological. The function of truth "is to regulate conduct—the conduct of the understanding as well as to adaptation to a perceptual environment" (3, p. 124).

The thought process is not arbitrary, inasmuch it is checked not only by the success of the conduct to which it leads, but also by its own postulates. These postulates of truth, or laws of thought, are: (1) the law of consistency (including identity and noncontradiction); (2) the law of totality (expressed as a command to look for connections among facts); (3) the law of duality (consisting in the universality of the subject-object relation for experience, and its restriction to experience); and (4) the law of finitude (limiting knowledge to what is finite, and assigning what is beyond to faith). Although these postulates are justified pragmatically in that successful knowing presupposes them, Boodin insisted that they are *discovered* in the thinking process, not arbitrarily devised for it. "(T)hought is an activity of the will, predetermined as regards its form by certain presuppositions which are posited by the will to think" (3, p. 155). Paradoxically, the postulates of truth are both *a priori* and hypothetical. "While they are *a priori* and necessary postulates from the point of view of formal knowledge, from the point of view of reality they must be treated as hypotheses to be verified in the procedure of experience" (3, p. 152). Thus there are no *a priori* valid metaphysical postulates. "(T)he only possible ontological necessities are the necessities of facts—of the conditions which we must meet in realizing our purposes, what reality must be taken as in order to satisfy the demands of the will" (3, p. 152). But since our knowledge is fragmentary, even these necessities, Boodin conceded, are hypothetical.

Furthermore, on the side of content, truth consists in a relation of agreement between judgment and its objects. Requiring more than internal consistency and intelligibility, "(v)alidity can only be stated as the agreement of an idea or belief with its reality" (3, p. 210). "To correspond or agree means to realize my purpose or at any rate to be able to act as if my hypothesis were true. Correspondence . . . has a twofold significance, the *instrumental* relation of the knowing attitude to its object and that of *sharing*, to use a Platonic term" (3,

p. 217). When the object of truth is physical, the relation is instrumental, for two reasons: (1) the facts which themselves *know* no system are arranged systematically to suit our purposes, and (2) our knowledge never grasps the real object in its entirety (3, p. 219). When the object of truth is a psychological unity or a social ideal, the relation of correspondence is sharing. As Boodin remarked: "We must imitate, not merely externally, but share and acknowledge, soul confronting soul, the individual's own meaning in its unique wholeness" (3, p. 220). Regardless of the sense of correspondence, the test remains the same—the agreement of our purposes and hypotheses with the ongoing of experience. Thus Boodin's voluntaristic pragmatism is balanced by his realism of objects. Even though he looked upon the object-construct of the scientific context as an instrument by which we cope with our own world, there yet remains the real object: "that which we must meet, to which we must adjust ourselves in order to live to the fullest extent" (3, p. 269).

THEORY OF REALITY

Pragmatic realism had posited the existence of objects (or processes) with which the knower must come to grips if his knowledge is to succeed. Now these objects exist not in isolation but in contexts, of which Boodin differentiated three. Objects (or processes) "figure in the world of interacting energies, with their causal and space relations; they figure in social contexts—in science and institutions, which we must imitate and react upon; they figure in the special context of each individual, as he tries to appropriate the processes as part of his world of meanings" (3, p. 276). And he added: "The persistent effort to see the various contexts of the world of objects as one pattern, the divine love for the wholeness of things, we call metaphysics" (3, p. 288). This conception of metaphysics as synoptic, however, did not preclude its pragmatic character. On the contrary, Boodin insisted, "Metaphysics means the systematic difference that facts make to each other and to our reflective procedure. It is what facts must be taken as in the *entirety* of our experience and not merely for a conventional purpose" (3, p. 292).

A *Realistic Universe* is system-building in the grand style of traditional metaphysics, but it is executed according to the requirements of a pragmatic method. Conceiving reality as "the differences it makes to our reflective purposes," Boodin offered the ultimate set of differences comprising reality. On analogy with the thought of Spinoza, these "*summa genera* of differences not further reducible" Boodin called attributes, and he identified substance with the epistemological postulate of totality—namely, that "the facts are part of one world in such a way that every fact can, under certain conditions, make a difference to other facts" (4, p. 385). Furthermore, the attributes are not parallel but overlap. Reality itself is individual yet presents us with irreducible differences with which we must cope when we try to realize our purposes. Boodin discriminated five ultimate attributes: being (stuff or energy), time, space, consciousness, and form. In one sweep, then, he believed he had arrived at a position which discards dualism and absolutism, the rival metaphysics that have dominated modern philosophy—dualism because more than two attributes are acknowledged; and monistic absolutism because substance, no longer regarded an empirically or dialectically confirmed ontological fact, is reduced to an epistemological postulate of totality. Boodin's metaphysics is, therefore, the theory of the five attributes, hailed in his opening chapter of A *Realistic Universe* as "the Divine Five-Fold Truth."

Being

By "being" Boodin meant "the stuff character of reality. This stuff is capable of making definite differences under statable conditions to other stuff" (4, p. 391). The attribute of Being does not denote "static, inert 'being,' but constellations of energy, conscious and unconscious" (4, p. 3).

This theory of being, termed "pragmatic energism," involves (1) the replacement of the idealistic equation of absolute substance with experience by the realistic conception of experience as transitive and dependent, and (2) the substitution of dynamic energy for static substance. In regard to the first point, the idealistic equation of experience with absolute substance, accepted as an epistemological postulate but rejected as metaphysically real, becomes an ideal for realization, experience being viewed as presupposing transexperiential contexts to guarantee both the communion of diverse experients in an objective space and the continuity of processes independently of their being experienced (4, pp. 16 ff.). Hence experience is not being, but an adjectival transaction in being. In regard to the second point, Boodin drew upon the sciences to support the equation: "Being = energy" (4, p. 32). Substances, he asserted, "are mere abstractions of the relative uniformities and constancies, physical and psychological, which we observe in the stream of processes" (4, p. 27). Hence not substances in the traditional sense, but energy systems are the simplest units of reality. What is energy? "Energy is what it does" (4, p. 53).

All energy systems contain three necessary factors: certain variables, the form or organizing relation of the system, and recurrence, the last-named being the pragmatic equivalent of substance (4, p. 37). Energy systems are empirical, and in consonance with the pragmatic method, which stipulates that realities consist in the differences they make to us in the realization of our purposes, three types of energy systems are distinguished: the material, the electrical, and the mental (4, p. 55).

Within the complex totality of these interacting, overlapping energy systems we may discern, again in accordance with pragmatic procedure, things, qualities, and relations. Things, though each evinces its own center of energy, are individuated "by the purposes which select them and which they fulfill" (4, p. 69). So are qualities, which belong to things yet vary with the change in contexts to which the things belong, and relations, which designate the connections, pragmatically ascertained, that conjoin things within contexts. Boodin defined "qualities" as "certain permanent expectancies which we have with reference to things under definite conditions" (4, p. 89).

Consciousness

Boodin defined the attribute of consciousness so as to avoid the reductionisms of materialism and the extravagances of idealism without succumbing to dualism. Unlike the materialist, who looks upon consciousness as an ineffectual epiphenomenon magically emerging from complex material organizations under certain conditions, Boodin conceived consciousness as a universal constant, thus sidestepping the insuperable problems of its origin. As he wrote: "logically it is simpler to assume the presupposition of consciousness than to derive it from nonconscious processes. It is easier, for epistemological purposes, to suppose that consciousness is a constant, rather than that it butts in; that it shines upon the just and the unjust, the simple and the complex, and in all kinds of weather, and that the difference in its effectiveness is due, not to it, but to the energetic conditions in the universe" (4, p. 142). And unlike the idealist, who treats consciousness as a condition for all reality, Boodin emptied consciousness of causal efficacy and even deprived it of the capacity to create meanings and cognitive contexts (4, p. 122). Consciousness, therefore, is the attribute whereby energy becomes aware of itself as meaningful (4, p. 123). And unlike the dualist, who is beset by the problem of explaining the transmutations and transfers of energy concomitant with the interactions of consciousness and material systems, Boodin eluded this difficulty by not treating consciousness as an energetic system (4, p. 128). Now, since for Boodin being is identical with energy and consciousness is not energy, it follows that consciousness is non-being, just as time, space, and form will prove subsequently also to be attributes of reality which are properly non-being.

What is the pragmatic meaning of consciousness? Boodin answered: "(I)t makes only one difference to reality. Under certain energetic conditions, it makes the difference of awareness" (4, p. 135). In its most generic form, consciousness is pervasive sensitivity of energy systems to one another throughout the whole of nature; it is, more specifically, epitomized in the energetic context of active mind. There is, then, a distinction between mind and consciousness: "(C)onsciousness and mind are conceptually separable facts, . . . consciousness is a fact superadded upon the contents of mind and their relations, under certain energy conditions of complexity and intensity; and . . . this consciousness when so added, does not *make* the will attitudes or perceptual contents nor does it add the *relations* of meaning to the contents" (4, p. 132).

Mind, on the other hand, is "a distinctive type of energy, however ignorant we may be of its relation to other energies" (4, p. 117). The essence of mind as energy is conative constitution or will: "In answer to the question: What is mental? we must say, then, that the will in its various stages of organization is mental" (4, pp. 173-174).

Space

Space is an ultimate attribute which must be acknowledged if our purposes are to be realized. But space as an attribute of reality is distinguished from serial or mathematical space, which is purely ideal or conceptual (4, p. 208). In contrast with ideal, mathematical space, real space is known through *a posteriori* empirical investigation. Real space is defined "as a limit of exhaustion and as the absence of resistance," reached by a process of abstracting away all contents (4, p. 397). Real space, moreover, is empirically required to account for motion and distance. The objective reality of empirically evident motion as the translation of an entity from one place to another presupposes the objective reality of the medium of motion—i.e., space (4, pp. 229-230). The empirical evidence that entities exist without fusing, yet are related to each other in terms of distance, also confirms the objective existence of the medium of external relatedness —i.e., space. From these considerations Boodin concluded that space is a real attribute.

The properties of real space are: externality, dimensionality, homogeneity, homoloidal structure, continuity, infinity, conductivity, temperaturelessness (4, pp. 234-243). Since real space is interpreted by means of empirical methods of observation, the properties listed above are subject to modification as demanded by new theories.

Einstein's theory began to have great influence after the first edition of A *Realistic Universe* had appeared. Nevertheless, Boodin was convinced that he had good reasons for not revising his own theory on its account. He argued first, that Einstein's theory is a mathematical conception of space which restrictively identified space and gravitational field; and second, that the specific tests met by Einstein's theory can, as A. N. Whitehead had shown, be met also by adhering to a concept of invariant space in line with Boodin's theory of real space (4, pp. xxxi-xxxiv; cf. 5, Part III).

Time

Although space is the ultimate attribute of reality which expresses the translation of a being from one position to another without affecting its nature, time is the ultimate attribute of reality which denotes the processes of transformation of beings. Time pertains to passage and change, so that as an attribute of reality time is tantamount to flux or "fluency of process" (4, p. 264).

Boodin's commitment to flux, however, did not obliterate his recognition of constancy. Indeed, he proposed a reconciliation of the ancient antinomy between constancy and change, by pragmatically accepting constancy as representative of features of energy systems and change as the attribute of time. The alternative, rejecting either change or constancy, would be a conception of reality inadequate for successful adaptation on our part (4, pp. 262-263). Time, for Boodin, though empirically confirmed as the flux attribute of reality, is neither Bergsonian substantialized time nor mathematical, serial time: "The flying, fleeting, evanescent character of experience, it seems to me," wrote Boodin, "is the primary character of time. The serial character is secondary, and is the result of *a posteriori* construction, necessitated by the real time character" (4, p. 265).

Incorporating the theory of time presented in *Time and Reality*, Boodin construed time as dynamic non-being. "That does not mean that time is unreal. What time *does* is something positive. It is responsible for passing away and novelty; it creeps into the intended reality and so makes necessary new judgments. What I mean by placing it under the category of non-being is, that it is not a thing or energy, though it makes positive differences to the world of energy" (4, p. 268). Boodin, moreover, emphasized the pragmatic difference time, as dynamic non-being, makes to knowledge. He summarily stated the relation of time to judgment as follows: "Time is that attribute of the real subject-object, which makes incompatible judgments (i.e., different judgments as regards the same aspect of reality at the same point) necessary" (4, p. 277).

Form

Reality, as we have seen, is a flux of energetic centers spread out in space and characterized by sensitivity or awareness. Empirically, human experience embodies the attribute of consciousness and encounters directly the attribute of space in its "sense of extensity with complex instinctive coordinations," the attribute of time in its "sense of duration with complex structural adjustments for measuring the flight of the time-process," the attribute of form in "the feeling for form with its tendencies and its sanctions in social institutions, to meet the demands of the universe upon us" (4, p. 334). These tendencies and demands, relevant to our thought activities, our aesthetic appreciation, and our conduct, crystallize in the ideals of Truth, Beauty, and Virtue. With respect to these ideals of life Boodin argued that they are identical in form "or the demands which they set to the concrete will," but are differentiated by the contents of the areas of life to which they apply (4, p. 307). The ideals of life are expressions of the attribute of form.

Metaphysically, the attribute of form is Boodin's answer to the question: "Does the process have direction, or is there validity in the flux?" It is the affirmation of holistic philosophy to the effect that form is "a part of the executive constitution of nature" (4, p. liii). "Form has to do, not with transformation, but with *formulation* —with the possibility of defining our situations in terms of clear and distinct principles" (4, p. 330). The primary differences between metaphysical systems pivot upon the acceptance or rejection of form (4, p. 338). If form is not accepted as a fundamental attribute of reality, then regardless of the conception of stuff that is adopted, the consequent cosmological theory would interpret the world as devoid of a standard to guide and evaluate its processes. Thus there would be no guarantee that the ultimate ideals are valid, and since the invalidity of these ideals is inadmissible on the grounds that their collapse would remove the possibility of truth and value even for the philosophy which expressed their nonoperancy, form as an attribute of reality must be acknowledged. "(T)he Ought" itself is defined as "the consciousness of the form character of the universe" (4, p. 356).

Like consciousness, space, and time, form is not-being; but its role is different from the dynamic not-being of time and the medium for relatedness and distance that is space. Form, as nonspatial and nontemporal, transcends the flux of energy, although it is, in a sense, ingredient in the flux as direction and order. Upon form depends the creativity of the flux, so that for Boodin "(f)orm is creative, but it creates not by production, but by elimination. It is creative as the artist is creative, i.e., by selection" (4, p. 333).

THEORY OF THE COSMOS

Boodin's theory of the cosmos is, in his own terms, *"empirical realism* and *cosmic idealism"* (5, p. 7). By "empirical realism" he meant to designate his method, a method which prescribes strict attention to the sciences. By "cosmic idealism" he meant to express the conclusion to which this method led him in cosmology—namely, to the conviction that in the flux of matter control and direction are exercised by form, Spirit, or God, guaranteeing the preservation and ultimate triumph of the highest ideals to which man aspires, the fundamental constitution of the cosmos being revealed by and exemplified in the highest organic types. In this real way, Boodin's philosophy fulfilled his hope "to combine the Greek love of Form with the modern respect for process" (5, p. 91).

Evolution

Boodin's cosmology gives special attention to the biological theory of evolution. His treatment of evolution springs from a consideration of two seemingly incompatible principles of science. One principle, the second law of thermodynamics, projects a world run out of energy, a cosmos dissipated, exhausted, reduced to nothing in the far distant future. The other principle, the theory of evolution regnant in the life sciences, portrays nature as a scene bursting with the perennial emergence of new forms and novel crystallizations of energy. Whereas on the one hand the prospect is that nothing will come of all that now is, on the other hand the outlook is the continuous creation of new being, rising ever higher and higher in the scale of perfection until Deity itself comes to be. Not only is the scientific philosopher confronted with a grave contradiction of principles; he is faced, on either side of the dilemma, with an implication which violates what Boodin regarded as "perhaps the most momentous hypothesis in the history of science," i.e., Leucippus's statement that nothing happens without a reason (5, p. 47). Boodin's solution of the dilemma was to formulate a theory of evolution which, instead of taking either the downward process of the second law of thermodynamics or the upward process of the theory of evolution as a principle sufficient to explain nature and its laws, subordinated all change, including evolution, to the governance of cosmic structure.

This solution has induced R. F. A. Hoernlé to remark that a more accurate title for *Cosmic Evolution* would have been *Cosmic Structure* (11). A cosmos structured by permanent coexistent levels of energy is neither dissipated by an endless loss of energy nor enriched by utterly accidental emergents. As Boodin said: "We may be sure that in a self-sustaining cosmos there must be an upward as well as a downward path and that therefore the levels of energy are eternal" (5, p. 112). Hence the cosmos is a closed whole from which neither energy nor matter escapes; it is a spatiotemporal dynamic equilibrium. By "dynamic equilibrium" Boodin meant "not merely that as the quantity or intensity of energy varies in any one part of the cosmos there must be corresponding variation in intensity in other parts of the cosmic field, but . . . also that the variation of phases and types of organization in one part will tend to produce corresponding variation in other parts" (5, pp. 114-115). Every element or part of the cosmos, moreover, exists within a cosmic field, and this field, a region of the cosmic structure, determines the state of the element or part. The universe, as self-moving and self-maintaining, is, in the words of Boodin, "a closed system, curved on itself so that nothing can escape in the void," and within its system there is "a *balance* of exchanges and rhythms . . . , so that the shifting of potentials and the shifting of structure in any history is controlled by adjustment within the cosmic field" (5, p. 116). Because the cosmos has a constant structure in dynamic equilibrium, Boodin compared it to an organism. He wrote: "We may think of the universe as a sort of organism or superorganism" (5, p. 35).

Boodin's holistic interpretation of the cosmos logically entailed a redefinition of evolution. In *Three Interpretations of the Universe* he distinguished three theories of evolution: preformation, emergence, and creation.

Preformation is "the notion that evolutionary development is latent in the process so that later forms and stages are really an unfolding or making explicit what is already present in the earlier stages of the same history" (6, p. 13). The theory of preformation originated in the thinking of Plato and Aristotle; was continued in the Middle Ages in the writings of Scotus Erigena, Cusanus,

Bruno, and Boehme; and is found in the modern period in the systems of Leibniz, Schelling, Hegel, Schopenhauer, and even, according to Boodin, in the work of A. N. Whitehead. Preformationism is credited with properly stressing the structures in nature, and with having a rational simplicity, both of which make it amenable to the scientific mentality and have enabled it to prevail. Against preformationism, however, Boodin charged: "It has failed to take time seriously. It has done its business with a spatialized time, and has eliminated real time with its novelty and contingency. The real world is too pluralistic and indeterminate to be fitted into one rigid scheme. It is far more interesting and more tragic than that" (6, pp. 87-88).

For Boodin emergence meant "the appearance of new characteristics and structures with no apparent guidance from within or without" (6, p. 13). As "preformation" is the original meaning of evolution, "epigenesis," signifying the intrusion of novelty into process, is the old word for emergence (6, p. 136). Boodin distinguished two theories of emergence: materialistic and hybrid. Whereas materialistic emergence, as expressed in the works of Lucretius, Democritus, Feuerbach, Engels, and Broad, "holds that everything happens by blind combinations of the elements of matter or energy, i.e., without any guidance" (6, p. 95), hybrid emergence, as expounded by Herbert Spencer, S. Alexander, and C. Lloyd Morgan, restricts the process of emergence to the phenomenal order of appearance, implying that there is an order which guides or underlies the process (6, pp. 128 ff.). Although Boodin admitted that emergence had done philosophy a service by taking time seriously and by calling attention to novelty in nature, he judged it inadequate as a principle of explanation, despite its validity as a description of what happens. "An explanation is not a mere statement of an occurrence, but of the *how* and *why* of the occurrence. We want to know how the elec-

tron, the atoms, the molecules, organisms, mind can occur in our world. This means an inquiry into the structure of a world which makes such things possible" (6,
pp. 137-138).

This "inquiry into the structure of a world" led Boodin to embrace a theory of creation. By "creation" he
meant "the occurrence of new forms, characters and
stages under the guidance of an actuality which controls
and animates the course of history. According to this
view the later stages are not pre-existent, but are due to
an impetus from outside the particular history. They presuppose the interaction of the particular history with an
actuality which foreshadows the future stages of the evolutionary process either existentially, or eminently (i.e.,
as capable of producing them because it implies them
and more besides). Thus creation is epigenesis or emergence (in recent terminology) together with control
from a higher level" (6, p. 13). Rejecting monistic theories of creation, as upheld by Origen, St. Augustine, St.
Anselm, and St. Thomas, because they are based on the
dogma of creation *ex nihilo,* which "lies outside the field
of a rational philosophy" (6, p. 488), Boodin adopted a
dualistic theory of creation, as intimated in the first chapter of Genesis and elaborated by Plato in the *Timaeus.*
Now this theory agrees with emergence in acknowledging the importance of novelty, with preformation in em-
phasizing structures and wholes, and with traditional
creation theory in recognizing that "the universe cannot
be understood without creative genius."

In *Cosmic Evolution* Boodin called his theory "cosmic
interaction." As he succinctly put it: "Determination by
adjustment is the master-key to the universe" (5, p. 429).
And he gathered empirical evidence, cited scientific theories, mined the history of philosophy, employed logical
argument, and engaged in effusive rhetoric to support
his theory of cosmic interaction. According to this theory,
the universe as a whole does not evolve; rather all its

levels coexist, and evolution in one part of the universe stems from the responsiveness of this part to communication of form by some higher level. He wrote: "The universe cannot be understood as one history proceeding from chaos to cosmos by chance combination of elements and natural selection. Rather must we understand reality as a rhythm of multiple histories which exist at different levels and which interact. The order of evolution at lower levels must be determined by interaction of the lower level with the higher levels" (5, p. 98). And he added: "The past, present, and future levels of the developmental history of our earth may be conceived to exist in their generic structural characteristics yonder in the various histories of the cosmos as the various stages of a human individual in their generic features coexist in the overlapping generations of the race" (5, p. 100). Viewing "the problem of evolution from the cosmic instead of the geological point of view," Boodin observed: "All the cosmic generations coexist in the depths of space" (5, p. 103). Likewise, viewing the evolution of life upon the earth, he concluded that its course was stimulated and guided by changes in the crust of the earth, the earth itself altering in response to its cosmic environment. "Thus in the history of the earth the various types and stages of life and intelligence have emerged as creative adaptations to the impulses of the cosmic environment" (5, p. 123).

Matter

Boodin's idealistic interpretation of evolution as "cosmic interaction" did not exclude the concept of matter. Instead, he took to task those idealistic philosophies which either negate matter as non-being or find in it solely the source of evil. In fact, he defined evolution as "an adaptive organization of matter to respond to its cosmic field," and spoke of it as "the incarnation of the energy patterns of the cosmic environment into material bodies" (5, p. 94). Although he recognized matter as a sluggish inertia principle, he still credited it with the docility necessary to fulfill its role of storing the energy patterns and the complex conditions upon which the evolution of cumulative adaptive structures depends. The function of matter in cosmic evolution, therefore, is fundamental, but instrumental. "It is through the medium of matter, in its progressive organization, that quanta of higher levels of energy are captured and held for the time being in the organization of individual history. Matter is the instrument of energy exchange from the cosmos to the individual and back again" (5, p. 257).

Has matter a character apart from its role in cosmic evolution? Here Boodin's answer agrees with the teachings of contemporary physics, as his metaphysics of pragmatic energism foreshadowed. As he briefly put it: "The fundamental unit of energy is the quantum, the rhythmic measure according to which all exchanges of energy take place; and the unit of matter is the electron" (7, p. 91). "Nature . . . consists of pulses of energy— quanta of radiation, positive and negative electric charges—within an electromagnetic field and a gravitational field" (6, p. 489). Matter construed as energy, in line with recent physical theories, never exists as mere matter, but "always . . . in various stages of organization" (5, p. 109). Since, according to the physicists' conceptions of the molecule, the atom, the table of elements, matter universally displays "a marvelous hierarchical organization" (5, p. 103), Boodin concluded that matter, too, "is an evolution, the result of interaction" (5, p. 108). Unable to impute the uniformity of the constituents and the structure of matter to chance, he was persuaded that "Matter owes its regularity, unity and dynamic structure to the fact that it is enveloped by mind, i.e., controlled by mind" (7, p. 34). "Matter runs its course within the field of spirit" (7, p. 37).

Mind

"(H)igher in the scale and more valuable than matter," mind, too, has a primary role to play in cosmic evolution. But mind, Boodin stressed, is "not more real than matter," since it "requires the organization of matter for its realization as much as matter of a lower order requires mind for its guidance," both mind and matter being "aspects of the hierarchical organization of the cosmos" (5, p. 128). Mind is not inert: "I am not interested," confessed Boodin, "in mind as an emasculated ghost" (5, p. 242). Rather mind is "a field of energy, which in turn owes its characteristics to the interaction of the life stream with the structure of the cosmos" (5, p. 218). This does not mean that mind is reduced to or wholly derived from matter. As an energy pattern mind is superimposed upon organic patterns just as these are superimposed upon inorganic patterns. Thus, even though human mind evolves as the specific response of organic matter to the stimulus of the cosmic environment under certain conditions, mind as an existent level of energy in the cosmos does not evolve. As Boodin observed: "From the point of view of cosmic evolution, it would be truer to say that the body is evolved for the mind or, in the language of Plotinus, that the soul makes the body, than to say that the mind is a mere function of the body" (5, p. 185).

According to Boodin, the milieu of mind is threefold: (1) the individual inner complexity of mental states, (2) the social synthesis of individual minds, and (3) the cosmic milieu of mind with nature and society (5, p. 200). The second milieu listed above is the topic discussed and investigated in Boodin's *Social Mind*. Boodin, in fact, used "the expression, social mind, for the synthesis of individual minds into wholes, with new properties" (8, p. viii). He contended that "there is a genuine social unity, distinguishable from what we call the unity of individual experience, and if not more real, at least more inclusive than this" (8, p. 141). Thus the study of mind, instead of investigating individual isolated minds, a topic properly explored by physiology (5, p. 161), should start with "the postulate of intersubjective continuity as an elementary fact," that is, "the immediate consciousness of mental responsiveness" (8, p. 141). Mind energy, then, is correctly construed as will energy permeated with social significance and valuations: "Mind is essentially a system of intersubjective meanings and valuations, and of controls as resulting therefrom" (5, p. 162). A paradox underscored by Boodin is that mind, though originally intersubjective, has socialized itself into privacy (8, p. 142).

Intersubjective continuity does not suffice, however, to constitute a social mind. Examples of social minds are race, nation, family, and religion. In addition to intersubjective continuity, other elements requisite for the existence of social mind are the sense of reciprocal response to a common situation and the fusion of several individual minds into a whole dominated by a particular quality rising to a specific intensity. Social minds differ, therefore, by degrees, some being more inclusive of members, others more uniform in quality, others more intense as unities. Moreover, social minds exhibit the capacity "to overlap in a hierarchy of greater and greater complexity" (8, p. 181), and from this characteristic the prospects for world order emerge. Boodin's remedy for the present crisis in civilization is the development of social minds that are moral unities capable of directing the social unities that embrace increasingly large masses of individual minds and of employing these social groupings as instruments to higher ends without shattering or diminishing those personal values indispensable to morality. Hence upon the evolution of higher social minds, both moral and personal, hinges the resolution of those conflicts that menace contemporary civilization (8, pp. 459-479).

God

The creative advance of evolution does not stop with the genesis and growth of social minds, nor is the hierarchy of energy levels that comprise the architecture of the cosmos topped with the type of social mind that exhibits itself in human history. "The whole process of evolution," Boodin wrote, "is a process of spiritualization" (6, p. 499). A nisus toward divinity is manifest in nature because "divinity, the supreme organization of harmony, beauty, goodness and love, is active throughout the cosmos, stimulating the evolution of every part in the direction of divinity. As light stimulates towards the adaptation to seeing light, so divinity stimulates towards communion with itself" (5, p. 123). Similarly, within the individual person God is present, but not as a comforting acquiescence and resignation; rather, God is felt in us as "a divine restlessness which spurs us on so long as we truly live. When it deserts us, we are already dead. Be productive and be productive for the common good— that is the eternal commandment" (9, p. 103).

God therefore guides the creative process of evolution within the cosmos and is the presence that urges each part to respond by further creation. At first, then, Boodin's answer to the question: What is God? is framed according to his conception of evolution as the cosmic interaction of levels of existence. He wrote: "God is the highest level of the cosmos. There can be no question of the existence of God, for whatever the quality of the highest level to which we strive to adapt ourselves in our best, this is God. God is for us the unique and perfect realization of matter" (5, p. 129).

But it would be a mistake to view Boodin's God as the final state of matter in an evolutionary cosmology.

Not Samuel Alexander, but Plato of the *Timaeus* is the
forerunner of Boodin's cosmogeny. An ultimate dualism
is posited, with matter and spirit coeval principles. For
"Spirit and matter have complementary properties. Matter is characterized by inertia, spirit by spontaneity; matter by entropy, spirit by creativeness" (7, p. 115). The
difference between matter and God is illuminated in
many passages where Boodin distinguished matter from
space and expressed himself in a fashion explicitly influenced by Henry More and the Cambridge Platonists.
Space, as conceived in *A Realistic Universe*, becomes an
absolute field identifiable in principle with the spiritual
field (7, p. 129). Further, this absolute space, or spiritual field, "prescribes the architecture of all subordinate
fields, which in turn make their variant individual adjustments according to their own relativity" (7, p. 69).

Hence "God is the real life of space, present to everything, everywhere and always, in its creative activity" (7,
p. 150). But God is more than space, just as being is
more than one of its media. "God is the spirit of the
whole which, in the words of Clement of Alexandria,
'gives spiritual tone to the universe'" (7, p. 74). And
He dominates the cosmos, in the language of Plato, not
by despotic power but by persuasion (7, p. 96).

Although Boodin advised that we think of God in
terms of the highest values we know—"personality, creative intelligence, creative beauty, creative goodness, and
creative love" (7, p. 46)—he was aware that his redefinition of God, required by modern science and altered social conditions, necessitated a reinterpretation of His attributes. For if God is defined as "pervasive energy
which is present everywhere by its activity . . . that spiritual power that works for the good—a leaven, a catalytic
agent which works constructively in our world for order,
unity and harmony" (9, p. 74), it follows that the traditional attributes of omnipotence and omniscience must
be modified. Accordingly, God must be understood "as

limited in His effectiveness by our willingness, by our co-operation or opposition. Our attitude makes a real dif-ference to God's activity" (9, p. 79).

Nonetheless, Boodin's admission that God's power to direct the cosmos toward the realization of maximal val-ues is contingent upon the variant responsiveness of the parts did not diminish his optimism about the outcome. He never glossed over the reality of cosmic tragedy: "the life of nature is a tragic life without hope. Nature ever consumes itself in restlessness; and those that live the life of nature are ever carried hither and thither, in futile motion, by the winds of their desires" (7, p. 202). But whereas contemplation of the tragedies of nature breeds melancholy, sensitivity to the creativity within na-ture and to the spirituality of this creativity engenders joy. "Laughter like music," he wrote in hyperbolic prose, "runs through all creation. Creation is a choral dance" (7, p. 210). Indeed, the failure of nature to satisfy the craving of the human spirit testifies to a field of spirit which, though immanent in the creative processes of na-ture, yet transcends it. Thus, just as the cosmos, in one sense, is "an aesthetic process of realization" (7, p. 115) exhibited in the vast architecture of nature and its proc-esses, so too, in another sense, the cosmos is an infinite society of spirits. As Boodin wrote: "With my beloved teacher, Josiah Royce, I believe that I am a member of a universal spiritual community and that it is my vocation to participate creatively with the eternal Spirit of truth, goodness and beauty, in companionship with all spirits that create in like manner, to spiritualize this temporal world. And I take courage from the faith that, however confused and discordant the life of this world may seem, there is ever present, like a Pilgrim Chorus, the eternal harmony of the Spirit of the Whole; and the music of this in my soul—distant and faint though it often seems—is the inspiration to strive to bring more harmony into a chaotic world" (7, p. 75).

NOTES TO CHAPTER 4

1. *The Posthumous Papers of John Elof Boodin* in *Studies in Philosophy* (Berkeley and Los Angeles: University of California Press, 1957).
2. John Elof Boodin, *Time and Reality* (New York: The Macmillan Co., 1905); *Psychological Review*, Monograph Supplement, Vol. VI, No. 3 (Oct. 1904).
3. John Elof Boodin, *Truth and Reality: An Introduction to the Theory of Knowledge* (New York: The Macmillan Co., 1911).
4. John Elof Boodin, *A Realistic Universe* (New York: The Macmillan Co., 1916); 2d rev. ed. (New York: The Macmillan Co., 1931). Quotes in the text are from the 2d edition.
5. John Elof Boodin, *Cosmic Evolution: Outlines of Cosmic Idealism* (New York: The Macmillan Co., 1925).
6. John Elof Boodin, *Three Interpretations of the Universe* (New York: The Macmillan Co., 1934).
7. John Elof Boodin, *God* (New York: The Macmillan Co., 1934).
8. John Elof Boodin, *The Social Mind: Foundations of Social Philosophy* (New York: The Macmillan Co., 1939).
9. John Elof Boodin, *The Religion of Tomorrow* (New York: Philosophical Library, 1943).
10. John Elof Boodin, "Nature and Reason," *Contemporary American Philosophy*, G. P. Adams and W. P. Montague, eds. (New York: The Macmillan Co., 1930; reprinted Russell & Russell, Inc., 1962), I, p. 138.
11. R. F. A. Hoernlé, Review of Boodin's *Cosmic Evolution*, *Journal of Philosophy*, XXIV (1927), 160-163.

Chapter 5

THE VALUE-CENTRIC
PHILOSOPHY OF
WILBUR MARSHALL URBAN

THE CRISIS IN VALUES

"The greatest spiritual adventure of my life" is what Wilbur Marshall Urban (1873-1952) called "the long night in which, as a student in Germany, I first read through the *Genealogy of Morals.* . . . In the grey light of morning I found myself surveying the wreckage of my beliefs in a curious mood, one in which a profound sense of loss was not unmixed with a sense of profound exhilaration—of a great task to be undertaken." From that moment he knew "that not only was the problem of values my problem, but also that it was destined to be the key problem of the epoch in which I was to live" (1). Urban's devotion to this single task animated and encompassed a creative philosophical career that reached over half a century and affected every domain of philosophy.

Urban, the son of an Episcopal clergyman, acknowledged his father as the source of his philosophical interests. Educated at the William Penn Charter School in Philadelphia and later at Princeton University, Urban studied at various times in Germany at the Universities of Jena, Leipzig, Munich, and Graz, and received his doctorate at Leipzig in 1897. He taught at Princeton, Ursinus, and Dartmouth, before he was called to Yale. For Urban, nurtured on religion at home and subjected to the concern with values that prevailed in Germany as a consequence of Nietzsche's challenge and of the birth of psychological and sociological investigations of values, the entire philosophical enterprise was intensely and passionately practical. He did not consider philosophy a profession of interest solely to a diminishing minority of academic specialists. For him it was a solemn undertaking in defense of values. Not only did he hope to check the corrosion of traditional values mirrored by philosophical modernism and culminating in incessant wars and social upheavals; he even wished to convert the contemporary crisis in values into a pivotal epoch of revaluation and regeneration. As Urban's preoccupation with the survival of civilized values deepened in face of the rising tide of troubles, his expectations of a happy resolution dimmed. Exhorting philosophers to quit the narrow technical quibbles that bedevil them and to tackle the problems of men, he pleaded: "If ever philosophy needed the freeing of its energies for the larger problems that concern our peace, it is now" (2, p. 9). Yet he never proposed that speculative philosophy be forsaken for political ideology or social engineering. On the contrary, "the genuine problems of speculative philosophy" must be confronted, since only through correct theory are the rectification of practice possible and the problems of men solved. It is because speculative "philosophy is always the epitome" of culture that it is indispensable (2, p. 239). The conservation and advancement of values by philosophy is tantamount to their realization and enshrinement within civilization as a whole.

Despite constant concern with values throughout over half a century, Urban's genius proved sensitive to the shifting currents of contemporary philosophy. German psychology and phenomenology were influential at the turn of the century, and their influence is obvious in his early works: A *History of the Principle of Sufficient Reason* (3) and *Valuation: Its Nature and Laws* (4). When after World War I naturalism, bolstered by process philosophy and evolutionary cosmology, challenged the great tradition on such key issues as being, knowing, and the status of mind and value, he elaborated and defended *philosophia perennis* in *The Intelligible World* (5). When during the same period the epistemological disputes between idealists and realists exhausted philosophy, he sought to transcend the conflict in *Beyond Realism and Idealism* (6). When in the 1930s logical positivism and linguistic analysis first rose to threaten the entire framework of traditional philosophy and to impugn the objectivity of values, he replied with *Language and Reality* (7). And when after World War II existentialist theology and atheistic naturalism decried human reason and values, he grappled with the problems of natural theology in *Humanity and Deity* (8). Central to all these undertakings was Urban's concern with values.

The "value-centric predicament" Urban embraced as inescapable in philosophy. He accepted Josiah Royce's formulation of it (9): "the question, 'How ought I to conceive the real?' is logically prior to the question, 'What is the real itself?' . . . the ought is prior in nature to the real; or the proposition, I ought to think so, is prior to the proposition, this is so" (5, pp. 61-62). To Royce's statement he added: "the very distinction between truth and falsity, between appearance and reality themselves, depend upon certain ideals or norms of truth and reality. Every judgment that something exists presupposes the meaning of it as true. It is because

meaning lies above all being, and because meaning is
inseparable from value, that the value-centric predicament cannot be escaped" (5, p. 64). It is the persistent
elaboration of the value-motif in all areas of philosophy
which determines the unique quality and distinctive
unity of Urban's thought. Urban intended first to formulate a general theory of value, and then to reinterpret
all the major areas of philosophy in terms of it. He desired, therefore, neither Nietzschean transvaluation of
values nor Deweyan reconstruction in philosophy, but
rather the revaluation of values and the revival of philosophy. What he hoped for was nothing less than the
conservation and regeneration of the traditional value-
commitments which he believed were fundamental to
Western civilization.

THE GENERAL THEORY OF VALUE

Phenomenology of Valuation

To formulate a science of values within the limits of
psychology and phenomenology was the aim of Urban's
first major work, Valuation. Dedicated to James Mark
Baldwin, who influenced the work, Valuation also
manifests the impact of the German and Austrian ex-
ponents of Wertlehre. Brentano, Ehrenfels, Kraus, Krei-
big, Kruger, Lipps, Meinong, Schwartz, Simmel, and
Wundt are all cited. Meinong in particular is singled
out since his program, "the value problem before the
forum of psychology," stated in Psychologische-ethische
Untersuchungen zur Werttheorie, had caught Urban's
attention (as had Nietzsche's Genealogy of Morals) as
early as 1897, while he was a student at Jena (1, p.
359).

Viewed a half century later Valuation is a difficult
book. In method it is phenomenological and genetic.
Phenomenologically it explores and describes the psychological phenomena of worth (or value) experi-

ences present in consciousness; genetically it traces the development of these experiences, the higher from the lower, and explicates the psychological processes which must be postulated to explain the genesis. And although its language and science are outmoded, it remains a landmark in the history of American philosophy as the first book wholly devoted to value theory. All the fields of value, economics, ethics, aesthetics, social morality, religion, were investigated to ferret out their interconnections and their common laws (if any), and to explain the levels of value and the criteria and nature of preferences between them. The term "axiology" was introduced in *Valuation* (10).

Urban strove to overcome the dichotomy of fact and value, of description and appreciation. Neither could be reduced to the other, since reduction of value to fact, appreciation to description, would impugn the normative control of values, whereas the converse reduction would rule out science. Yet a science of values requires that somehow values be facts, appreciations be descriptive. Urban met the requirement by construing description and appreciation as overlapping in valuation. Every value experience evaluates: it not only feels and desires but also cognizes its object; it contains a noetic feature. Every value experience is an appreciative description in the sense that intrinsically it is a feeling-attitude containing reference to some object it cognizes. By hierarchical ranking of the value objects without the imputation of metaphysical reality, a general theory of value, beginning with psychological descriptions of feelings and desires as appreciations, is axiological, i.e., normative, capable of the reflective evaluation of values, within the limits of phenomenology.

The psychology subservient to phenomenology invested Urban's theory with a scientific appearance. Tracing values back to funded affective-volitional meanings, Urban distinguished between the value object, the value experience, and the causal determinant of the value experience. Value experiences are causally determined by the valuing subject's psychological condition, his character or personality. Yet they exhibit an autonomous structure analyzable quantitatively in terms of degree of depth and breadth and qualitatively in terms of direction and reference. Sharply discriminated from the surrounding sensation feelings, value experiences directionally exist within a positive-negative range of quality describable as pleasantness-unpleasantness and referentially involve value objects beyond themselves. Inasmuch as phenomenologically a value experience is a feeling-attitude meaning some value object, it includes cognition of this value object as presumed, asserted, or assumed to exist. It also includes a conative disposition to actualize it, enjoy it, and so on, thereby establishing tensions or movements of repose and expansion within the experience of the valuing subject. From these referential aspects of value experience, Urban contended, arise the fundamental feelings of obligation and aesthetic enjoyment. This does not mean that values are to be reduced to or identified with value experiences. Phenomenologically, values "are *what* we feel about the object, not *how* we feel" (4, p. 56).

Urban's phenomenological psychology of valuation is genetic in methodology, sketching the progression of value experience from its origin in simple appreciation to the higher and more complex stages of characterization and participation, each stage indicating a different rank of value objects. Whereas appreciation refers to "condition worths," e.g., food, sex, or economic good, which satisfy the purely individual, subpersonal and subsocial organism, characterization and participation refer to personal and impersonal or over-individual values, respectively. Characterization imputes worth "to expressions of feeling or acts of will as manifesting certain dispositions of the personality" (4, p. 233), and participation ascribes value "to an act, not because it expresses a personality, but because it is instrumental to certain social, over-individual ends, and satisfies certain impersonal demands" (4, p. 234). Since characterization and participation refer to ideal objects such as persons and communities, awareness of such objects is, according to Urban, initiated in the individual value experiences of simple appreciation and generated by feelings of sympathy and faculties of projection. Where, for instance, Nietzsche could detect no basis in healthy human nature and consciousness for the traditional values of personality and community, Urban sought in *Valuation* to record genetically the evolution of the highest phases of value consciousness from the most primitive phases of simple appreciation, to interpret the movement of valuation as a progressive ascent in awareness of value culminating in participation in the loftiest and most universal values.

Axiology and Phenomenology

In *Valuation* axiology is defined as "the reflective evaluation of objects of value. We not only *feel* the value of objects, but we evaluate these objects and ultimately the feelings themselves" (4, p. 16). Thus axiology ascertains the criteria governing the establishment of a hierarchy of value objects, and as epistemology does for factual judgments, it also investigates value experiences to determine the criteria of validity for value judgments. Although for both factual and value judgments objectivity is the condition of truth or validity, in the case of value judgments the objectivity is of a special sort, tantamount to over-individual control. In this sense value is a norm. Now whether values *qua* norms are facts (i.e., exist) is bracketed, since value judgments do not entail that values exist but rather that they ought to exist and even that will ought to be exerted to realize them. Hence, for

Urban, the objectivity of values as norms pivots on their sufficiency.

Are certain values to be preferred over others? Can such preferences be justified by reasons? Will the rationally preferred values be efficacious in respect to wills?

Urban's phenomenology of valuation never satisfactorily answered these questions. It failed, in fact, to uncover absolute values fixed eternally for all men and all occasions, although it did discover "practical absolutes," moments of intense value-consciousness when certain ideals confound all distinctions of the intellect and impose themselves upon the agent as absolute. These practical absolutes, however, neither correlate with an ontological situation independent of the valuing subject nor comprehend all the dimensions of value. Such correlation and comprehension would, of course, constitute sufficiency. But since objective ontological correlation required, for Urban, a met-empirical will beyond all empirical wills to establish continuity between individual value experiences and reality and to posit an identity between this met-empirical will and the empirical wills when the latter are engaged in valid valuations, it cannot be assured by phenomenology. Similarly, a supreme moment of experience in which all valid values coalesce is beyond the scope of phenomenology. Naming such a moment "the Beatific Vision," Urban concluded: "Whether it is attainable or not, and if attainable capable of being held, it is not for us to say" (4, p. 428).

Despite its technical ingenuity Urban marked *Valuation* down as a failure, confessing that, though unquestionably important "as a stage in the forming of my philosophical creed," it "has always been a source of real embarrassment for me. For it turned out, as is often the case, that its completion marked the passing beyond the stage which the book itself represented" (1, p. 360). And he ascribed the main fault to the presuppositional method. Genetic explanation of valuation demanded

not merely a description of how a given worth experience is caused by preceding ones and in turn causes suc-
ceeding ones in a strictly mechanical chain, but also
an appreciative interpretation of the value goals or ends
toward which the efficiently caused value experiences
aimed. Therefore Urban had devised a special form of the
genetic method—the presuppositional method, which
for him stood midway between the causal mechanism
and the value teleology. Accordingly, the interpretation
of the data of valuation stressed presupposed psychological faculties and processes whereby value objects functioning as final causes were nevertheless "constructed"
from data involved in the strictly mechanical chain. A
halfway house between normative interpretation and
causal explanation, *Valuation* collapsed before the problems of axiology. "I can only say that when I came to
the fundamental problems of the last chapters I found
the method breaking apart in my hands . . . what I was
feeling after was such a phenomenology as was much later developed by Spranger and Jasper [sic], but which
was possible only after value theory had developed far
beyond the point which it had reached at that time"
(1, p. 361). Now regardless of where Urban expressly
put the blame for failure and whither he anticipated
success, the actual course of his philosophical development reveals a gradual abandonment of phenomenology
and steady movement toward metaphysics.

Axiology and Metaphysics

In 1913 Urban returned to Europe for study with
Meinong at Graz. There he fell under the spell of Rickert
and Husserl. When a few years later he made a fresh
start on the problems of axiology, the influence of Rickert was unmistakably present. Three papers which appeared in the *Journal of Philosophy* in 1916 and 1917
are the important products of this transitional period
(11). But the intellectual tendencies and theses crystal-

lizing in Urban's mind found their most mature statement in *The Intelligible World*.

In *The Intelligible World* axiology is broadly defined as inquiry into *"the metaphysical status of value"* (5, p. 134), entangling a host of psychological, epistemological, and ontological problems. Inasmuch as the phenomenology of valuation had already demarcated the value object from the value experiences, and since in recognition of the normative quality of value Urban, like G. E. Moore, ruled out definitions of value in terms of interest or satisfaction (maintaining, in fact, that values are indefinable), the focus of inquiry shifted from psychology to epistemology and ontology.

Urban scrutinized the value judgment, contending that the value predicate expresses not only a qualitative essence but also a particular relation between this essence and existence. Thus to judge a thing beautiful or a person noble is to ascribe a quality which is "worth existing" or "ought to be." Urban singled out "this double character of the value judgment, this unique bearing on existence" as constituting "the *differentia* of the value judgment" (5, p. 142). Like the existential judgment, moreover, the value judgment does not merely conjoin a subject and a predicate; it contains a distant "reflexive act," so that while an existential judgment reflexively "recognizes or acknowledges 'that it is so,'" a value judgment "acknowledges 'that it ought to be,' or 'is worthy to be.' This meaning, ought to be, this unique bearing on existence, is an object solely of acknowledgment" (5, p. 144). Neither intuiting nor indicating a special quality, valuation is noetic in the sense that it assents to a form of objectivity. In brief, a value "is not an *entity* to be pointed to; it is a *meaning* to be acknowledged" (5, p. 146).

Axiology and epistemology, furthermore, are involved in a circle. For just as "valuation is noetic . . . cognition is valuational" (5, p. 148). Logic and knowledge "presuppose that truth is better than error, reality better than unreality—in other words, that such distinctions are value distinctions" (5, p. 148). The circularity of valuation and knowledge, of axiology and epistemology, Urban summed up in two "equally incontestable" theses: "Knowledge, in any intelligible sense of the word, is impossible without *acknowledgment*, acknowledgment of the values presupposed in any distinction between the true and the false, the real and the apparent. But it is equally true that there is no acknowledgment without knowledge in some sense of the object or objective acknowledged" (5, p. 147).

The epistemological topics lead directly to ontology. Every existential judgment establishes the existence of its object only when it is valid, i.e., possesses truth value. The epistemological discrimination between "judgments of value" and "judgments of fact" enhances admission of the autonomy of values, since it signifies that "the *values are there*—independently of our scientific and theoretical judgments about the world" (5, p. 143). Thus value is "an *objective*, or a unique form of objectivity" (5, p. 143). And since ontological predicates like "exist" or "subsist" are inadequate to describe the oughtness of value, "In the case of value *its being is its validity*" (5, p. 145). Hence Urban's philosophy belongs to the Platonic tradition which exalts the Good above being and knowing, but in placing values "above all ontology" Urban gave Platonism an Hegelian slant since he meant "that their acknowledgment . . . is the necessary condition of all intelligible communication—even . . . of the communication of the ontological predicates themselves" (5, p. 145).

The priority of value over being is the source of the antinomy of axiology. On the one hand, Urban's thesis that value transcends being borders on negative ontology, since it posits "a sphere the peculiar character of which is not completely characterized by its determination as being" (5, p. 155). The contrast between value and reality, ought and is, validity and being, constitutes the condition indispensable for "all willing. . . . If fact and value were identical there would be no will and no event" (5, p. 159). On the other hand, the separation of value and reality, ought and is, validity and being, "is ultimately contradictory and makes all our thinking and its communication unintelligible" (5, p. 152). For existence and truth are themselves axiological determinations. In another sense value and being must not be regarded as strangers: "things do have to be in relations of value, as well as in other types of relations, to be things in the full sense of our experiencing them as things" (5, p. 157). Value is not "a mere addendum to something which is by its own nature without value, but . . . the very substance and essence of the thing" (5, p. 160).

Essentially what the antinomy of axiology represents is the systematic tension resultant from Urban's struggle to synthesize coherently the Platonic transcendence of value over being and the Hegelian immanence of value within being. Value transcends being insofar as being is less than what ought to be, is phenomenal, and to the extent that it is permeated by will, strives to realize value. Simultaneously value is immanent in being insofar as being itself is a value-determination, is intelligible, and to the extent that it is understood, what is is what ought to be. Thus "the intelligible world" is both Plato's Heaven of the Forms and Hegel's community of Absolute Spirit. Discursive thought cannot press further than the paradoxical axiom of the duality-yet-inseparability of value and being. As Urban put it: "If there are any points where these two (value and being) come together, where they fuse in one experience—and I think there are —we can know them only in trenching on the mystical and can communicate our knowledge only in figures and symbols" (5, p. 159).

REVALUATION IN PHILOSOPHY

Urban believed that his axiology distilled the irrefutable quintessence of *philosophia perennis*. Hopeful that axiology would be better developed in future years, Urban especially looked forward to the eradication of defects in the phenomenology of valuation and the formulation of a correct theory in consonance with psychological science. Meanwhile, he was satisfied that his version of axiology as the metaphysics of value was not only true in the main, but was also the very heart and spirit of traditional philosophy. By means of this metaphysical axiology Urban sought to revaluate and revitalize modern philosophy, to divert it from contemporary deviations, and to return it to the highways of *philosophia perennis*. His enterprise encompassed ethics, epistemology, philosophy of language, logic, cosmology, and theology.

Ethics

Axiology as reflective evaluation received immediate application in Urban's textbook on ethics (12). In it ethics is defined as "in the last analysis, just the science of systematized valuing; or, otherwise expressed, the valuing activity of man made systematic" (12, p. 8). As systematic valuing, ethics explores the values of things, activities, persons, and ascertains their relative values. It discovers, in other words, "that one thing is better than another" and therefore "that thing ought to be rather than the other. The forms of conduct or behavior which have this character of *oughtness* are then called standards or norms" (12, p. 9). Hence ethics is a normative science.

A norm weds theory and practice. Practically it "controls action through consciousness and value and *through the sense of obligation or 'ought' that arises from this consciousness of value*" (12, p. 11). Theoretically a norm is "a truth also, or a form of knowledge. If I come to learn that one act is better than another, that men have rights to certain things and ought to have them, that is knowledge (and not mere opinion) just as much as learning the laws of nature is knowledge" (12, p. 12).

The concept of value was rendered more specific in content. Urban repudiated the commonplace view that "value is that which satisfies human desire" (12, p. 16) on the grounds that only those values which *also* further or conserve life are deemed valuable; and he also rejected this survival-value view, because life itself is not intrinsically valuable but acquires its value from the kind of life it is. What he advocated was an ethics of self-realization: *"that alone is ultimately and intrinsically valuable that leads to the development of selves, or to self-realization"* (12, p. 18). Of course, Urban did not propose self-realization at the expense of community values. He wrote: "the very relations of a man to others are part of his intrinsic selfhood, it is only in the realizing of functioning of these relations that the realization of the self is achieved" (12. p. 128).

Urban unveiled the content of the value concept in a scale of values. By the application of three principles: "instrinsic values are rated higher than instrumental or extrinsic; permanent values higher than transient; productive higher than unproductive" (12, p. 170), he sketched a value hierarchy of three main ranks: the organic values of the body, economics, and recreation at the base; the hyperorganic social values of association and character next; the hyperorganic spiritual values of intellect, aesthetic enjoyment, and religious feeling at the apex (13). Finally, Urban maintained that this system of values "furnishes norms of action, principles of choice. We have only to see and acknowledge the right order of values to be under obligation to choose according to that order. There is, so to speak, what the philosophers call an *a priori* relation between value and obligation, that is a relation that is both universal and necessary. The proposition that the greater good ought to be chosen rather than the lesser, is axiomatic. No reason can be given for this other than the fact that the opposite is repugnant to reason and can not be given an intelligible meaning, or, as the philosophers used to say, 'can not be conceived' " (12, p. 176).

Epistemology

According to Urban, knowing and valuing are interlocked. Just as valuation includes noetic features—the cognizing of the value object during the act of acknowledgment—knowing contains valuational features. "The very fact that we must know, and that we recognize and acknowledge that 'must,' indicates that prior to the activity of knowledge, that which constitutes its very driving force, is the acknowledgment of truth as a value and of the obligation to seek it as one of the supreme goods of life" (2, p. 16). By exploiting the axiological structure of knowing in *Beyond Realism and Idealism* Urban strove to overcome the epistemological impasse of contemporary philosophy. Epistemologically both idealism and realism, he argued, "are constituted, so to speak, by certain empirically and logically unsupported judgments of value, and it is the acknowledgment of these values which constitutes the driving force of idealism and the resistance of realism" (2, p. 17). "For the realist 'the peculiar significance' of knowledge—its inmost value—is conceived to be lost if the object of knowledge is not held to be independent of the knower, however that independence be conceived. For the idealist, on the other hand, the real significance is lost if the object of knowledge is not in some sense mind-dependent, however that mind-dependence may be conceived" (2, pp. 16-17).

Thus Urban diagnosed the epistemological controversy as springing from rival conceptions of genuine knowledge and so from prior evaluations of knowledge. This does not mean that idealism and realism are arbitrary; on the contrary, they are both "necessary *life forms* of the human reason. In a sense they are intellectual transmutations of the will to life itself. The cry we must know is a form of the cry we must live" (2, p. 25). Urban credited idealism as "the driving force of all vital culture— that which creates, . . . revives and reforms" and realism as "the stabilizing element in culture—that which restrains and conserves" (2, p. 25). So they must be reconciled; otherwise life decays, culture topples, and philosophy perishes. Only through appeal to values, however, can realism and idealism be reconciled, and then only if their two separate minimal demands are met. Now realism is satisfied when it is admitted that "the very purpose and meaning of knowledge is to be true to something beyond it" (2, p. 97), whereas idealism imposes the axiological demand that "meaning . . . cannot ultimately be separated from value . . . that the two notions intelligibility and value are inseparable" (2, p. 64). Since Urban regarded these seemingly incompatible demands to be mutually supporting, an epistemological counterpart to the antinomy of axiology disclosed as inescapable in the metaphysics of value, he advanced an "idealistic philosophy along realistic lines," maintaining both that thought is directed toward an object beyond itself and that this objective for thought is inseparable from value.

Philosophy of Language

Urban's philosophy of language, heavily indebted as it is to Cassirer's philosophy of symbolic forms, is original by virtue of its dependence upon the value theory. Urban, in fact, defined the philosophy of language as "concerned with *the evaluation of language as a bearer of meanings, as a medium of communication and as a sign or symbol of reality*" (7, p. 37). Citing "the history of

European culture" as "the story of two great opposing valuations—high and low *evaluations* of the Word" (2, p. 23), Urban espoused the former, the idealist, rather than the latter, the naturalistic, evaluation. Meanings, rather than ideograms, phonograms, or language behavior, comprise the focal point of the idealist view. As Urban stated in *The Intelligible World*: "*Back of the concept of meaning lies the concept of value, and the two concepts cannot be separated*" (5, p. 61). The idealist approach, in effect, locates the meanings conveyed by language within a speech community united by common orientation toward values.

Meanings originate in values. As animals attend to discriminable features of their experiences for cues to action, so men apprehend sense data whose meanings derive from behavior aimed at values. This involvement with values, apparent at the level of perception, is intensified at the level of language and semantic meaning. "The essence of semantic meaning is its intentionality" (7, p. 125). Because intentions are acts of minds, and because minds, being purposive, have intentions which subserve or are identical with these purposes, intentions involve values. Moreover, intentionality entails the *suppositio*, and the *suppositio* in turn is value-centric. Intentionality, embodied in discourse consisting in a triadic relation between (1) individual speaker or hearer, writer or reader, (2) the speech community, and (3) reality, includes "a context or universe of discourse presupposed. That is the supposition, and this supposition, as part of the intentionality, must be apprehended and *acknowledged* if understanding is to be possible" (7, p. 125). Inasmuch as ordinary language is elliptical, it is constant witness to a context dependent upon acknowledged, implicit suppositions.

Discourse is meaningful insofar as the speech community mutually acknowledges certain suppositions. "The condition of the meaningfulness of an assertion or proposition is, then, *not* that certain entities about which the assertion is made exist, in the sense of being empirically verifiable, but that the universe of discourse in which these entities have their existence is mutually acknowledged" (7, p. 201). "In every proposition the circumstances of its enunciation show that it refers to some collection of individuals or possibilities which cannot be adequately described or defined, but can only be indicated as something familiar and mutually acknowledged by both speaker and hearer. At one time it may be the physical universe of sense; at another, an 'imaginary' world of some play or novel; at another, a world of validities or values, as in ethical discourse" (7, pp. 203-204). Thus the traditional values, acknowledged in literature, religion, and philosophy, have an ontological claim equal to that of the empirical facts of scientific discourse, and even, in some respects, superior to those facts, since science itself is shaped to promote certain values. Furthermore, there are supposed entities inescapable for all intelligible discourse: the Self, Others, and the World; and these are "not so much objects of *knowledge,* in any narrow or sectarian sense of that word, as objects of acknowledgment . . . values and validities" (5, p. 48).

Urban viewed with alarm the modernist inclination to restrict language to a merely empirical employment, to discount discourse about values as cognitively meaningless, and to trivialize the symbolisms of art, religion, and metaphysics, thereby facilitating the imminent destruction of the values they represent. He urged a high evaluation of the Word.

Logic

For Urban logic, like ethics, is a normative science, constituting the morality of thinking. But Urban's distinctive contribution to logic lay in his interpretation of self-reference in philosophical argument (14). All metaphysical propositions are self-referential: by virtue of their universality they contain their enunciators within their ranges of meaning. They are either *a priori* when their denials lead to self-contradiction, or inadmissible if they themselves lead to self-contradiction. But it must be understood the resultant self-contradiction or self-refutation is essentially an *argumentum ad hominem*. For example: "Whoever claims that there is no valid knowledge, in this very claim expresses a 'case' of knowledge for which he presupposes objective validity. So far he contradicts or refutes himself. X makes the assumption A, that he possesses no valid knowledge. This has as its consequence merely that X himself can have no valid knowledge of this assumption A, for if he had this knowledge he would possess in it a case of valid knowledge. It is not the assumption A (that X possesses no valid knowledge) that contains a contradiction, but rather a further assumption B (namely, that X possesses a valid knowledge of A). From this contradiction there follows as a consequence, however, not the falsity of A, but merely the falsity of B" (5, p. 45).

By interpreting self-reference as essentially *ad hominem* Urban concentrated on the individual man stating the argument and presumably seeking values, at least truth-value. Since no man can allow what is incompatible with his nature as a seeker of values, Urban concluded that whatever a man discovers to be axiologically intolerable is logically unintelligible. The logical validity of all theory, therefore, pivots on man as value seeker. So completely do values dictate theory that man's very conception of the cosmos is obliged to conform to the conditions of his willing. Unless the primacy of values is acknowledged philosophically, philosophy is meaningless, for unless the world has meaning and value for philosophy, philosophy as an activity undertaken in the world is meaningless. And to condemn the world as meaningless or valueless is to stand self-refuted, since if the condemnation is true, then the condemner is doing what is meaningless. Further, to the extent at least that the condemnation is true and meaningful, so is the world.

Cosmology

Urban's cosmology, presented in *The Intelligible World,* is an attempt to "restate some very old things in a new way" by "shifting . . . the philosophical center of gravity from being to value" (5, pp. 174-176). Abjuring modernist tendencies to submerge man and his values within an alien scheme of evolutionary naturalism, Urban argued that, since life is intelligible by virtue of its ideals or values, "a world, in order to be an intelligible context for such a life, must . . . be one in which the values, by which the individual life is lived, have their counterpart in an order of values that is cosmic" (5, p. 183).

Urban urged the revaluation of the categories of traditional cosmology—space, time, substance, and cause —by reference to axiology. Space and time, traditionally looked upon as appearances, are construed as phenomenal of values which are atemporal and aspatial. Existents exhibit meanings and values which are there, for acknowledgment, beyond space and beyond time. Space and time, nevertheless, are necessary forms for the existence of values. "The inmost meaning of time is the inalienable difference between that which is and that which ought to be, and, conversely, it seems, the inmost meaning of value is bound up with its expression in the time form" (5, p. 262). " 'It takes time' for new qualities to emerge in the inorganic and organic world. It takes time for human meanings and values to be realized" (5, p. 262). Even the category of substance is viewed as "a value category. The retention of the meaning and value of the 'individual' is the axiological basis of substance in its meaning of thinghood, the retention of the meaning and value of the universal the basis of substance in its sense of essence, the retention of the meaning and value of concrete totalities the basis of its use of important or characteristic elements" (5, pp. 283-284).

But nowhere is Urban's originality more remarkable than in his axiological revaluation of causation. To be axiologically intelligible, the principle of causation must, in some fundamental way, fuse efficient and final causes, origin and destiny. Harking back to ideas adumbrated in his doctoral dissertation, Urban maintained that "the ultimate cause must contain *eminently* all the reality, meaning, and value of the effect. The less can be derived from the more, never the more from the less" (5, p. 216). He affirmed: "The intellect is ultimately oriented towards value, and this orientation requires that the 'sufficient reason' of any reality shall retain the reality of the thing to be explained. . . . Now the meaning and value of anything (and therefore its nature) can be expressed only in terms of purpose or finality. Consequently, its ultimate origination, its *sufficient* reason, requires that this element of finality shall be included in the notion of cause or ground. Causality and finality must in some way be brought together in a more ultimate concept" (5, pp. 216-217).

Grounded in the principle that each thing has a sufficient reason, and conjoining origin and destiny, intelligible causation cannot be contradicted. The putative experience of development, whereby the posterior seems to rise higher than the prior in value and being, is discounted by means of the category of potentiality: the posterior is simply potential in the prior. For Urban, the meaning of potentiality "is simply the postulate, or insight, that in the interpretation of any process it is the process as a whole that is to be considered if we wish to know the nature of reality revealed in it. In other words, the concept of potentiality merely maintains that any valid speculative derivation presupposes the retention of the meaning and value of the thing to be derived" (5, pp. 279-280).

Evolution, survival, and history are revaluated in light of intelligible causation. Viewed as more than a sheer sequence of accidental happenings, evolution exhibits purposive development. Unless the evolving subjects actualize values beyond time and beyond space, nature would be the scene of futile exfoliation of species and individuals under the sway of death. But the axiological bleakness of such an outlook rules it out for man, who therefore must acknowledge a higher destiny. Similarly, history, which is the record of the development of whole nations, i.e., "value totalities or individualities" (5, p. 375), witnesses to progress in the sense that its intelligibility presupposes "a consistent or continuous advance through time" toward the attainment of "an absolute standard, apprehended, however dimly, by man" (5, p. 370). Thus purposive evolution, human survival, and historical progress are transcendental necessities. Unless they are posited, natural, social, and individual processes are absurd, meaningless sequence; but since striving human agents in quest of values deem such sequence unintelligible by virtue of its axiological intolerability, Urban concluded that the transcendental forms are justified philosophically.

To secure the progressive realization of these forms in and through time-bound processes Urban adverted to Hegelianism, construing the subject of development as timeless and spiritual. For, he held, that development, whether individual or universal, particular or cosmic, natural or historical, "requires *a subject of such a nature that by its successive changes new conditions of further changes in a fixed series are continually introduced, and that this series leads ultimately to an end in which the original disposition or potentialities are completely realized.* It is not by itself, but by virtue of the permanent nature of the developing subject, that each particular stage is the cause of the next. This alone is intelligible causation, and intelligible causation can never be thought as anything but realization or development of the Idea" (5, p. 327).

Theology

Humanity and Deity presents Urban's revaluation of traditional theology. Against both atheistic humanistic naturalism and antihumanistic theological existentialism, Urban advocated a natural theology starting from acknowledged human values. He wrote: "the essence of religion cannot be separated from man's consciousness of value without losing its meaning. The initial *datum* of all religion is the acknowledgment of value, and . . . from this all religious thought proceeds" (8, p. 75). Natural theology, the rationale of man's religious experience and the elucidation of its presuppositions, is therefore governed by the primacy of value as its cardinal principle. "The underlying postulate of all thinking about God, His attributes and His acts, is . . . the identity of God with the Sovereign Good, and of the inseparability of the latter from being" (8, p. 156). Natural reason, to which all proofs of God's existence appeal, is, indeed, described as having "by nature (a) native and intrinsic reference to the Good or value" (8, p. 159).

The ontological argument, understood as the " 'initial datum' of the other proofs" (8, p. 170), in effect avers "the identification of God with the Highest Good and the identification of *ens perfectissimum* with the *ens realissimum*" (8, p. 165). Only by carrying "in our minds already an intuition of perfection" can we ascribe the quality of divinity to the entity whose existence is demonstrated cosmologically from perceptible motion, causality, and contingency (8, p. 173). It is, then, the fourth way, "the anthropological proof," which Urban regarded as the mainstay of the Thomist argument. "We experience degrees of Good—distinctions of more or less, of better or worse—and from these we argue to the Perfect Good presupposed" (8, p. 174). In this sense humanity is the key to Deity: "Humanity and Deity, like the inside and the outside of the curve, like the mountain and the valley, are apart from each other unthinkable" (8, p. 49). "If . . . there were not from the beginning the moral or value consciousness of man, with its coimplicates of perfection and of *ens perfectissimum*, the movement of thought which we call the theistic argument would never get started at all" (8, p. 171).

Grounding traditional theology upon axiology, Urban undertook to formulate the demonstration of God's existence in terms of values. He differentiated two distinct but related arguments—from values and from meaning. "The argument from values starts . . . with the initial acknowledgment of the intrinsic values—of beauty, honour and intelligence—upon which the goods of life depend for their significance; with the initial assumption that the values are *there*. . . . As genuine values . . . they are unintelligible, 'impossible,' unless they have their origin and consummation in a being religion calls God" (8, p. 195). The argument from meaning runs thus: "If the world has a meaning, God, the Supreme Spirit, must be its origin, ground and goal. But the world has meaning indubitably. Therefore there must be a ground and goal of the nature described by religion as God" (8, p. 198). Thus the theistic argument begins with man and acknowledged human values. Because God alone can account ultimately for these values, men must perforce acknowledge His existence.

CONCLUDING REMARKS

Broad in scope and ample in content, Urban's philosophy manifests a distinctive unity by virtue of its value-centricity. Organized around values without unfolding in a linear order, Urban's philosophy furnishes not only a general theory of value but also the revaluation of all philosophical disciplines. Unquestionably the enormous compass of this intention and the efficacy of its execution mark an important chapter in recent American thought. More than any other philosopher of the period Urban shifted the philosophical argument for idealism to the field of values. Just as philosophers were becoming aware that the criteria of meaningful discourse raise a major and significant philosophical problem, he insisted upon the intelligibility of the idealist program as regards values and the unintelligibility of the alternatives. He advocated an intimate connection between knowing and evaluation and emphasized the primacy of evaluation. As Urban said: "we cannot detach meanings and values from mind without becoming unintelligible" (15).

A repeated maxim of Urban is that what is intolerable from the standpoint of value is unintelligible from the cognitive standpoint. For truth is a value to be sought and cherished. In this connection Urban's favorite form of argument is: Acknowledge this, or else beware of the horrible consequences. Its cogency optimistically depends upon the supposition that man has the ability to avert the consequences and the allied supposition that the world somehow sustains the desired acknowledgment. And yet, paradoxically, it is just this optimism that lends peculiar force to this value-centric philosophy. Whatever the logical merits of his argument, Urban was confident that men would withdraw from the destruction of civilized values once they envisioned the horrors such destruction entails. Whether, of course, he was right in supposing that the cosmos would nurture man's highest hopes and that philosophy could sound the clarion call and rally men behind the Good, only time will tell.

NOTES TO CHAPTER 5

1. W. M. Urban, "The Logical Foundations of Democratic Dogma," *The Rice Institute Pamphlet*, XXX (1943), pp. 97-98, substantially a paraphrase of "Metaphysics and Value," in *Contemporary American Philosophy*, G. P. Adams and W. P. Montague, eds. (New York: The Macmillan Co., 1930; reprinted by Russell & Russell, Inc., 1962), Vol. II, p. 359. Citations in the text will be to the latter.

2. W. M. Urban, *Beyond Realism and Idealism* (London: George Allen & Unwin, Ltd., 1949).

3. This book is Urban's doctoral dissertation (Ph.D., Leipzig, 1897). Originally printed in Philadelphia in 1897, it was issued in 1898 as the first number of Volume I of *Princeton Contributions to Philosophy*, edited by A. T. Ormand, when Urban was Reader in Philosophy at Princeton. While its avowed theme is the record of use of the principle of sufficient reason in German philosophy, it obliquely discloses how purely logical restrictions wrenched reason from its broad vision of value and being. At moments Urban's dissatisfaction breaks through, since logic, narrowly conceived, leaves values out of account. Indeed, this immature essay concludes with an antinomy between logic and value: "Perhaps all these *worth* categories might be found to have a 'sufficiency' of their own, and the abstraction by means of which we come to a critical understanding of the logical Law of Ground, may only serve to bring the antithesis more plainly to our consciousness. At all events the critical results cannot be undone" (p. 88).

4. W. M. Urban, *Valuation: Its Nature and Laws* (London & New York: Swan Sonnenschein and Co., Ltd., and The Macmillan Co., 1909).

5. W. M. Urban, *The Intelligible World* (New York: The Macmillan Co., 1929).

6. Though published in 1949, the book was probably written in the thirties, as evidenced by the fact that Urban refers to books of that period as if they had recently appeared. See John E. Smith, "Beyond Realism and Idealism: An Appreciation of W. M. Urban, 1873-1952," *The Review of Metaphysics*, VI (1953), 347. At any rate Urban's concern with this topic can be traced back to an early article, "Beyond Realism and Idealism vs. Two Types of Idealism," *Philosophical Review*, XXVII (1918), 63-71. And the formulation of the argument for the meeting of apparent extremes reflects the influence of Bosanquet.

7. W. M. Urban, *Language and Reality* (London and New York: The Macmillan Co., 1939).

8. W. M. Urban, *Humanity and Deity* (London: George Allen and Unwin, Ltd., 1951).

9. The quotation is from Josiah Royce, *Lectures on Modern Idealism*, J. Loewenberg, ed. (New Haven: Yale University Press, 1923), p. 237. Urban also cited as the source for the term "value-centric" E. G. Spaulding, *The New Rationalism* (1918), pp. 206 ff.

10. On p. 16. The term had been previously employed by Paul Lapie in *Logique de la volonté* (1902) and E. von Hartmann in *Grundriss der Axiologie* (1908), according to E. S. Brightman in his article, "Axiology," in the *Dictionary of Philosophy*, D. D. Runes, ed. (New York: Philosophical Library, 1942), p. 32. Apparently, however, Urban did not know about these earlier occurrences of the term. In 1930 he claimed: "The term 'axiological' was coined by me wholly independently, and, so far as I know, it occurs in no earlier literature" (*Contemporary American Philosophy*, p. 361, n. 1). Yet later he referred to the "almost simultaneous appearance in many quarters" of the new term "axiology." "The rapidity with which the new term was adopted also made it clear that in it had been found a means, not only of clarifying many issues that had been confused, but also of unifying a field of investigation which had gradually become one of the central interests of modern philosophy." See "Axiology," in *Twentieth Century Philosophy*, D. D. Runes, ed. (New York: Philosophical Library, 1943), p. 53.

11. See "Value and Existence," *Journal of Philosophy*, XIII (1916), 449-465; "Knowledge of Value and the Value Judgment," *ibid.*, XIII (1916); and "Ontological Problems of Value," *ibid.*, XIV (1917), 309-327.

12. W. M. Urban, *Fundamentals of Ethics* (New York: Henry Holt & Co., 1930).

13. See the table in *Fundamentals of Ethics*, p. 169.

14. Professor F. B. Fitch of Yale University, a close student of Urban, has developed this aspect of Urban's thought within mathematical logic, resulting in a symbolic logic without the theory of types. For Urban's favorable comment on Fitch's work, see *Humanity and Deity*, p. 209, n. 1.

15. W. M Urban, "Philosophy of Spirit: Idealism and the Philosophy of Value," *Contemporary Idealism in America*, C. Barrett, ed. (New York: The Macmillan Co., 1932), p. 106.

Chapter 6

DeWITT H. PARKER'S
METAPHYSICS OF VALUES

INTRODUCTION

In *The Self and Nature* DeWitt H. Parker (1885-1949) described "the method of metaphysics" as "radical empiricism extended through the imagination" (1, p. vi). A generation later, in his mature system, *Experience and Substance*, Parker cited approvingly his early description of the procedure of metaphysics (2, p. 9). Taking experience as given, and viewing it as a fragment of a wider reality, metaphysics is radically empirical. Yet its empiricism is oriented toward analysis. It probes into the omnipresent features of given experience to uncover what is universal and permanent in the particular and transient. Metaphysics therefore unfolds the categories of experience, and so it becomes speculative. It employs these categories, forms of the eternal embedded in experience, to envision the given experience in the wider context of the reality beyond and to interpret this reality in terms accessible to experience. Thus metaphysics flies from the given experience upon the wings of imagination to speculatively grasp the world picture.

DeWitt Parker's career as a philosopher was remarkably rich. His academic credentials were excellent. In 1902 he entered Harvard, and for the next six years he studied under Royce, Santayana, Palmer, Munsterberg, James, Perry, and Holt. After two years on the faculty at the University of California, he was called to the University of Michigan, where he taught philosophy for the rest of his life. His creative works tended to center on the philosophy of values, and among the philosophers studied in the present volume he is the foremost contributor to the fields of aesthetics and the philosophy of art. Although Parker was concerned both with the analysis of given experience to provide the metaphysical categories and with the formulation of a cosmological scheme based on these categories—a concern that is evidenced in such extensive works on metaphysics as *The Self and Nature* (1917) and *Experience and Substance*(1941)—he was preoccupied with no area of given experience more than with value experience, as manifest in the titles of his books: *The Principles of Aesthetics* (3), *The Analysis of Art* (4), and *Human Values* (5). In his intellectual autobiography Parker confessed that this interest in "the general nature, classification, and criticism of Values" came as "a result doubtless of ethical problems raised by the Great War" (6). On two occasions, at least, Parker promised in print to write a volume on the metaphysics of value (5, p. 12, n. 1; and 2, p. vii). Unfortunately he never did so, although at the time of his death he was at work on such a volume (7). Professor William K. Frankena of the University of Michigan has edited this manuscript and published it as *The Philosophy of Value*, the title Parker himself had chosen (8). Later, the excluded chapter stating Parker's metaphysics of values was published (9).

The primary purpose of the present chapter is to revivify the total structure of Parker's thought, for he was a philosopher of exceptional talents. He possessed a literary style of unusual warmth and sensitivity, clarifying abstract questions with illustrations drawn from intimate contact with life. When the dominant temper was naturalistic and antimetaphysical, Parker elaborated and ably defended a metaphysics of voluntaristic idealism (10). The second purpose of this chapter is to reconstruct Parker's metaphysics and to explore its bearing on and implication from his theory of values. Although Parker never fulfilled his intention to complete a metaphysics of value, the outlines of such a theory may be gleaned from his published writings, and in this field his contribution is unique and comprehensive. Value experience involves categories which, being universal and eternal, are metaphysical; and to Parker belongs credit for elucidating these categories. To deny the relevance of metaphysics to values, he would have argued, is to be blind to the way such categories as substance, time, space, and causality pervade value experiences. Moreover, value experiences occur in the wider context of experience and reality. And Parker's philosophy, instead of retreating from the demands of a speculative view, has aimed to formulate this wider context in which values are possible and come to exist.

THE GENERAL THEORY OF VALUES

Parker proposed to formulate a general theory of value, one which defines the "*generic* concept" of value (8, p. 5). Expressing a universal which is embodied in all species of value, this theory is designed to grasp the nature of value, free from the bias that affects an axiology expounded from the standpoint of a specific type of value, whether aesthetic or moral.

Further, the examination of specific values from the perspective of the general theory illuminates the continuity of values and suggests how moral and aesthetic features, prominently displayed in particular values, nevertheless run together in all values. In *Human Values* Parker had declared "that there is no separate moral interest or value, but that, on the contrary, morality is indissolubly connected with every branch of human activity" (5, p. vii). Similarly, aesthetic features pervade all moral values. "The aesthetic experience realizes in little . . . the value of the mind as a whole—harmony. Beauty is the type of the good" (5, p. 322).

Besides elucidating the generic concept of value, Parker sought to determine the status of value in the world and to open the way for a juncture with independent metaphysical investigations to ascertain the nature of the world which allows value this sort of status. Finally, because Parker held that the existence of values is disclosed only in expressions, he inquired into the nature and role of value statements, determining whether or not they are cognitive, the extent to which they are cognitive if cognitive at all, and the function they perform if not cognitive.

Generic Value

Parker's analysis of value yielded as universal features six essential factors and six dimensions. The essential factors actually constitute the specific values encountered directly in concrete experience, while every value exemplifies the dimensions. Together the factors and the dimensions of value make up its generic concept, providing the investigator with an instrument for the understanding of experienced values detected by empirical inquiries.

Essential Factors of Value. First of the essential factors is *desire.* It is "a vectorial experience . . . asymmetrical and directed . . . like movement and like time . . . It is also a tense experience; we can . . . compare it to coiled spring. . . . Finally, it is an efficacious experience, an activity, one which changes or might change the course of events" (8, p. 91). Value consists in precisely the satisfaction of desire, and when desire is frustrated, the result is evil.

Second, value experience involves *a goal or objective* as an essential factor. This is "never an object but an activity or passivity, usually with reference to an object. It is not the bread that I want, but to eat the bread" (8, p. 92). Satisfaction consists in the realization of the objective.

Third, value experience requires *an object.* "The energy of desire flows through and around the object and is released by it" (8, p. 95). This does not mean that the value is identical with the object. Rather the relation between object and satisfaction is causal. Thus "complementary object" is distinguished from "means object," the former directly causing the satisfaction, the latter being necessary to produce the complementary object. Moreover, Parker held that in some instances value experiences are objectless. He seems to have meant first, that some values are enjoyed gratuitously without prior consciousness of a desire with an objective, e.g., my pleasure in the scent of flowers drifting through the window of my study; and second, that some satisfactions, especially aesthetic values, are uncaused by purely physical objects, e.g., my pleasure in hearing the symphony. In this context the second is the more important contention. For Parker an aesthetic object is not a physical object. As he bluntly put it: "Aesthetic facts are mental facts" (3, p. 7). The physical work of art is "an aesthetic instrument," but "the aesthetic object," i.e., the experience of value, belongs to the world of imagination (5, p. 324). Parker's distinction between the values of real life and of imagination pivots on his conception of complementary objects as either physical or imaginative. Values of real life—health, comfort, ambition, love, ethical value, knowledge, and efficiency—draw "their complementary objects from the environment, physical and social, and depend for realization upon adaptation to it"

(5, p. 48). In the case of values of imagination, dream, play, art, and religion, Parker wrote: "I do not so much conform to a given environment as create one of my own, and instead of employing real things as complementary objects, I make use of . . . 'substitute objects' —objects of make-believe or of faith, rather than of belief, and belonging not so much to the real as to the imaginary or 'ideal' world" (5, p. 48).

A fourth essential factor of value experience in the case of conscious intelligent experients is *judgment* "concerning the fitness of means objects or the complementary object for the realization of the goal" (8, p. 99).

Fifth is "*the assuagement of desire through the realization (verification) of the objective*" (8, p. 100). An active or passive experience, my own or another's, results in the realization of an objective, an activity or passivity, which satisfies the initial desire.

Sixth, the value process is accompanied by "*anticipatory and memorial satisfactions*" (8, p. 102), the former adding incitement to the process of realizing the objective, the latter enriching it with echoes of past satisfactions.

The Dimensions of Value. Besides explicating the six essential factors constitutive of values, Parker analyzed the "multidimensionality" of value itself. Each of the six dimensions brings into focus "a range of variations of a kind which may occur independently of another range and may or may not be susceptible of serial order" (8, p. 104). First is *intensity.* As intensity characterizes separately the desire and the satisfaction, there is usually, though not strictly, a correlation between the intensity of the initial desire and the intensity of its satisfaction (8, p. 105). *Duration* is second. To be enjoyed a value must last awhile, its echoes in subsequent experience evincing its persistence (8, pp. 105-107). *Volume* is the third dimension of value. Evident in the difference between the value in drinking water and that in drinking coffee, volume "depends rather upon the complexity of the pattern of desire than upon the complexity of the pattern of the object, although the two are roughly correlative" (8, p. 107). *Quality* is the fourth dimension pertinent to value. Values manifest qualitative variations not reducible to a single kind, say, sensual pleasure, because "the satisfaction is colored by the activity, and itself becomes different according to the difference in the activities" (8, p. 108). Fifth is *height*. Despite recurrent philosophical attempts to reduce the height of value to volume or quality or to some complexity of the other dimensions, Parker was convinced that, in view of the traditional acknowledgment of a hierarchical ranking of values, "there is some unique dimension of values, referred to by the term 'height,' which is an intrinsic attribute and not a mere evaluation or rating" (8, p. 111). The sixth dimension is *harmony*. It consists in "precisely the co-operation of diverse strains of desire toward a single goal or satisfaction" (8, p. 115).

The presence of the dimensions in value experiences accounts for norms. Consequently, the identification of value with satisfaction is rendered consistent with normative ethics. "All values are 'moral' in the broadest sense, since they are normative or imperative" (5, p. 199). Reflection on the dimensions of values in connection with both the desires they satisfy and the considered means for their satisfaction produces the principles of evaluation or criticism: principles of success, of interrelation with other interests, of adequacy (5, p. 89; cf. 8, pp. 157 ff.). These principles are in effect expressions of higher order desires. "A standard is an objective of desire, but of a desire of higher order, a desire regarding desires and satisfactions of a specific sort; and like all such objectives, more permanent than those of lower order" (8, p. 150). Moreover, "there are no separate desires, since all are interwoven in the matrix self, the desire of highest order" (8, p. 155). This self, the in-

herent life plan of an individual subject, is tantamount
to the norm which, establishing the complex objective
of the totality of one's desires, subordinates and inte-
grates all component desires and satisfactions. By reference to this desire of highest order all desires may be
criticized. Hence "only desire can judge desire" (8, p.
156).

However, recognition of norms springing from values
identical with the satisfactions of selves does not suffice
for morality so long as the satisfactions are egocentric,
for "in the case of morality, man is pursuing a goal that
cannot be identified with his own satisfaction" (8, p. 239).
Why, then, be moral? Neither fear of consequences nor
desire of approval, though constraining the disruptive
desires of men to some extent, exhausts the meaning of
morality. Rather, the moral interest is born of another
source—the self-transcending efficacy of love. "Love may
be defined," Parker wrote, "as any activity which finds its
end and value in the maintenance and increase of value
to another mind" (5, p. 177). Through love men are
able to find vicarious satisfactions in the satisfactions of
others. Hence, "morality depends, in the last analysis,
upon love" (8, p. 269).

The Status of Value

Parker not only described and defined value and its
dimensions; he also sought to ascertain its status. Value
theorists have, in the main, advanced three conceptions
of the status of value: objectivism, relationalism, and
subjectivism. Parker's position is a species of subjectivism,
stated and defended in the context of a criticism of the
alternative theories.

Objectivism defines value as a transcendent "ought"
whose being is its validity (W. M. Urban) or as a property resident in objects (G. E. Moore, C. I. Lewis).
Whereas, from Parker's standpoint, a theory such as
Urban's fails because, segregating value norms from ac-

tual processes of desire, it neglects the immanence of value in actual experiences of satisfaction, the equation of value with properties resident in objects is ruled out by the definition of value as the assuagement of desire (2, pp. 304 f.; 8, pp. 51 ff.). G. E. Moore's conception of generic good as non-naturalistic and indefinable contains additional faults, since value is definable ostensively as *this* experience of enjoyment, and analytically as the assuagement of desire (8, pp. 44 ff.). C. I. Lewis's conception of value as a potentiality residing in objects to produce experiences of inherent value is rejected because Parker's penchant for the radically empirical rules out potentiality as a nonempirical mode of being, a recrudescence of barren Aristotelianism (8, pp. 38-39).

Although Parker's theory is sometimes misrepresented as relationalism, he dismissed relationalism, just as he repudiated objectivism. In the development of relationalism, R. B. Perry's naturalistic definition of value as the object of any interest has figured prominently. Against this position Parker's objections are several (8, pp. 34 ff.). First, some value experiences—for instance, music—are devoid of objects, so that occasionally the objective of desire involves no object but inheres directly in the subjective process of enjoyment. Second, the ambiguous formula of value as the object of interest, while seeming to bridge the span between the inner and the outer worlds, is actually a sham. Once precisely interpreted, it falls on one side or the other, since the only sort of relation that holds between an object and a value satisfaction is a causal relation, in itself devoid of value. Thus the definition of value as any object of interest proves, according to Parker, to be an untenable halfway house between objectivism and subjectivism. If it means that the objects of interest have objectively the properties which satisfy the interest, it collapses into objectivism and is open to the objections previously mentioned. If it means that the interest endows the object with value, then either the term "object" in the formula signifies a concept akin to Parker's concept of "objective," or the expression really means that value is the satisfaction of an interest with which the object is causally associated. Now if the first alternative (equating Perry's object with Parker's objective) is the acceptable specification of the formula, then, paradoxically, value would pre-exist the process of its realization; it would be enough to be interested in a value to enjoy it; and the role of the objective as a guide for action would be gratuitous. Hence the formula collapses into an absurd subjectivism, or the second alternative, identifying value with the satisfaction of interest or desire, is adopted.

This leads directly to Parker's type of subjectivism. "Values belong wholly to the inner world, to the world of mind" (5, p. 20). But this does not impugn the operancy of norms partially immanent in all values, nor does it collapse values into fleeting episodes of epiphenomenal consciousness. The inner world in value experience extends from the initial impulse of desire, to the apprehension of an objective through the realization of which the desire is assuaged, to the reflective consideration of the complementary and extrinsic objects, if any, requisite for the realization of the objective, to the active or passive process of realizing the objective, finally to the climactic satisfaction which constitutes the value.

More important, however, the assignment of values to a subjective status does not signify that they are psychical accidents in an indifferent, perhaps hostile world. Parker posited an intimate connection between value and existence. He distinguished two broad streams in the history of philosophy: one springing from the tradition established by Leucippus, Democritus, and Lucretius, the other stemming from Socrates, Plato, and Aristotle. Whereas the former looked upon value as "an incidental, purely contingent aspect of reality" and regarded the world empty of value until life and consciousness began, the latter have asserted that "value is essential to reality, and (that) the very conception of existence apart from value is meaningless" (2, p. 292). Parker's theory belongs to the second stream. "The unity of value and existence," he held, "follows directly from the conception of existence as a system of experiences, together with the insight that volition is primary in experience" (2, p. 292). Thus fact, the stuff of scientific objectivity and the exclusive principle of metaphysical naturalism and materialism, is an abstraction from value-drenched existence.

Value Expressions and Knowledge

Since in Parker's theory values are deemed to be subjective, it is no surprise that expressions of value, the only mode by which privately felt values can be publicly displayed, receive close attention. When the philosopher's special interest in knowledge theory is added, it is natural that the question of the cognitive character of value expressions should come to the front.

If the cognitive is equated with the factual and its articulation is restricted to descriptive statements in which the terms designate empirical objects accessible to public verification, then the subjectivity of value precludes the possibility of value judgments being cognitive, i.e. true or false, though of course statements about value expressions could be cognitive. Despite the similarity of grammatical form between factual statements and value expressions, the ascription of value to an object really signifies the existence of a subjective satisfaction (5 pp. 412-413; 8, pp. 61 ff.). Further, to read value expressions as reports of private feeling is to mistake their role. As illustration Parker chose the statement: "I love you." Of course, this statement may be understood as the report of a psychological state of affairs, describing the feeling of love by the speaker for the hearer, so that it is true or false, depending on whether or not the speaker is lying. However, occurring in the context of lover speaking to beloved, "The expression 'I love you' is part of a process that includes the love of the lover. Indeed, his love is part of the very content of the expression, literally part of its meaning" (8, pp. 75-76). Accordingly, "value statements . . . are vectorial currents of feeling which overflow into expressive media and as such are neither true nor false" (8, p. 68).

Parker divided value statements into two classes: lyrical and practical. Lyrical statements simply communicate feelings without intending to cause action. Interjections, declarative expressions of feeling, and aesthetic objects are all lyrical statements (11). Practical expressions, like lyrical ones, communicate feelings, but in addition they are intended to induce or prevent action. Commands, entreaties, and legal and ethical expressions are practical statements. The volitional character of ethical statements is manifest in instances of moral conflict. A hardened criminal may not feel at first that theft is wrong, and no description of facts may move him, unless he can be stirred by appropriate exhortations to feel sympathy for his victims or to apprehend that thievery does not promote his own interests. Recognizing the volitional basis of ethical and legal statements, Parker refrained from the naturalistic reduction of morals to social science. He attributed Dewey's faith in social science as the ultimate instrument for the eradication of moral conflict and evil to a rationalism outdated by contemporary realities (8, p. 51). He insisted that morality is not a matter of knowledge alone. The public world is the product of the desires of men, desires which clash despite the accumulation of knowledge, and which can be reconciled (though never completely) by the efficacy of love (8, pp. 174 ff.).

Parker's theory of value expressions has, therefore, obvious affinities with current noncognitivism or emotivism in values (12). Nevertheless, it is distinctive in three important respects.

In the first place, corresponding to every value expression are "one or more conditional predictive, empirical propositions" (8, p. 87), which state the physical properties of objects that causally produce satisfactions. The correlation between value statements and factual statements, giving rise to "the persistent confusion between the two types," simultaneously "shows that values do not exist in some hypostatic realm of their own but have firm residence in the world of fact—in existing desires and in prevalent conditions for their realization" (8, pp. 87-88).

In the second place, Parker conceded a cognitive element in value expressions. "Expression may contain self-knowledge, but knowledge by acquaintance, not knowledge by description. And in knowledge by acquaintance what is known is what is present to the concepts that know it" (8, p. 77).

Art illustrates perfectly the combination of knowledge and feeling in expression. Art objects are substitute objects for the imaginative satisfaction of desires which exceed what can be gratified in real life. But unlike other modes for the imaginative satisfaction of desire—dream and play—art is expression which clarifies and socializes the private possession into "the dream for all men and the surcease of superabundant desire" (4, p. 30). Since no object in the world is more beautiful than the human body, which crystallizes the promised gratification of countless human desires (3, p. 227), the artists' preoccupation with representing it is understandable. But if Renoir's bathers satisfy imaginatively insatiable desires for erotic play, what impulse is fed by Rodin's statue of the old courtesan? Parker's answer to this question not only broadens the conception of the imaginative satisfaction art provides; it also sheds light on the cognitive role of emotive expressions. The representation of ugliness, pain, or evil in art meets Dionysian, moral and cognitive needs in man (4, pp. 122 ff.). It fills Dionysian desires of lust, hate, and cruelty within the imagination and without spilling over into the world of real life. By doing so, it meets the moral demand of purging men of these base impulses by subordinating them in release to the mastery of form that art involves. In satire it urges men to direct moral reform. But neither the harmless indulgence of base impulses nor the moral fervor for reform explains the expression of evil in art objects such as Rodin's statue or the great tragic dramas. Here the justification is the cognitive insight man gains through the art. "Man has the pressing need to come to some certain understanding with himself concerning life as a whole, and particularly concerning the most baffling element of all, evil. Man must face the facts, all the facts, and find a way of living at peace with them and himself" (4, p. 122).

In the third place, the cognitive character of value expressions is linked with the entire theory of knowledge. For knowledge is itself a value satisfying desire; it illuminates action with a plan that anticipates the series of actions and events necessary to achieve a goal (5, p. 245). Its success turns on its adjustment to the objective situation. Though ministering to the multifarious desires of men, knowledge can do its job only if it eschews wishful thinking for a realistic appraisal of the objective situation. There is, then, a desire for knowledge: "The tendency to believe in accordance with evidence —or the tendency to adjust action to its conditions, which is intelligence—is itself a desire on an equal footing with other desires" (5, p. 254). In this sense, there can never be a conflict between desire and reason as something which is not desire, for reason is itself a desire (5, p. 255). Just as facts may be looked upon as a kind of abstraction, so judgments of fact—knowledge in the narrow scientific sense—prove indispensable for a lucid understanding of the skeletal network of causal connections immanent in a value-drenched existence.

METAPHYSICS OF EXPERIENCE

Parker's philosophy of values is intricately interwoven with metaphysical propositions. First, it is grounded in presuppositions of a metaphysical character. In probing into the particular, concrete experiences, metaphysics unfolds the underlying generic forms or universal categories—substance, causality, relation, time. The involvement of these categories in the philosophy of values has been evident throughout the previous discussion. Not only does the propriety of undertaking a theory of generic value hinge upon a metaphysical doctrine of the relation between universal and particular, such that universals, while detachable from particulars in meaningful concepts, exist solely in the concrete particulars; also, the description of the experiences of value, attending to the essential features and dimensions of value, makes use of the generic concepts which metaphysics examines and interprets. To be enjoyed, values must endure awhile, and to exhibit the dimension of harmony, they must be amenable to interrelation. Hence an acceptable metaphysics posits a theory of time which allows a past moment to "echo" in its successors (2, pp. 131 ff.) and a theory of relation which accords the equal reality of relations and terms related (2, p. 205). Moreover, the fact that complementary objects cause satisfactions injects consideration of causality. Causality is a metaphysical category necessitating animistic interpretation (2, pp. 270 ff.) if the subjectivity of values is to be guaranteed, for it supposes that causality of external origin is prompted by the desires of beings similar to one's self and is directed toward satisfactions of value. Finally, the definition of value as the satisfaction of desire depends upon a metaphysics of the self.

Second, Parker's philosophy of values culminates in metaphysics in that it suggests definite conclusions about the nature of the world. Although Parker's cosmo-logical theses were allegedly reached independently of value considerations, the coherence of both aspects of his philosophy affords collaborative support. After all, the fact of values, defined as the satisfactions of desires, evinces a kind of world in which selves with desires exist and in which the desires are not wholly futile—a kind of world, in short, which is amenable to a spiritualistic in-terpretation. "The unity of value and existence," to re-peat a quotation, "follows directly from the conception of existence as a system of experience, together with the insight that volition is primary in experience" (2, p. 92).

The Self

Parker's metaphysics is a metaphysics of experience: to be is to experience or to be an element of experience (2, p. 48). Hence experience cannot be an accident of some crude material, the secretion of the life process at an advanced stage of biological evolution. Nor is it a diaphanous stuff of fragile duration, a gratuitous flash of quality in a void. On the contrary, experience is sub-stance. But before demonstrating the equation of experi-ence with substance, Parker offered a preliminary descrip-tion in which he brought to the forefront a novel and complicated theory of the self, a theory adumbrated in and presupposed by the philosophy of values.

According to Parker, "the term 'experience' is a gen-eral term like 'water'; for even as, not water, but this pool or this cupful exists, so, not *experience*, but this or that center of experience exists" (2, p. 27). The first note-worthy fact about experience, then, is its centricity. "Ex-perience falls into distinct wholes" (2, p. 26), and "there is no additional operation between wholes of experience" (2, p. 27). These centers of experience, also called "wholes" or "monads," are "like circles that are never concentric or coincident, never lie wholly one within an-other, but may overlap or be tangential" (2, p. 27). Thus "the centricity of experience is the same as ego-centricity" (2, p. 47), and the key to a proper understanding of experience is the unique "self" or "ego" that constitutes the core of each center of experience.

Parker's concern over the nature of the self harks back to his early essay in metaphysics, *The Self and Nature*, and his adherence to former conclusions is evident in the treatment of the wholes of experience. These wholes are analytically divided into activities and sensa (2, pp. 28 ff). The sensa are factors of experience which overlap; and the contiguity of consciousness with its environment is the coincidence of sensa as events of consciousness with sensa as surfaces of objects, i.e., other wholes of experience (1, pp. 53 ff). In the rhetoric of Parker: "Perception is a contact with an alien reality—a chance embrace of strangers, involving no fatal entanglements" (1, p. 54). At the heart of each center of experience is the cluster of activities indicative of the self: "apart from the activities there is no self" (2, p. 29). One type of activity is expression, "the giving of meaning," of which perception is an example, for "perception is the activity of giving 'thing' meanings to sensa. . . . Perception is, as Berkeley called it, a natural language, with ordinary sensa taking the place of words" (2, p. 30). Another type of activity is conception. "Its effect is to enlarge experience vicariously by presenting absent existences as if they were here and past ones as if they were present" (2, p. 31). The third type of activity is volition, "the guidance of experience from within" with some objective intended (2, p. 32). Of the three types of activities, volition is basic: "all acts are acts of volition" (2, p. 33). Thus Parker's description of experience discerns the existence of centers or wholes, then segregates sensa from activities within each whole, next places these sensa under the control of external centers (countercontrol), then defines the self as the core of activities, and finally locates the basis of all activities in volition. Hence the metaphysics of experience is a metaphysical voluntarism.

But to regard being as wilful subjects and their volitions does not afford sufficient stability, unless the agents of desire intend more than the gratification of passing whims. Toward a stabilizing of the voluntarism Parker, in his mature system, distinguished between the focal and the matrix self (2, pp. 41 ff.). "The focal self is an event, coming and going, one of a series of events flashing into and out of existence" (2, p. 43). It "consists of that activity, or complex of compresent activities, now in operation" (2, p. 43). The focal selves, however, "do not rise from a vacuum, but appear against a background more stable than themselves, and whatever intelligible relations they possess among themselves they derive from the matrix from which they emerge" (2, p. 43). Now Parker did not mean to shatter the self into one matrix and many focal entities. "There is but one self: the focal self and the matrix self are only two aspects of a single fact. The matrix self is a layer of deeper significance that continues and endures from one ongoing activity to another, but it cannot exist unless there is a focal activity that carries it on" (2, p. 45). The matrix self, the essential self which preserves the unity of meaning that overarches all the focal selves flowing by, imparts stability and continuity. The matrix self is, indeed, "the life plan" (8, p. 126), upon which the organization and criticism of values fundamentally depend.

Experience as Substance

Parker defended his metaphysics of experience as substance by demonstrating that experience meets the four criteria of substantiality developed in the history of philosophy: "to be substance means to be subject but never predicate, to be independent, to be causally efficient, and to be conserved through change" (2, p. 49).

The proof that experience is subject assumes that to be is to be subject or predicate. The distinction between subject and predicate marks off the unique, unrepeatable factors from the generic, recurrent factors of existence. Therefore, to "assert that substance is absolute subject . . . (is to) mean that there are factors of existence that are unique; hence, while substances may be designated by proper names and partly described, they cannot be adequately described" (2, p. 51). Now it is evident, according to Parker, that the individual monad that I am, as well as the particular events that I experience are unique. For while you and I may hear the same song, the concrete events of hearing a song occurring in you and me are absolutely unique, so that they are subjects, not predicates. Similarly, the monadic centers of experience are unique and therefore subjects, for "while there might possibly be another person just like myself—although this is doubtful—there could not be another me" (2, p. 55).

Second, experience is independent. By "independence" Parker meant with Aristotle "self-existence, that is to say, existence that is not intrinsically—as distinguished from causally—founded on the existence of other things in the way that the existence of relations and universals is founded on the existence of individuals," although he recognized that "independence now means . . . , in addition, absence of causal determination from outside" (2, p. 51). "If we view experience strictly from the inside, ignoring what we may know about it through its discoverable relations to other things, it does not reveal itself as being intrinsically based on anything other than itself, either as a whole monad or in its elements. . . . Experience comes to us not like a relation, like an adjective that needs its perch on a substantive, but as a self-subsistent kind of entity, standing on its own feet. The only intrinsic dependence that a monad reveals is dependence on other monads—social dependence—the *I* on the *you;* the *you* on the *me,* but the entire circle of monads is not revealed as depending on anything known to be different in kind from experience" (2, p. 56).

Experience meets the third qualification of substance, namely, causal efficacy. Causal efficacy supplements independence, for while internal determination suffices for the latter, external determination of events outside the monad is requisite for the former (2, p. 52). Parker located causal efficacy within experience "in two broad classes of events: events inside a monad determined by something in that same monad, and events in one monad determined by something in another monad" (2, p. 57). Within consciousness one is aware of the coming to be and the passing away of a series of events, displayed against the background of a relatively constant item of experience, "in such a way as to fulfil its objective or intent" (2, p. 57). "In every phase of experience we find a relatively constant factor generating events within experience which fulfill its intent" (2, p. 58). As for external determination, some events in a single consciousness can be explained only by reference to the intentions of other consciousnesses. "When I listen to the impassioned orator or the inspired creative musician I experience sounds that no intention of mine could possibly produce. And all communication, if on a lower plane, is of the same nature: a creative process starting in one mind yet having effects in another mind, through which it is understood" (2, p. 58).

Finally, experience possesses the fourth characteristic of substance: conservation through time. This criterion does not require that substance be eternal: "all that we can rightfully demand is that it should persist through a succession of events, in relation to which it may be said to endure" (2, p. 53). Experience meets this qualification. First, experience contains universals which recur at different times and places; these universals are conservative features of experience. Second, "experience is conserved through the matrix self" (2, p. 60). This self "has no existence independent of a stream of experience, and could not possibly be embodied in any other center; it is, therefore, not a universal, but a deeper stratum of individual existence within the ongoing pulse of experience, a true *res cogitans* which abides as the more superficial layers overlying it are sloughed off" (2, p. 68).

Hence Parker concluded that experience, conceived not as a succession of discrete entities but as "a process of accretion and attrition around a central core that remains relatively but literally invariant" (2, p. 69), is substance. And because of his manner of describing experience, his metaphysics, though based on experience, is neither a phenomenalism nor a skepticism; rather it is a spiritualistic monadism oriented toward the realization of values. So, though a monadism, this idealism supposes that the monads are not simply located in absolute isolation but that they partially overlap to form neighborhoods of satisfying cooperation or battlegrounds of frustrating conflict. "All reality is a dynamic process produced cooperatively by the desires of monads. Being is secondary to doing, and doing is the creature of desire" (2, p. 350).

The Omega System

Within individual consciousness philosophical investigation has discerned a layer of selfhood below the focal selves that pass by. Within the system of interrelated monads science discovers the existence of different levels of experience—the sociological dependent on the psychological, the psychological on the biological, the biological on the physical, the macroscopic physical on the microscopic physical. In its form as well as its existence each level is determined by the level below, except the "final lowest level" which is undetermined by anything below and which, for want of more precise information, Parker called the "Omega system" (2, p. 320).

In two respects the Omega system is eternal. By contrast with the transiency of all things, lives, and systems of ideas, "only the Omega system of the physical world is a type of being that is not known to be transitory" (2, p. 321). First, dialectical considerations confirm that the Omega system is everlasting. It could not have had a beginning, since that whence it came would then be tantamount to the Omega system. Nor can it end, since that whither it passes would, in turn, be tantamount to the Omega system. Nor can it change, since change presupposes the persistence of something that does not change, in this case "the Omega system, an eternal present, existing at all moments of time" (2, p. 323). Second, the eternal character of the Omega system is also revealed in connection with historical propositions (2, p. 323; 13). The truth of all propositions is in correspondence with a reality external to them. However, as the events represented by historical propositions, being past, no longer exist, these propositions must refer to the echoes of the past events, and these echoes must exist in the Omega system. "It must bear on its face the scars and wrinkles of every event" (2, p. 324).

Since metaphysics is based on experience, and since the description of experience detects the fact of centricity, the Omega system can be speculatively portrayed only in the terms of concrete experience (2, p. 327). Paradoxically, the dependence of human consciousness on lower levels of existence is rendered compatible with a spiritualistic interpretation of the universe because the ultimate level, the Omega system, is grasped in spiritual terms. The Omega system is Parker's alternative to evolutionary naturalism, or emergent materialism. With religious sentiment Parker agreed, "the control of the Omega system is exerted by a single Will" (2, p. 341). Just as all the activities within a single monad spring from its volitions, its desires for satisfaction, so all the changes that occur in the natural world, even those determined from below, are due to the satisfactions in the Omega system sought by "a will at least as complex as that of man" (2, p. 344). Underlying and controlling all the levels of desiring is the Omega system, whose long-range plans, its volitional preconditions of all events to come, are approximated by the laws of physics. This system is the cosmological equivalent of God, but an immanent God "with the same ideals that we have" (2, p. 350).

From the standpoint of the Omega system, the fact of death, so troubling to a philosophy which defines value as satisfaction, yet refuses to succumb to pessimism, may be justified. As new monads need fresh opportunities and forces in the physical world desire satisfaction, other monads perish (2, p. 356; 1, p. 314). However, Parker was never persuaded that all the evil in the world could be so easily explained away. "We can find the root of evil," he confessed, "but not the justification of it" (1, p. 312).

Religion is born of man's awareness of evil and is rooted in his interest in survival: "the background of every religion is a great pessimism" (5, p. 360). Religion imaginatively compensates for defeat and disillusion, though it demands, in addition to imagination, a faith which approximates the kind of belief appropriate to things of the real world. The uniqueness of religion is that it "represents an effort to bring the two worlds, of fact and of imagination, together" (5, p. 49). Acknowledging evil, religion nonetheless effectively strengthens "man's motives for living against despair" (5, p. 360). "It has given him something of more value in the struggle for existence than any single victories—the conviction, tonic for all his endeavors, that in the long run he cannot fail" (5, p. 361). Thus religion is a kind of belief determined by value. "So long as an imaginative interpretation of reality in terms of desire is required to provide men the confidence necessary to carry on with serenity, religion will exist" (5, p. 369). Moreover, theology, defined as "an interpretation of the universe favorable to man's wishes, but not capable of any direct

verification or refutation" (5, pp. 362-363), comprised
for Parker the primary task for religion in the future.
"Faith will proclaim, as against every form of naturalism, the existence of a supreme and enduring value, to
which all who labor in love may contribute. The tragic
harmony which a man may realize in his own life through
faith, he will ascribe to the universe" (5, p. 373).

Parker's account of the Omega system in *Experience
and Substance* is his sketch of the theology justifiable by
"a radical empiricism extended through the imagination." Parker did not deny the existence of evil. Rather
he located the root of evil in the heart of the Omega
system, for just as the desires of the system are dissociated
to crystallize into the finite monads that throng the
world, so in the beginning these desires are incompatible.
God, therefore, is responsible for evil. "The primary material of the world was once a part of God, and in it lay
hidden the competition and disharmony that are the
root of evil" (2, p. 357). Still Parker recommended not
despair but arduous moral struggle. "In the creative process, in which we are co-workers with God, we are given
the opportunity for victory and love, for beauty and for
virtue. . . . To ask for more is to ask for what God himself cannot give" (2, p. 358).

CONCLUSION

Parker developed his philosophy of values in full awareness of its metaphysical underpinning. His philosophy is
a profound and original humanism which embraces a
"naturalist" value theory founded on a metaphysics of
explicit monadic idealism. Like the naturalists, Parker
identified values with the satisfactions of desire. He
traced the origin of values from basic organic needs and
presented a theory of the continuity of biological, moral,
aesthetic, cognitive, and religious values, which made
possible the formulation of a general theory of value

with specifications in all these areas. Like the emotivists, who followed upon the heels of the naturalists, Parker held that value expressions are primarily noncognitive, expressing private feelings and intending to excite corresponding feelings in others. Thus he doubted the efficacy of rational, scientific methods in the field of values. He did not, of course, disregard the normative component of value. On the contrary, he maintained that every satisfaction involves a normative dimension, determined by its position in and coherence with the basic system of desires defining the self. Accordingly, rational methods do not get to the heart of the matter of moral conflict and evil. Parker conceived the world as a system of monadic selves each willing its own satisfactions, such that the satisfactions of some are the frustrations of others. Good and evil are interlocked. Love may assuage the hurt by enabling the individual self to find value in the satisfactions of others. Love is man's main practical stay against despair of the evil that undermines and overwhelms him. Philosophy is also an aid. Theoretical knowledge of the Omega system, interpreted as Divine Will underlying the physical universe, may guarantee the preponderance of good over evil. But Parker, despite this idealism, never wavered in his conviction that the world contains ineradicable evil. Art in its highest moments makes it possible for man to face evil, and religion imbues men with faith in a victorious good despite the appearance of things. But in the final analysis the highest end of human life is a harmony which Parker described as tragic.

The supreme end for man, Parker saw, is a kind of harmony. Neither the harmony of sublimation of desires nor the harmony of their integration encompasses the supreme harmony, though both are subsumed as subordinate methods of limited effectiveness. Sublimation alone fails because it cannot eviscerate the lower desires without shattering the whole fabric of human existence.

And despite the recognition that the good life is the happy integrated life (8, pp. 133 ff.), integration does not suffice, since it does not reckon with the human condition in a world where good and evil are entwined. The good life prevails through conflict, suffering, and waste. "None of life's values would have the poignancy which they possess were they not set off against contrasting values," Parker wrote (5, p. 401). And he surmised: "In the end, it may be true that life is better because of death" (5, p. 402). The highest good for man, he therefore contended, is "tragic harmony," a harmony "not merely founded upon . . . but inclusive of evil" (5, p. 404). Tragic harmony dwells in the concrete wholes of experience manifest as moods of resignation, defiance, good humor, and faith. "There are, it is true, some lives that have the radiant and symmetric harmony of a star. But for most men the ultimate value is some tragic or comic victory which finds expression in a mood of resignation, defiance, faith, or humor, akin to a melody of Mozart or Beethoven. This victory each man builds in his own way out of the smooth joys or sharp stones of his adversity. For all men the ultimate value, and hence the categorical imperative, is in its complete essence so personal that it is mystical" (5, p. 408).

NOTES TO CHAPTER 6

1. DeWitt H. Parker, *The Self and Nature* (Cambridge: Harvard University Press, 1917).
2. DeWitt H. Parker, *Experience and Substance, An Essay in Metaphysics* (Ann Arbor: University of Michigan Press, 1941).
3. DeWitt H. Parker, *The Principles of Aesthetics* (Boston, New York, Chicago, San Francisco: Silver, Burdett and Company, 1920); 2d ed. (New York: F. S. Crofts and Co., 1946). All references here are to the second edition.
4. DeWitt H. Parker, *The Analysis of Art* (New Haven: Yale University Press, 1926).
5. DeWitt H. Parker, *Human Values, An Interpretation of Ethics Based on A Study of Values* (New York: Harper &

Brothers, 1931); reprinted (Ann Arbor: George Wahr, 1944). All references will be made to the Wahr papercover, litho-printed edition (1947).

6. DeWitt H. Parker, "Empirical Idealism," in *Contemporary American Philosophy*, G. P. Adams and W. P. Montague, eds. (New York: The Macmillan Co., 1930; reprinted by Russell & Russell, Inc. 1962), Vol. II., p. 165.

7. Parker did write an article entitled "Metaphysics of Value," *International Journal of Ethics*, XLIV (1934), 293-312. The article appears to be the first of a series, but to my knowledge the sequel was never published, but the same ground is covered in *Experience and Substance*, Chap. 15, pp. 292-312.

8. DeWitt H. Parker, *The Philosophy of Value*, with Preface by William K. Frankena, ed. (Ann Arbor: University of Michigan Press, 1957), Professor Frankena states that since the final projected chapter of the book had not been written at the time of Parker's death, editorial considerations prompted the omission of the introductory chapter and the reduction of other references to metaphysics, although he points out that Parker, keenly disposed to metaphysics, would not have taken this elimination of metaphysics lightly.

9. DeWitt H. Parker, "The Value Situation: Basic Categories and Attitudes of the Value Situation," *Review of Metaphysics*, XIII (1960), 555-596.

10. Perhaps it should be recalled that Parker edited the Schopenhauer *Selections* for Scribner's Modern Students Library.

11. For Parker works of art are linguistic expressions. Hence a monograph in aesthetics is a contribution to philology. See DeWitt Parker, "The True, the Good, and the Beautiful," *University of Michigan Contributions in Modern Philology*, No. 11 (July 1948).

12. See DeWitt Parker, "Discussion of John Dewey's 'Some Questions about Value,' " in *Value, A Cooperative Inquiry*, Ray Lepley, ed. (New York: Columbia University Press, 1949), pp. 233-244, and "Rejoinder by Parker," pp. 451-454.

13. See Parker, *The Metaphysics of Historical Knowledge*, in *University of California Publications in Philosophy*, Vol. 2 (Berkeley: University of California Press, 1913).

Chapter 7

THE CRITICAL
REALISM OF
ROY WOOD SELLARS

INTRODUCTION

Twenty years ago the voluntaristic idealist, DeWitt H. Parker, said: "No American has done more persistent and original thinking on fundamental philosophical problems during the last thirty years or so than my colleague, Professor Sellars" (1). High praise, indeed, in view of the thoroughly different philosophical standpoints of these two philosophy professors at the University of Michigan. For whereas Parker is associated with metaphysical idealism, value theory, and aesthetics, Roy Wood Sellars is linked with critical realism, evolutionary naturalism, ontological materialism, socialism, and naturalistic humanism.

Born in Canada in 1880, Roy Wood Sellars entered the University of Michigan at the age of nineteen, and except for a few periods of study away, he has passed his life "in the little city of Ann Arbor, in the usual academic fashion" (2, p. 262). With the University of Michigan as his anchorage, he has written ten books, contributed chapters to as many more, and has published scores of articles and reviews which express a sober and independent philosophy that has won for him the esteem of his fellow philosophers (3), and which have exerted considerable influence on recent trends in American philosophy.

Sellars' first book, *Critical Realism* (4), completed in 1913 and published in 1916, has been singled out as the work "which gave name and direction to the second phase of realism in America" (5, p. 447). A septet of prominent philosophers: Durant Drake, Arthur O. Lovejoy, James Bissel Pratt, Arthur K. Rogers, George Santayana, Roy Wood Sellars, and C. A. Strong banded together to produce the second major co-operative volume in the development of American realism: *Essays in Critical Realism* (6).

Evolutionary Naturalism (7) was the first published attempt to build a cosmology upon the epistemology of critical realism, although later, with varying degrees of success, other critical realists were to undertake similar enterprises, the most notable being George Santayana's *Realms of Being*. It was also the first serious effort by an American thinker to formulate the type of evolutionary cosmology which, labelled "emergent evolution" and backed by the prestige of its British proponents, S. Alexander and Lloyd Morgan, was to dominate so much Anglo-American philosophy during the third and fourth decades of the present century. Not satisfied with presenting the principles of critical realism and evolutionary naturalism merely for professional philosophers, Sellars sought to express them in terms comprehensible to undergraduate students of philosophy in three textbooks in philosophy: *The Essentials of Logic* (8), *The Essentials of Philosophy* (9), and *The Principles and Problems of Philosophy* (10). The last work, "partly revision, partly supplementation" of *The Essentials of Philosophy*, contains ideas and principles relevant to Sellars' cosmology that are worthy of consideration by the most advanced students of philosophy.

Nor did Sellars halt with epistemology and cosmology; he also ventured into ontology. Constructive and polemical, *The Philosophy of Physical Realism* (11) presents a materialistic ontology in which the unfashionable concept of material substance is defended against positivism and process philosophy. In this connection Sellars has recently joined V. J. McGill and Marvin Farber to edit a collection of essays, *Philosophy for the Future* (12), which, as its subtitle declares, is in quest of a "Modern Materialism."

Expert in epistemology, cosmology, and ontology, abstruse branches of philosophy which are seemingly unconnected with the problems of men, Sellars has nonetheless devoted much of his thinking to these problems. In *The Next Step in Democracy* (13) he has openly advocated socialism, and in *The Next Step in Religion* (14) and *Religion Coming of Age* (15) he has upheld the unorthodox position of humanistic naturalism in religion. As a long-time leader in American humanist circles, Sellars is the author of the first draft of the humanist manifesto and a co-signer of the published document (16).

EPISTEMOLOGY: CRITICAL REALISM

Critical realism followed upon the heels of neorealism. Before and after the publication of *The New Realism* (1912) various thinkers attacked the epistemological monism of neorealism on the grounds that, unless ideas as mental events are distinguished sharply from the external objects of which they are the vehicles of knowledge, the explanation of error is difficult, if not impossible (17). Here arose the opportunity of critical realism. In contrast with neorealism's concepts of mind, critical realists, according to Durant Drake, "emphasize the duality . . . between the cognitive state which is the vehicle of knowledge and the object known," although as realists they also contend: "What we perceive, conceive, remember, think of, is the object itself (or, on occasion, the mental state introspected, remembered, or conceived), which is independent of the knowledge-process, and beyond which there is nothing else" (6, p. 4, n. 1).

Distinguishing between ideas *qua* the contents, characters, essences, sensa, or images given in immediate apprehension or intuition and real things *qua* objective existents that are somehow known but not immediately given to the mind, the majority of the critical realists revived the dichotomy of *essence* and *existence,* so that the most astute critic of recent epistemologies has interpreted critical realism as the replacement of ideas with essence (18, II, Chap. xii). For Sellars, however, critical realism did not involve the doctrine of essence. He has explicitly repudiated the essence theory on the ground that it failed to "carry with it the solution of the mechanism of knowing," and he has confessed that it "seemed to me . . . something of a verbal short-cut . . . (since) the apprehension of the right essence at the right moment was left somewhat of a miracle" (11, p. 60). For Sellars the cardinal principle of critical realism is not the doctrine of essence, but rather its emphasis upon "the reality and significance of another kind of knowledge than that of the intuition of character-complexes—a knowledge which presupposes this givenness of characters as a foundation, and yet goes beyond it in affirming physical existents of which knowledge is possessed" (6, p. 189).

From Natural to Critical Realism

A noted historian of American philosophy has aptly observed: "Underlying all the subtleties of Sellars' analysis of knowledge is a profound regard for the view of the plain man" (19, p. 294). *Critical Realism* opens with an exposition and criticism of the plain man's outlook on knowledge. Sellars has called "(t)his attitude toward the physical world, in which it is considered independent of the event of perceiving and hence common . . . that of Natural Realism" (4, p. 3). Springing not from logical or factual considerations, but simply from the practical life and instinctive nature of man, "Natural Realism, in the form in which it is a true description of our ordinary outlook on nature, is a flat epistemological dualism in which there is no peculiar, non-physical relation between the individual and the object—the two terms of the dualism" (4, p. 4). Natural Realism is the starting point of philosophy, since philosophy is properly a reflection upon experience, articulating its implicit theories and, through criticism, eradicating conflicts and contradictions. Strictly speaking, the attitude of the plain man toward knowledge falls short of the explicit harmony Sellars imparted to Natural Realism, although, once expressed, Natural Realism emerges not only as "the matrix of realistic theories of all sorts" (4, p. 4), but also as deeply marked by inadequacies and contradictions which have persuaded idealists of the inherent untenability of realism. "These inadequacies and contradictions concern (1) the fact that perception has conditions which do not appear in that which is immediately perceived; (2) the distinction between appearance and reality, a distinction which is held by the plain man along with the immediacy of perception, although the two cannot be reconciled; (3) the lack of concomitant variation between things and that which is actually perceived; (4) the difference between the perceptions of individuals; (5) the explanation of images, dream-life, and memory; (6) the synthetic or composite character of that which is perceived and the presence in it of inferential elements" (4, p. 7). But these difficulties, which furnish arguments for the idealists, do not justify the total abandonment of realism; rather, they require that realism be critical.

First of all, science starts from the base of Natural Realism and comes in time to adopt a critical attitude. Named "Scientific Realism" (4, p. 26), this attitude demands the employment of exact methods of measurement and instruments of discovery to avoid the peculiarities of personal observations. In large measure scientific realism has inspired a representationalism (e.g., Locke's) in epistemology, according to which ideas, the effects in minds causally induced by external objects, copy the primary qualities, *viz.*, the extension, mass, motion, figure, number, of external objects, but do not resemble the secondary qualities of these objects, *viz.*, the powers of the primary qualities to induce sensations of color, sound, taste, odor, temperature, in the subjects. Although this representationalism is unsound, scientific realism is correct to insist that the information of science be "not penetrated by the relativity to the human organism characteristic of percepts" (4, p. 30). Thus scientific realism, while beginning with Natural Realism, comes to outgrow it. Initially a sophistication of Natural Realism, scientific realism, adhering to the causal theory of mental events, ushers in what Sellars has termed "The Advance of the Personal" (4, p. 49) and so opens the way for idealism.

"The Advance of the Personal" signifies "the movement of the inner, personal sphere upon the outer, common sphere" (4, p. 49). Though misused by the idealists who attempt to absorb the external world into the personal sphere and treat the former as a construction from the latter, "The Advance of the Personal" need not lead to the relinquishment of realism. As Sellars has said: "Because appearances are personal and intervene between the individual percipient and the physical thing, it does not follow that we have any less reason to believe in the existence of the physical thing. An effect cannot be more real than the cause. So long as we retain the contrast, we must remain realists" (4, p. 52). But he continued: "If realism is to be saved, it must disembarass itself of its immediatism; *i.e.*, the physical object can no longer be regarded as immediately present in perception" (4, p. 58). The problem then arises: How can we know external objects if they are not immediately given?

The Principles of Knowledge

In *The Philosophy of Physical Realism*, his latest major work, Sellars has formulated "the conditions, mechanism and essential nature of human knowing" (11, p. 67) economically in six general principles:

1. "Human knowing is conditioned in a perfectly natural way as regards both external controls and internal operations" (11, p. 67). Here Sellars focused attention on the naturalistic setting of the knowing organism, stressing not only the external stimuli affecting the percipient organism, but also the active response of the organism. Taking advantage of the findings of biopsychology, Sellars viewed "the patterned stimulus . . . as only the *occasion* of perceiving," adding: "Perceiving is a directed activity" (11, p. 69). That meanings obtrude upon and affect the perceptual experience explains, moreover, the tenacity of natural realism, according to which "the object of perceiving is regarded as given in experience" (11, p. 70).

2. "Though conditioned causally and resting on neuromuscular mechanisms, human knowing is yet knowing" (11, p. 70). Knowing is an achievement which depends upon the natural organism, just as seeing depends upon eyes. This dependence upon the organism in no way obstructs the possibilities of knowledge as judged by its own relevant tests.

3. "The causal theory of perception should be restated as the causal theory of sense-data and not of perceiving" (11, p. 72). Here a word of caution concerning terminology is in order, since in his early writings Sellars used the term "perception" or "percept" to mean direct awareness of the data of consciousness. Despite the possibility

of terminological confusion, however, Sellars' thesis has been constant and is clear. The immediate contents of consciousness, available to direct apprehension or intuition, are the effects of the confluence of external physical and internal organic causes. They are not the objects we perceive but the means whereby we perceive objects. How can we be sure that we perceptually know objects through these causally produced sense data? As answer Sellars has suggested "a return to a causal theory of sense-data in terms of reproduction of pattern and a judgmental, denotative theory of perceiving" (11, p. 110).

4. "Knowing must be studied at its various levels as a characteristic claim of the human knower" (11, p. 73). At its origin and in its most primitive form, knowledge is founded on "all our adjustments to external things" (11, p. 86). Even the subject-object contrast of knowing has its naturalistic basis "upon a stimulus-response polarity which is defined by movement and delicate motor adjustment" (11, p. 87). And because of this anchorage of knowing in an organism responding to external stimuli, knowing admits of degrees of adequacy to the objects of knowledge. Perception therefore is supplemented and corrected by conception, since "the external world does appear in perception—but darkly" (11, p. 96). But when we move on to conception, especially of the scientific variety, a serious challenge confronts epistemology, inasmuch as "the world *as conceived* in it [science] differs so markedly from the same world *as perceived*" (11, p. 97). And Sellars has met the challenge by adhering to realism: "I hold to our usual belief that we are dealing in these two cases with literally the same external world. It is the theory of the critical realist that we have to do here with levels of knowing and that, in science, we have a closer approximation to external fact than in perception. . . . For us, atoms, electrons and protons are as real as chairs and tables" (11, p. 97).

5. "The act of cognition is complex and appears in

consciousness as an interpretation of an external object in terms of logical ideas" (11, p. 74). The data immediately apprehended are in cognition referred to, or predicated of, external objects; or, rather, external objects are interpreted by means of sense data or logical ideas which are intuited. These data and ideas are events, particulars, not essences. Sellars has written: "They are *points of departure for predicative interpretation of objects* and not themselves such predicates. When I assert that an object is blue, I am not assigning to it my sense-datum as such. Rather am I characterizing it in terms of a property thought by means of a specified predicate founded on the sense-datum" (11, p. 154).

6. "Things are selected as objects by the mind and are not in the mind. This signifies that knowing involves a peculiar transcendence" (11, p. 76). Knowing is an activity which, in disclosing objects by means of ideas, is about external things and consequently transcends the cognitive organism (11, p. 78). Sellars has traced transcendence back to biological mechanisms. As he has said in a recent article: "(T)he sensory complex arises in the brain under patterned stimulation of the sense organs and has the role of guidance of response. Such guidance is a transcending role and rests upon the control by the object of the pattern applied to it. Because the mechanism is there, we do not need to get mystical about transcendence" (20).

The Theory of Truth

Throughout this discussion of the principles of critical realism there is visible the vigor of Natural Realism, chastened somewhat through consciousness of its critical defects. Nonetheless, for Sellars the fundamental postulate of realistic epistemology remains: the claim of knowledge to reveal external realities. "This postulate, if challenged, is confirmed by the success of our critical thinking" (2, pp. 272-273). The tests for knowledge are four: "(1) the consilience of established facts; (2) the logical coherence of ideas; (3) agreement of investigators; and (4) guidance and control over nature" (2, p. 273). But these tests, while ascertaining the truth of knowledge, do not add up to the nature of truth. Truth consists essentially in correspondence, not of appearances with things, but of the reproduction of the order of things in the order of our ideas (21).

Alleging that the doctrine of correspondence entails the supposition that perceptions are appearances of things, Roderick M. Chisholm has charged Sellars with resorting to a "locution (which) . . . is misleading" (3, p. 42). But Sellars, it should be recalled, has never accepted the copy theory of traditional representationalism, for he finds difficulties in endeavoring to render the exact nature of correspondence intelligible. "We should realize," he has confessed, "that no dialectical answer will do justice to the problem" (7, p. 37). Clarification of the concept of correspondence requires concentration on the psychophysical situation in which mental events occur as organic responses to external stimuli. "The datum is a correlated response to the stimulus. And it is this *differential correlation* that makes the present content valid material for knowledge of the physical world" (7, p. 37). Thus elements in consciousness need not be supposed to copy elements in physical things. What goes on in knowledge is the reproduction of "the characteristics of things" in respect to their "structure and connections" (7, p. 37). Viewed from the other side: "The pattern of nature can be worked out through an inferential study of the pattern of appearance" (7, p. 183).

Attention to structure and connection has moved Sellars in the first place to adopt the correspondence theory of the nature of truth. But underlying this motive is his basic loyalty to Natural Realism, which finds expression in his emphasis upon the referential character of knowledge. Truth, accordingly, is a property of propositions when "they give knowledge of the object denoted, that is disclose its characteristics and relations" (11, p. 125). That ideas afford knowledge implies, therefore, that they correspond to external things. "We can infer correspondence from the fact of knowledge and not knowledge from the discernment of correspondence through comparison" (11, p. 282). With this view of truth Sellars has kept abreast of more recent treatments of truth by analytic philosophers. In particular, he has noted that the semantic conception of truth, according to which the term "true" is assigned to sentences whenever they are accepted as informative, is merely preliminary to further philosophical investigation. Since for Sellars "correspondence is an implication and not a test," he has contended that his "analysis fits in with the semantic theory of truth. The difference is that the philosopher has to explore the epistemology of the situation" (22). Thus critical realism establishes a link with current analytic philosophy (23).

As Brand Blanshard has commented, critical realism is a compromise between realism and idealism (18, I, p. 416). Indeed, Sellars has been explicit in his offer of "a view of knowledge which would include and satisfy the idealistic motives, yet grant all that realism could rightly demand" (4, p. 154). The historic relation of critical realism to neorealism has been mentioned. Insufficiently appreciated is Sellars' conscious opposition to the Chicago School which propounded a theory of logic and knowledge as much neo-Hegelian as pragmatic. As Sellars later put it, his *Critical Realism* "was exercised chiefly with the then Chicago School" (24, p. 544). This school he attacked for three reasons: First, it failed "to give existential status to the term 'experience,' " since it never sought to answer "the question, Whose experience?" (24, p. 544). Second, it reduced knowing to "a forward-looking reference," neglecting the reference knowledge makes to past or coexistent objects and events

(24, p. 544). Third, like idealism it rejected "as illusory, . . . independent and transcendent objects" (24, p. 544). For Sellars the heart of knowledge lies in its claim of reference, or (to use the term favored by critical realists) transcendence. Transcendence, moreover, is nothing mystical, but rather is "an epistemological category developed around facts about the mechanism of perceiving and knowing in general. It expresses the realization that the object known is not given as the sense-presentations and concepts are, that knowing is *through* concepts and directed at what is intended but not given" (24, p. 547). Thus critical realism makes connection with topics in phenomenology and existential philosophy.

Building upon idealism and realism and revealing affinities with current philosophical tendencies such as analysis, phenomenology, and existentialism, critical realism is nevertheless unique. In regarding the contents of consciousness as mental events and not as the properties of things, Sellars agrees with idealism, but in holding that these mental events reveal the properties of things and that we know things by means of them, he upholds realism. And this realism is but a logical development of Natural Realism. While analytic, existential, and phenomenological philosophies often appear remote from the outlook of the plain man, critical realism is a philosophically respectable formulation of this outlook. As Sellars said in the concluding paragraph of his first book: "(C)ritical realism exists already preformed, as it were, in Natural Realism, that is, in the plain man's outlook. Our task has been to clarify it and make it conscious of itself" (4, p. 282).

COSMOLOGY: EVOLUTIONARY NATURALISM

Of his cosmology Sellars has remarked that it may be "called, indifferently, evolutionary naturalism, emergent evolution, or emergent materialism" (15, p. 141). But since he has favored the term "evolutionary naturalism" to designate his theory of the world, an understanding of this theory may be furthered by a clarification of the concepts "naturalism" and "evolution." By "naturalism" Sellars means "the self-sufficiency and intelligibility of the world of space and time" (7, p. 2). Naturalism, then, involves ontological categories such as space, time, and material substance, and leads to ontological materialism. Unfortunately, Sellars' concept of "evolution" is one which at least one sympathetic critic of his thought, Bahm, has charged with obscurity (3, pp. 1-2). As Sellars himself has said: "The evolutionary naturalism which the keen eye can discern is like a statue hidden in the marble" (7, p. 19). Nonetheless, the concept of evolution is that which differentiates Sellars' naturalism from past naturalism. "(P)ast naturalism did not take evolution seriously nor did it take mind seriously" (7, p. 16), Sellars has argued, adding: "Evolutionary naturalism is not a reductive naturalism" (7, p. 19). As a cosmological theory which squares with facts and scientific principles, evolutionary naturalism can explain these facts and principles better than can supernaturalistic idealism (spiritualism), mechanical materialism, or metaphysical dualism. In furnishing such explanation, it must, according to Sellars, first "do justice to the different kinds of process, inorganic, organic, mental and social, which exist in our world; second, it must make comprehensible the efficacy of mind and consciousness" (10, p. 211).

Creative Process and the Integrative Levels

Because change is essential to evolution, evolutionary cosmologies are usually associated with process metaphysics. "The principle of evolution means, in the first place, the reality of basic alterations all through the universe. It stands for the acceptance of *process* in the place of fixed and static things" (10, p. 271). Although this usually means that substance as a metaphysical category is discarded, Sellars has firmly defended substance. A few sentences will suffice to underscore the primacy of substance in his evolutionary naturalism: "(C)hange presupposes an endurant which can change" (11, p. 303). "(C)hange is never the vanishing of primary being but only an alteration of pattern. Such a view of the secondariness of change has always been one of the meanings of substance" (11, p. 304). Evolution, then, is change which occurs within substance.

Further, evolution is more than change. "Evolution implies novelty" (7, p. 161). For the creation of novelty change must be cumulative. "The new arises from the old by cumulative change" (15, p. 176). Minimal changes accumulate and generate differences of degree which, intensified and augmented, become accentuated not only in particular things but in kinds of structure in nature, engendering thereby a hierarchy of beings and levels of causality. Structure, or organization, is the key concept. Accretion and agglutination fail to explain wholly the novelty produced by cumulative changes. Formal as well as material elements are involved. "It is the organization which is novel and with which new properties must be correlated" (7, p. 332). The principle of evolution as cumulative change must therefore be supplemented by the principle of organization (10, p. 274). With its portrayal of nature as undergoing cumulative change in which emerge new patterns or novel organizations, evolutionary naturalism is not reductive. The mistake of traditional naturalism was its claim that science could proceed simply through the analysis of every natural thing or event into its simplest elements, and so "science often forgot the fact of synthesis" (7, p. 16). Creative synthesis, however, does not suggest for Sellars monistic idealism. Though it introduces novel organizations within the cumulative change of nature and reinforces the continuities of nature, "there is nothing in this definitely localizable, creative synthesis which points to the cherished notion of the objective idealist that the universe is an individual" (7, p. 215). On the other hand, the facts of creative synthesis rule out the traditional outlook of reductive materialism. "Integration, configuration and wholeness are more significant for nature than science was ready to admit. Nature seems able to form systems which have a measure of internal unity and are not mere collocations of self-sufficient units" (10, p. 288). The theory that cumulative change involves patterns or organizations which account for the emergence of new levels of reality without culminating in the sort of organic individuality posited by monistic idealism is called "organicism" (10, p. 288).

Sellars has compared the general plan of nature "to a pyramid of a tier-like structure. A process of creative organization led at each stage to the advent of gradients or levels above" (10, p. 363). At the base there is inanimate nature, matter and its organizations into molecules and atoms; then there is animate nature, living things of all grades and kinds; next there is mind, a novel pattern which emerges within the life of specific organisms; and finally, there is society, an organization of living organisms having minds (10, p. 345). Since each level of integration in nature involves new capacities and has its own laws and categories (10, p. 372), the endeavor of the traditional mechanical materialist to account for the behavior of entities at higher levels solely in terms of factors at lower levels is necessarily foredoomed. Yet this does not mean that the higher levels are unrelated to the lower levels. On the contrary, all the levels of nature together comprise a hierarchy. "There is novelty of an undeniable sort at every level of reality" (7, p. 319), and this novelty does not emerge from nothing. "Evolution means that there are levels in nature, that the higher is the outgrowth of the lower, that A and B integrated are more than A and B separate" (7, p. 329). It also means that "(t)his rise to higher levels must rest upon and but carry out the potentialities of the lower levels" (7, p. 335). Although "the higher order implies and includes the lower order" (7, p. 261), it is impossible to deduce the higher levels from the lower ones. Further, each level has its own laws: "the laws of nature form a hierarchy in which different levels are discontinuous" (10, p. 364). Regardless of this logical discontinuity of the levels of nature and causality, a discontinuity which science must recognize, there is a genetic continuity which admits both identity and difference. As Sellars has put it: "The identity . . . is the objective significance of organization. The differences consist in the rise of kinds and orders of organization. It is with this that we must correlate new properties" (7, p. 332).

Mind

Since life is a new gradient, biological categories cannot be reduced to those of chemistry and physics. In the light of the genetic continuity of the levels of nature, however, they "must fit into the *outlines* of the categories of physics and chemistry. Here, also, we must have structure, relations, events, and energies. A *living thing must be a spatio-temporal system*" (10, p. 290). The synthesis of matter into distinctive organic patterns is creative, and so the novelty of life emerges. As Sellars has said: "The organism is not a mere aggregate. It is an organization in which there is differentiation of function" (7, p. 329). The concept of organic function is the key to Sellars' theory of mind. Although this theory goes back to his *Critical Realism*, where epistemological motives placed the knower and his mental contents in a natural setting which stimulates him and to which he responds, it calls for a cosmological basis which evolutionary naturalism supplies. First of all, the substantialist conception of mind is discarded. "Mind must be thought of as a term for systematic tendencies and operations which have slowly come to pass in the organic world. . . . It is a

term for functions" (10, p. 322). Not a substance, mind
is a physical category: "The mind is the brain as known
in its functioning. It is the brain in its integrative capacities" (7, p. 300). Derided as the "under-the-hat" theory
of mind, it "makes mind local, emergent, physical and
conscious" (11, p. 411).

But if mind is a physical system, if "(t)he psychical is
literally in the brain as a quality" (11, p. 411) and "is as
extended as the brain-event to which it is intrinsic" (11,
p. 415), metaphysical dualism and its problems are once
for all superseded. Still it is necessary to specify the relation of consciousness to what Sellars has chosen to call
"the brain-mind," particularly since he has intended by
"consciousness" "the total field of a person's experiencing as it shifts and changes" (11, p. 407). In order to
render this concept of consciousness consistent with his
physical theory of the brain-mind, he has resorted to a
sophisticated version of the double-aspect theory, called
the double-knowledge theory (10, p. 338). Thus "what
we call consciousness is a patterned complex of events
intrinsic to the functioning of the brain-mind. In consciousness we are on the inside of these events; we *are*
the events" (10, p. 322). Ontologically, therefore, consciousness would appear to be a new category. "Consciousness is the qualitative dimension of a brain-event.
It is the patterned brain-event as sentient. It is because
of its status that we, as conscious, *participate in the being
of brain-events*. Here, and here alone, are we as conscious
beings, on the inside of reality" (11, p. 414). While at
first brain-events, patterns or organizations constitutive
of consciousness, may seem to be merely epiphenomenal
effects of the conjoint operations of external and internal
causes, consciousness is intrinsically cognitive, and issuing
from the response behavior of the organism, it is referential or transcendent. Sellars, then, is cognizant of the
extreme complexity of the ontological situation (25).
"It is in this respect," he has confessed, "that I come mid-

way between materialism and panpsychism. A brain-state is for me conscious content *plus*" (11, p. 420).

Purposiveness and the Limits of Evolution

In philosophy of mind, Sellars' rejection of epiphenomenalism, reductive materialism, and mechanism by no means implies adherence to vitalism or external finalism. But he has contended that, since the organism is a new organization or pattern of matter involving mind and consciousness, its behavior cannot be explained solely in terms of material components and antecedent history. "(A)n organism is a thickened system with definite trends. Its organic structure points it towards the future" (10, p. 376). Since its structure, as evolved through cumulative change, contains an internal teleology (10, p. 373), neither external pushes nor external pulls can exhaustively explain its behavior. Hence, purposiveness is a natural quality of naturally evolved organisms.

Professor Bahm has remarked that Sellars is not a thoroughgoing evolutionist in that evolution plays a restricted role in his cosmology (3, p. 5). First of all, Sellars is a materialist, so that there is neither evolution of matter from some nonmaterial stuff nor evolution beyond matter to some new being. "The evolutionary naturalist does not doubt that there are levels of integration in nature, but levels of reality is quite another, and very questionable, category" (7, p. 204). There is, then, no emergent deity in Sellars' cosmos. Nor does the universe as a whole evolve. Sellars has said: "I do not apply the concept of evolution to the universe taken as a superentity inclusive of and containing all others, but only to physical systems within it" (11, p. 3). In addition to these limits, according to which evolution is equated with changes within a continuant matter that can never be transformed into any nonmaterial being, the normal processes of nature are regular and routine, originating no novel patterns of creative synthesis. In brief, "cumulative evolution seems to be very local and exceptional" (11, p. 433).

ONTOLOGY: MATERIALISM

Sellars' critical realism contends that knowledge is an activity of sentient organisms within nature in quest of truth, i.e., of cognitive achievements in which the patterns of sense data and ideas within consciousness reproduce the organizations and connections of the things to which they refer. Sellars' evolutionary naturalism maintains that all organisms, including men with brain-mind, are products of natural processes in which syntheses and organizations of matter result in new gradients constitutive of distinctive natural levels with distinctive natural laws. Thus knowing as mental process is nonetheless an event or set of events within the natural order, and consciousness, though qualitatively felt immediate experience, is also the pattern of neural events occurring in the brain. Consequently Sellars, in contradiction to pragmatists, positivists, and other naturalists, has always urged not only that epistemology cannot be disregarded, but further that epistemology leads logically to ontology. For knowledge is not self-enclosed activity restricted to the mind; it intends, denotes, or refers to realities. This process of referential transcendence is effectuated through categories. The organism, stimulated by the environment, responds by means of appropriate capacities. These capacities are in fact cognitive ideas which order the data of consciousness according to patterns similar to the organizations of things, and hence they constitute the basis of knowledge. The study of these categories is the task of ontology.

Sellars defines categories as "the standard elements and distinctions" of knowledge (7, p. 79). They are not arbitrarily imposed upon discrete sense-data. "(T)he chief characteristic of the individual's field of experience," Sellars has said, borrowing a page from the *Ge-staltists*, is *"wholeness with patterns and meanings.* From the first, experience is categorized" (11, p. 141). Nor are the categories derived *a priori* from a transcendental ego; they evolve within experience of the world. They "have as empirical a foundation as do sense-data; and we should expect them to *manifest* the categorial structure of things, including ourselves. We think in the world and the world thinks in us. Or, to put it another way, thinking is an activity controlled by our nature and the nature of the world" (11, p. 214). *Evolutionary Naturalism* is, in large measure, a description of the empirical genesis of categories, tracing their foundation in experience and demonstrating that the dialectical puzzles raised by philosophers—*viz.*, Zeno's paradoxes and Kant's antinomies—are dissolved once categories are understood to be standard functions of cognitive activities within experience. In one sense categories are not literally real. "They are not physical things; they are not even peculiar elements of the physical world. They are characters of our knowledge about things. *It follows that the validity of the categories is bound up with the validity of knowledge"* (7, p. 79).

Ontological categories are, therefore, "fundamental concepts characteristic of our knowledge about nature" (7, p. 82). However, since categories are patterns which grow up within experience in response to the organization of things in nature, they duplicate the real patterns in nature. The primary ontological categories are: space, time, thinghood (substance), and causality (7, p. 80). Perhaps in reaction against the prevalence of process cosmology in recent American thinking, Sellars has tended to stress the importance of thinghood, or substance, as a physical category. He has called his ontology "physical realism," or "reformed materialism," or simply "materialism" (26). And he has on occasion been prepared to acknowledge and elaborate the affinities of his materialism with dialectical materialism, although he has expressed little sympathy for the dialectic in dialectical materialism (27). Since causality has already been discussed in connection with evolutionary naturalism, it is appropriate here to concentrate on space, time, and substance. Space and time are property-concepts which, according to Sellars, presuppose substance.

Space

Let us begin with space. "Space is a strategic category" (7, p. 84). The hostility of idealism to space is notorious, since judgments concerning space, such as those pertaining to position, size, contour, distance, and direction, are not only associated with the traditional theory of primary qualities upon which the doctrine of matter has hinged, but also they suggest, irresistibly in accord with natural realism, the structure of a system of realities lying outside the mind. Further, space is the focal point of a number of philosophical perplexities, for example, whether it is finite or infinite, continuous or discontinuous, and so on. In *Evolutionary Naturalism* Sellars' approach to the category of space is genetic, and, in spite of ontological inclinations, he was so preoccupied with critical realism and evolutionary naturalism that the reality-status of space is somewhat blurred. The development of the category of space from primitive types of spatial experience is depicted, beginning with sensational space, proceeding to perceptual space, moving on to conceptual empirical space, then to conceptual mathematical space, the last-named type of space being considered "an abstractive conception resting ultimately upon characters gotten in perception" (7, p. 93). The dominance of epistemological concerns throughout the discussion is further manifest in the thesis that the category of space obtains its total meaning from judgments which impute spatial properties and relations to things. As Sellars says: "Space as a category is not an external reality. To assert that the physical world is spatial, means, not that the physical world is *in* a non-dynamic receptaculum analogous to mathematical space, but that certain predicates are interpretative of its actual constitution and nature" (7, p. 99).

In *The Philosophy of Physical Realism* the ontology of space is in sharp focus. Here space signifies "the extensiveness of physical systems" (11, p. 317). "The ontology of space is the ontology of extensiveness and positionness as characteristics of the physical universe" (11, p. 318). This theory is "a relational, adjectival theory of physical space" (11, p. 319), for it conceives space to be a matrix of relations among extended things. But while Sellars' theory departs from the Newtonian conception of absolute space in that "it does not consider space a reality apart from the universe," it is nonetheless absolute as regards metrical, or operational, views: "The physical world is intrinsically spatial" (11, p. 317). Further, when insisting upon physical extendedness as the ontological basis for the category of space as physical, he has indicated how the paradoxes of Zeno and others may find their solution. Such paradoxes arise when mathematical distinctions are treated as if they were physical entities. Physical extendedness, the foundation of the category of space, moreover, entails the coexistence of substances, establishing the interrelatedness of material particles and the continuity of matter. As Sellars has said: "I am convinced that physical bodies are not cut off from one another in an absolute way, but retain touch with one another. . . . Relations are in some sense physically real" (11, p. 319).

Time

Time, like space, is a strategic category, since it discloses fundamental characteristics of reality. Yet it is, in Sellars' judgment, "a treacherous category" (11, p. 330). As in the case of space, so in the case of time, a genetic description of the emergence of the category is traced from its original appearance in sensory and perceptual experience through its ramification in the concepts of science and mathematics. Time is rooted in the experience of change: "The elementary experience which is at the foundation of what we roughly call time is the immediate feeling of change" (7, p. 105). "Time is the *fact of* change as a characteristic of our universe; it is eventness" (11, p. 246). The difference between space and time, despite their universality, is pointed: "When we think of nature in terms of it [space], we think of coexistent bodies whose parts exist alongside of one another. Time, on the other hand, signifies an order of change qualified by duration. Such change we think of as *in* bodies" (7, p. 118). This identification of real time with change implies that time is local. Time "is the process-aspect of reality, the dimension of alteration, of the vanishing and the arriving. Reality is an extended and variegated complex whose constitution shifts locally. It is this local shift which is real time" (11, p. 331).

Herein lies the justification for rejecting the question whether physical nature has a beginning or an end in time. "Instead of nature being in time, time (change) is in nature" (7, p. 121). "Nature will be grasped as a differentiated, stereometrical process, that is, time will become immanent in space" (7, p. 146). By equating time with change going on in material systems in determinate regions of space, Sellars has broken with much recent temporalistic metaphysics (e.g., Bergson's) and subordinates time to space. He has written: "After all, space, that is, existence, dominates the universe. No part of nature can get ahead of other parts of nature and leave them behind in time. I believe that temporalism has weakened our sense of existence as substantial" (11, p. 337).

Now space and time may be approached in two ways: the ways of science or ontology. As the approach of science, measurement "concerns itself with measuring, locating, dating, finding numerical laws," whereas the approach of ontology, while assimilating the data of science, "is intent on grasping the categorial structure of *being*" (11, p. 247). Sellars is convinced that the metrical and operational concepts of space and time utilized in science "must not be read too literally into nature" (11, pp. 247-248), but that they must always be checked against our fundamental experiences of the physical categories. Otherwise basic ontological categories, confirmed by experience, may be needlessly sacrificed to enable scientists to cope with significant but narrow problems of measurement. Thus Sellars has denounced various philosophical attempts to offer ontological interpretations of the concepts of space and time implicated in Einstein's theories of relativity (28). He has boldly proclaimed "that the Theory of Relativity represents a revolution in physics but not in philosophy" (11, p. 258).

Substance

In elucidating the ontological categories of space and time, Sellars has repeatedly alluded to the category of substance. Since recent philosophy has tended to denigrate substance in favor of process, Sellars' position is unfashionable, particularly as regards its materialistic doctrine of substance. In the crucial twelfth chapter, "A Defense of Substance," in *The Philosophy of Physical Realism*, Sellars has announced: "I shall argue that matter is ontologically real, is existent in its own right. And I shall think it in terms of the category of substance" (11, p. 278).

What, then, are "the essential notes" of the category of substance? Precisely they are "endurance and being," and in anticipation of possible objections, Sellars added that "there is nothing in these notes which excludes relations. Merely, things cannot be reduced to relations" (11, p. 276). Further, substances are not only related; they also change, although this recognition of process or change should not obscure Sellars' thesis that change takes place in substances. Hence substance is defended against *eventism*, the metaphysical doctrine that reality consists wholly of complexes of events (11, p. 8). His "technical point . . . is that eventness does not preclude endurance, but, rather, presupposes it" (11, p. 305). Change is the activation of an existing physical system; and events are changes located within such systems. Here, at last, the conception of consciousness as a pattern of events within the brain-mind receives its ontological basis. As regards the second essential note of substance, being, this is equated with matter. A vigorous proponent of materialism, Sellars has asserted: "I take the physical world to be another term for being or existence" (11, p. 285). Of course this materialism is not utterly monistic, since evolutionary naturalism posits heterogeneous gradients at different levels of nature, revealing a plurality of novel organizations of matter. Nor is matter an inert substrate. "The physical world is dynamic and concrete. . . . Material systems are extended, structured, massive, causally effective" (11, p. 286).

Material substances are not unknowable substrates. Metaphysical skepticism, traceable to Locke's doctrine of substance, which Sellars has sought to reform, is inconsistent with critical realism. "All knowing presupposes *being* and, in this sense, claims ontological reach. It is what exists that we seek to know" (11, p. 285). "Substances are continuants which can be made objects of cognition and which are self-existents" (11, p. 283). Yet pursuant to the requirements of critical realism, material substance is neither directly intuited nor inferred from ideas which copy it. On the contrary, knowledge of matter is attained through sense-data and ideas which in perception and cognition refer to the discriminable properties of things. Consider sense-data. According to Sellars, they are "internal *events* which flash within us a projection of the more stable structure of *things*" (11, p.

281). "They are *points of departure for predicative interpretation of objects* and not themselves such predicates" (11, p. 154). From this it does not follow, as
many materialists allege, that material being is "a quali-
tyless substratum," but it does follow that "we can never
intuit the existential content of the world" (11, p. 308).
Since the sense-data which natural realism hastily mistakes for the existential properties of things prove instead
to be events internal to consciousness, the conclusion
that things have no qualities may be easily, but wrongly,
inferred. "Certain that being must have its content,"
Sellars has nevertheless advised that "we must be satisfied to speak categorially of forces and energies in nature"
(11, pp. 308-309).

From sense-data, by means of which things are perceived, arise ideas and meanings, through which things
are known. Neither identical with nor copies of the existential contents of things, sense-data and conceptual
meanings are indicative of objective properties. Such
properties are, according to Sellars, intrinsic to the things
of which they are the properties. "A thing has no existence apart from its properties and its properties no existence apart from the thing. In other words, a thing and
its nature are inseparable. A thing is always a *that-
what*" (11, p. 161). Because we know the properties of
things through sense-data and concepts, it has been
tempting for the realistic proponents of essence to con-
strue these properties as essences, i.e., universal contents,
and to regard things as aggregates of essences. Sellars,
however, is openly hostile to the metaphysics of essences
and universals. A self-styled logical conceptualist and ontological nominalist, he has insisted: "Only individual
things are real . . . I believe in concepts but I do not
believe in universals as a peculiar kind of entity in external things which may be in many things at once and
give them an identity of nature" (11, p. 155). Just as
things are particular, so their properties are particular. In

ontology identity of characters is dismissed; in its place
similarity is substituted (11, pp. 171 ff.). The properties
or characteristics of a thing, such as magnitude, composition, patterns, and modes of behavior, are expressions of
the natures of things. "They are *that* about the thing and
its relations which can be manifested and deciphered.
It is this structural and relational form, or order, of the
physical world which makes it knowable" (11, p. 284).
Thus the nominalistic, materialistic ontology of physical
realism neatly complements the epistemology of critical
realism.

SOCIAL AND RELIGIOUS PHILOSOPHY:
NATURALISTIC HUMANISM

"Can humanism and values find elbow-room in naturalism?" is a question which, according to Sellars, can receive only a negative answer so long as naturalism is
reductive and its materialism mechanical (2, p. 282). Further, critical realism maintains in the theory of knowledge that since sensory qualities, the secondary qualities
of traditional philosophy, are excluded from, or at least
not ascribed to, physical things, such qualities are neither
identical with nor resemble the properties of things.
Further, since these qualities, functioning as sense-data,
merely indicate the real properties of things through
their patterns and organizations, these real properties are
better known in scientific cognition than in sense perception. Now with the removal of sensory qualities from
nature, there is heightened concern over just how values can be explained and located within the general
structure of the universe. However, inasmuch as evolutionary naturalism, though materialistic and critically
realistic, maintains the emergence of different levels of
beings and causality within nature, it clearly provides for
men and hence, for human values.

Value Theory

Central to Sellars' theory of values is his distinction between cognition and valuation, a distinction which Professor Frankena has cited to suggest that "Sellars is maintaining some kind of noncognitive theory in opposition to both intuitionism and naturalism in ethics, and was doing so as far back as 1925" (3, p. 66). Although Sellars has often made such statements as "cognition is not valuation and . . . valuation is not cognition" (10, p. 443), he seems to have been concerned to distinguish two kinds of judgment which he called "cognitional judgments" and "judgments of value." "In cognitional judgments we regard ourselves as characterizing the object, asserting what we regard as a disclosure of it. In judgments of value we are estimating it with respect to its *bearing* upon human life" (11, p. 446). In judgments of value "it is as though I sought a *power* in things which *could* have bearing on my life or on the life of others. It is as though I estimated it [some object] *with respect to* human living" (11, p. 444).

Values, like sense qualities, do not characterize physical things but indicate *capacities* of these things "to enter human life with certain consequences of importance to the self or to a social group" (11, p. 445). Values, then, are not the intrinsic properties of things. "There must be implied at least the *possibility* of connection with our lives. In other words, value is not an attribute, like size and composition, which is out there to be known. It is, to use G. E. Moore's term, not a natural property; that is, not the kind of property disclosable by sense-data" (11, p. 459). Value judgments deal "with the *powers* of things" to affect our lives "in desirable and undesirable ways" (11, p. 472). Although values are constituted by (consist of) such psychological factors as feelings, sentiments, desires, and interests (11, p. 445), this does not mean that values are restricted to what men actually desire and are interested in. Sellars has sharply attacked *Factualism*, namely, "the acceptance of valuations as brute facts with respect to which the question of validity and adequacy cannot be raised" (11, p. 451). For factualism "presupposes a dogmatic attitude of finality and disregards the possibility of new knowledge and creative development in experience" (11, p. 454). Normative judgments need not be merely imperatives allegedly enforced by the power of God, nor need the validity of norms be simply the coercion of police power and public pressures within society. Normative judgments of value, whether moral or aesthetic, are, according to Sellars' analysis, implicative. To judge that a given person ought to perform a given duty or that he should appreciate a given work of art is tantamount to expressing "a belief that certain likes and dislikes follow from a trained personality. I expect you to [do it or to] like it *if* you are the kind of person you might be" (11, p. 456).

Judgments of value, then, involve *double reference*—references to objects and references to persons (11, p. 472). Since, moreover, values are amenable to development, it follows that, anchored at one end in the nature of man and at the other end in the capacities of things, values evolve. Evolutionary naturalism treats society as an emergent, describing it as "*a new kind of thing*," which, although not a physical integration, is yet "a mentally mediated and historically developed integration of human beings which finds expression in cooperative, or joint, behavior and in personality" (10, p. 351). The medium in which values develop is society, just as society itself develops from natural human individuals, themselves comprising an emergent level in physical nature. At the level of man and society values may be said to exist. As Sellars has said: "Clearly values are intrinsic to reality at this high level. In values we are *in* culture, *in* civilization, *in* the very pulse of selective and creative human life" (29).

Democratic Socialism

According to Sellars, democratic society offers the most plausible promise of the evolution of values appropriate to the broadest human reach. Democracy, after all, is the political constitution of a society whereby the power of government comes exclusively from the people, who possess the ultimate sovereignty and express themselves through voting (13, p. 251). Within democratic society the evolution of values is consequently grounded in the actual aspirations and desires of all its voting members.

However, for Sellars, political democracy is not the final achievement of social evolution. Influenced by the social philosophy of Lester Ward and Charles Horton Cooley as well as by the writings of the British Fabians, Shaw, Wells, and the Webbs (12, p. 68), Sellars proclaimed that *The Next Step in Democracy*, to cite the title of the book he devotes to this topic, is socialism. This book, appearing in 1916, with Europe in the throes of World War I and America in uneasy and short-lived neutrality, went unnoticed. Read today against the background of the Russian Revolution, British socialism, and the American New Deal and New Frontier, it makes diagnoses and proposes remedies for the ills of our industrial civilization that are no longer radical. Nonetheless, it is imbued with a sense of moral fervor and redolent with righteous demands for social justice. Boldly conspicuous is Sellars' conviction, so widespread among intellectuals in the decades following World War I, that political democracy to fulfill its moral intention must evolve into the sort of economic democracy socialism provides.

According to Sellars' definition: "Socialism is a democratic movement whose purpose is in securing of an economic organization of society which will give the maximum possible at any one time of justice and liberty" (13, p. 9). Socialism, therefore, is democracy universalized. "While working for popular sovereignty, socialism always has in mind those broad human values to which it regards such sovereignty as a means. A people who achieved this formal democracy and allowed unjustified privileges to exist would be an ethically undeveloped people, a people whose development was, perhaps, legal and onesided and who were not conscious of the larger issues of life" (13, p. 252).

Religious Naturalism

With man firmly located within nature and with values wholly rooted in men and in human society, the question of the status and role of religion arises for consideration. Whereas tradition regards religion as faith in the causal efficacy of supernatural agencies that intervene in the course of nature and in the life of man, Sellars' evolutionary naturalism and his materialistic ontology rule out the existence of the supernatural. In fact, in *The Next Step in Religion*, he has taken pains to trace the evolution of religious ideas, originating in the primitive tribal life of men and developing through the ages in myths and rituals. After examining the evolution of Christianity and its theology, Sellars has noted how scientific thought banishes many of its fundamental dogmas, such as the creation of nature, the miraculous agency of supernatural beings, the immortality of human souls. Though a partisan of science and critical thinking, Sellars is not totally devoid of appreciation for traditional religions. His is not the method of the iconoclast coldly bent on discarding the ideas with the idols. Of Christianity he has said: "In the figure of Jesus, ethical and aesthetic idealization guided by religious emotion has created a personality of a peculiarly appealing type well fitted to remain as an ideal to foster and maintain the noblest tendencies. But this ideal has become practically self-supporting apart from its mythical scaffolding. Its real foundation today is in its appeal to sympathies, natural to social beings, which the spiritual evolution of humanity has developed and given content to" (14, pp. 96-97).

In accord with this high estimation of the ethical role of religions, Sellars concluded the second of his two books on religion with a section bearing the title: "Let Us Stand By the Churches But Demand More of Them" (15, p. 286). For Sellars has redefined religion, in consonance with humanistic naturalism, as *"loyalty to the values of life"* (14, p. 7). As "the strategy of human life" to conserve and create values "in the face of destiny" (15, p. 51), religion must adjust to every change in man's conception of his destiny. To acknowledge the exclusive validity of a materialistic naturalism and of a humanistic system of values does not necessitate the repudiation of the spiritual, but it does demand its reconception. As Sellars has said *"The spiritual is man at his best, man loving, daring, creating, fighting loyally and courageously for causes dear to him"* (14, pp. 7-8). Or as he put it in a later book, "the spiritual is an expression of human life as it develops in society" (15, p. 243). Thus the spiritual is naturalized and humanized, and religion "comes of age," with naturalistic humanism as its credo.

Being mature, the religion of naturalistic humanism will, Sellars contends, "still be a religion and will reflect man's strategy in the face of a changed interpretation of reality" (15, p. 184). First of all it will dispense with the God-idea, since the thesis of supernatural agency cannot be justified scientifically. "Religion began without gods and it may end without them" (15, p. 53). Second, it will discard the idea of immortality, since (evolutionary naturalism holds) the living soul is inextricably linked to the living organism, and the capacities of the living individual will be promoted to high levels of activity and value within society (15, p. 193). "The living soul is at once a living organism and a conscious self" (15, p. 195). Finally, in ridding religion of the God-idea and the idea of human immortality, humanistic naturalism passes beyond the pessimistic perspective of traditional naturalism, which judges the natural universe to be hostile to man and to human values. Humanistic naturalism neither elevates nature into a God to be worshipped and prayed to nor counsels despair over the career of man and the fate of human values in the natural universe. Rather, the religion of humanistic naturalism is a sober call to human action in behalf of human values. As Sellars has said: "Let man stand on his own feet and trust his own powers. The universe is not unfriendly; rather it is the natural scene of his birth and achievements. It is something within which to work in a human way, bravely, creatively, gently, wisely. Here is a new attitude, that of an adult shifting for himself, set on carving out his own fortunes, aware that life is not a path of roses, knowing that tragedy may claim him, and yet fighting a good fight for whatsoever things are honorable and of good repute. Here we have man and religion coming of age" (15, p. 156).

NOTES TO CHAPTER 7

1. DeWitt H. Parker, "Some Comments on 'Reformed Materialism and Intrinsic Endurance,'" *Philosophical Review*, LIII (1944), 383.

2. Roy Wood Sellars, "Realism, Naturalism and Humanism," in *Contemporary American Philosophy*, Vol. II, G. P. Adams and W. P. Montague, eds. (New York: The Macmillan Co., 1930, reprinted by Russell & Russell, Inc., 1962).

3. See *A Symposium in Honor of Roy Wood Sellars*, with contributions by Professors Archie Bahm, Roderick M. Chisholm, William Frankena, John Kuiper, Wilfrid Sellars, and Marten Ten Hoor, in *Philosophy and Phenomenological Research*, XV (1954), 1-97. Helpful to all students of Sellars' philosophy is Gerald E. Myers' "Bibliography of the Writings of Roy Wood Sellars," *ibid.*, XV, 98-103. See in connection with this symposium Roy Wood Sellars, "My Philosophical Position: A Rejoinder," *ibid.*, XVI (1955), 72-97.

4. Roy Wood Sellars, *Critical Realism* (Chicago: Rand-McNally & Co., 1916).

5. W. H. Werkmeister, A *History of Philosophical Ideas in America* (New York: The Ronald Press, 1949).

6. *Essays in Critical Realism* (New York: The Macmillan Co., 1920). Sellars contributed the chapter: "Knowledge and Its Categories," pp. 187-219.

7. Roy Wood Sellars, *Evolutionary Naturalism* (Chicago: Open Court Publishing Company, 1922).

8. Roy Wood Sellars, *The Essentials of Logic* (Boston: Houghton, Mifflin Co., 1917).

9. Roy Wood Sellars, *The Essentials of Philosophy* (New York: The Macmillan Co., 1917).

10. Roy Wood Sellars, *The Principles and Problems of Philosophy* (New York: The Macmillan Co., 1926).

11. Roy Wood Sellars, *The Philosophy of Physical Realism* (New York: The Macmillan Co., 1932).

12. Roy Wood Sellars, V. J. McGill, and Marvin Farber, *Philosophy for the Future: Quest of Modern Materialism* (New York: The Macmillan Co., 1949).

13. Roy Wood Sellars, *The Next Step in Democracy* (New York: The Macmillan Co., 1916).

14. Roy Wood Sellars, *The Next Step in Religion* (New York: The Macmillan Co., 1918).

15. Roy Wood Sellars, *Religion Coming of Age* (New York: The Macmillan Co., 1928).

16. "A Humanist Manifesto," *The New Humanist*, VI, No. 3 (1933).

17. Victor E. Harlow, A *Bibliography and Genetic Study of American Realism* (Oklahoma City, Harlow Publishing Company, 1931), p. 69.

18. Brand Blanshard, *The Nature of Thought* (London and New York: Allen and Unwin & Macmillan, 1939).

19. Joseph L. Blau, *Men and Movements in American Philosophy* (Englewood Cliffs, N. J.; Prentice-Hall, Inc., 1952).

20. Roy Wood Sellars, "Referential Transcendence," *Philosophy and Phenomenological Research*, XXII (1961), 6.

21. Roy Wood Sellars, "A Correspondence Theory of Truth," *Journal of Philosophy*, XXXVIII (1941), 653-654.

22. Roy Wood Sellars, " 'True' as Contextually Implying Correspondence," *Journal of Philosophy*, LIV (1957), 719-720.

23. See the remark of Sellars' son Wilfrid, professor of philosophy at Pittsburg and a leading analytic philosopher: "A discerning student of philosophy, familiar with the writings of Sellars *père*, who chances to read Sellars *fils*, and is not taken in by the superficial changes of idiom and emphasis which reflect the adaptation of the species to a new environment, will soon be struck by the fundamental identity of outlook. The identity is obscured by differences of terminology, method and polemi-

cal orientation, but it is none the less an identity." Wilfrid Sellars, "Physical Realism," A Symposium in Honor of Roy Wood Sellars, op. cit., p. 13.

24. Roy Wood Sellars, "Critical Realism and the Independence of the Object," Journal of Philosophy, XXXIV (1937).

25. See Roy Wood Sellars, "Panpsychism or Evolutionary Naturalism," Philosophy of Science, XXVII (1960), 329-350.

26. See such titles as the following articles by Roy Wood Sellars: "Why Naturalism and Not Materialism?" Philosophical Review, XXXVI (1927), 215-225; "Reformed Materialism and Intrinsic Endurance," Philosophical Review, LIII (1944), 359-382; "Critical Realism and Modern Materialism," Philosophic Thought in France and the United States, Marvin Farber, ed. (Buffalo: University of Buffalo Publications in Philosophy, 1950), pp. 463-482; and "The New Materialism," A History of Philosophical Systems, Vergilius Ferm, ed. (New York: Philosophical Library, 1950), pp. 418-428.

27. See Roy Wood Sellars, "Reflections on Dialectical Materialism," Philosophy and Phenomenological Research, V (1944-1945), 157-179.

28. See following articles by Roy Wood Sellars: "Reinterpretation of Relativity," Philosophical Review, XLI (1932), 517-518; "Note on the Theory of Relativity," Journal of Philosophy, XLIII (1946), 309-317; "Philosophy and Physics of Relativity," Philosophy of Science, XIII (1946), 177-195; "Gestalt and Relativity: An Analogy," ibid., XXIII (1956), 275-279; "Physical Realism and Relativity: Some Unfinished Business," ibid., XXIII (1956), 75-81.

29. Roy Wood Sellars, "Introduction," to C. Bouglé, The Evolution of Values, trans. by Helen Stalker Sellars (New York: Henry Holt and Company, 1926), p. xxviii.

Chapter 8

THE TEMPORALISTIC
REALISM OF
ARTHUR O. LOVEJOY

INTRODUCTION

"Not boldness, but circumspection, and again circumspection, and always circumspection" (1). That is the motto Arthur O. Lovejoy (1873-1962) recommended to his fellow philosophers in his presidential address to the Eastern Division of the American Philosophical Association. Observing that American philosophy from the turn of the century to World War I had undergone a revolution against the alleged certitudes of idealism and witnessed the rise of divergent realisms and pragmatisms, Lovejoy wondered whether philosophy must lose itself in incessant disagreement and fail forever to arrive at universally intelligible and definitely cogent results. He attributed the failures of philosophers to their confusion of the distinct activities of edification and of inquiry; and he undertook to specify the conditions for progress in philosophical inquiry. Above all he urged that philosophers pledge themselves to dispassionate, disinterested inquiry. Philosophers, he contended, must develop the habit of "logical observation." They must deliberately and systematically attempt to enumerate exhaustively all the elements that bear upon a philosophical problem. Philosophy, he held, is intrinsically a cooperative enterprise, since it requires more than one mind to advance toward the truth. Yet, he readily added, philosophical cooperation consists primarily in disagreement, for he quoted Harrington's aphorism with approval: "Truth is a spark to which objections are like bellows." Nevertheless, he seldom wavered from his conviction that truth would win unanimous assent. Philosophers, he advised, should adopt a common and an unambiguous terminology and should formulate a common set of rules for the purpose of philosophical discussions. They should treat individual problems in isolation and deal with general issues in piecemeal fashion. And finally, they should prepare an undogmatic, nonpartisan, comprehensive catalogue of philosophical considerations, organized according to the problems or theses to which they are pertinent. Thus the cooperative pursuit of objective truths would be facilitated, and progress in philosophical inquiry, based upon circumspection, would be attained.

Circumspection was the hallmark of Lovejoy's own work as a philosopher. Educated at the University of California and at Harvard during its "golden age," Lovejoy taught at Stanford, at Washington University in St. Louis, and at the University of Missouri before he was appointed professor of philosophy at Johns Hopkins, where he served as professor and professor emeritus from 1910 until his death in 1962. Lovejoy's contributions to recent American thought and scholarship exemplify the conditions he deemed indispensable to progress in philosophy. The most critical and erudite American philosopher of his generation, Lovejoy has won high position not only in philosophy, but also in the field of intellectual history, especially in English studies and comparative

literature. Indeed, the history of ideas, a whole new discipline with its own journal, has sprung up under his
aegis. At home in philosophy, literature, and science, he
could equally well distinguish the thirteen pragmatisms,
discriminate the varieties of romanticism, trace the influence of Platonic metaphysics on Western thought,
distinguish the divergent meanings of "nature" in ancient, medieval, and modern authors, blast the incoher-
ences of objective relativism or behaviorism, and pin-
point the ambiguities of relativity theory in physics.
Lovejoy's *métier* was the monograph, and it is impossible
to conceive the history of recent American thought without the steady stream of articles, critical and historical,
which flowed from his pen throughout the first half of
the twentieth century.

Lovejoy's work was widely recognized and appreciated
by his colleagues. He was elected to the presidency of
the American Association of University Professors and,
on separate occasions, to the presidency of the Western
and the Eastern Divisions of the American Philosophical
Association. He was appointed Carus Lecturer for the
American Philosophical Association, and his lectures
gave birth to his first and most important book of philosophy, *The Revolt Against Dualism* (2). He was elected
to deliver the William James lectures at Harvard. These
lectures gave rise to his second book, his greatest contribution to the history of ideas, *The Great Chain of
Being* (3). At Johns Hopkins University the members
of the History of Ideas Club, on the occasion of the
twenty-fifth anniversary of its founding, invited Lovejoy
to collect some of his papers for publication under the
sponsorship of the Club; the happy result was *Essays in
the History of Ideas* (4). And on two occasions Lovejoy's
work has been the topic of symposia, first in the *Journal
of the History of Ideas*, and recently in *Philosophy and
Phenomenological Research* (5).

Lovejoy's contributions to the history of ideas have

tended to overshadow his contributions to philosophy proper. In addition to his widely read *The Great Chain of Being* and his collection of oft-cited and discussed papers, *Essays in the History of Ideas,* Lovejoy has written three other major works on the history of ideas: *Primitivism and Related Ideas in Antiquity,* with George Boas (6); *The Reason, The Understanding and Time* (7); and *Reflections on Human Nature* (8). Although Lovejoy has sharply demarcated the method of the philosopher from that of the intellectual historian—the former being concerned solely with the logical considerations pertinent to the subject under investigation and the latter being concerned with the entire thought of the past relevant to the question under study—he has nonetheless paused in his historical inquiries to offer contributions to philosophy. *The Great Chain of Being* concludes with a philosophical afterthought on the result of historical investigations for philosophical cosmology. *Reflections on Human Nature* digresses from a recital of the thoughts of seventeenth- and eighteenth-century authors on moral philosophy to present, in Lecture III, Lovejoy's own views. *The Reason, The Understanding and Time* closes with an appendix which critically discusses Bergson's temporalism and suggests the major elements of Lovejoy's own temporalism. Yet, on the whole, the impression which these works leave on the reader is of an historian interested mainly in reconstructing and recovering past thoughts.

Despite the critical attention it spends on the theories of others, however, *The Revolt Against Dualism* is a major landmark in recent epistemology and philosophy of mind. W. H. Werkmeister has described it as "the most comprehensive and most systematic defense of critical realism as an epistemology" (9, p. 478). But having first been published over thirty years ago, its philosophical content tends to be obscured by the massiveness of Lovejoy's historical books and essays. However, the posthumous publication of *The Thirteen Pragmatisms and Other Essays* (10) has awakened appreciation of Lovejoy as a philosopher. This book brings together papers written during the first quarter of the twentieth century, including his contribution to the highly influential co-operative volume which defined a movement, *Essays in Critical Realism.*

It is the aim of this chapter to focus on Lovejoy's works as philosophy. It is possible to extract from his books and articles a closely reasoned position. Cogent and circumspect, this position is, in his own words, "a temporalistic realism" (11). Beyond the area of technical philosophy its most fruitful application is perhaps in the history of ideas. This chapter will explore: Lovejoy's temporalism; his realism, to be examined in connection with dualism; and his conception of intellectual history, considered within its philosophical context.

TEMPORALISM

Although Lovejoy has devoted uncounted pages to discussions of time, he has never elaborated his temporalistic philosophy. To see his temporalism whole it is necessary to draw together particular elucidations and theses from fugitive essays and chapters and to organize them systematically. Surprisingly, these scattered remarks on time and temporalism lend themselves to orderly presentation.

The Roots of Lovejoy's Temporalism

Lovejoy's temporalism grew out of his reactions to idealism, pragmatism, and evolutionism. As a student, first at California and later at Harvard, he had become acquainted with the idealisms of Howison and Royce. This acquaintance convinced him that, in addition to the crosswise pluralistic rejection of absolute idealism expressed by Howison, there was need for a lengthwise pluralism which, insisting upon the reality of externally related moments of time, would also undo absolute idealism—or, for that matter, any idealism which stressed eternity and neglected time (11, pp. 92-96). A more positive source of Lovejoy's temporalism was his belief in the actuality of evolution. After all, Bergsonism was in the air, and while a student at Harvard Lovejoy had studied James's philosophy and found in it the outlines of temporalism. Indeed, he went so far as to place James's pragmatism essentially within the compass of temporalist thought and to classify him as a French philosopher (12).

In his 1909 presidential address to the Western Division of the American Philosophical Association, Lovejoy discussed "the Obsolescence of the Eternal." He argued for a temporalism, exclusive of the eternal, by consideration of the question "whether a belief in the eternal character of 'ultimate' reality, or of any reality at all, is reconcilable with a belief in the actuality of evolution, in the most general sense" (13, p. 482). Evolution he defined as "a process of real temporal becoming," by which he meant "not only change, but also the emergence into existence, at diverse moments, of new items of reality which did not previously exist and which, therefore, by their appearance bring an actual augmentation to the total content of the universe" (13, p. 482). Eternity he defined "as neither everlastingness nor mere permanence through time, but timeless existence,—being that is without change in itself, or in any of its relations, and therefore without date,—entity to which the lapse of time cannot lend even an increment of age" (13, pp. 482-483). Attacking the doctrine of the eternal upheld by the neo-Kantian idealists, some of whom, e.g., McTaggart, had endeavored dialectically to refute the reality of time, Lovejoy denounced the eternal as "the characteristic but not incorrigible distemper of adolescent metaphysics" (13, p. 501).

In contending that the eternal is obsolescent in face of the idealistic arguments for the unreality of time, Lovejoy indulged in a sophisticated *tu quoque,* employing the same forms of argument, e.g., from the internality of relations and from the criteria of conceivability according to the laws of thought, which were dear to the hearts of the idealists. He advanced two main arguments against the idealistic doctrine of the eternal. The first argument is that, since the idealist philosophers who uphold the doctrine of the eternal expect it to make a difference in time, the eternal is brought into relation with the temporal, and consequently, this relation between the eternal and the temporal changes, i.e., temporalizes, the eternal. In sum, "the assertion of a real relation between an eternal and a temporal reduces the eternal to the temporal" (13, p. 496). The second argument is, in Lovejoy's own words, "a temporal form of the law of excluded middle." It is, he said, "impossible for us to conceive any concrete thing save as either *now* existing or not now existing,—as other than past or present or future" (13, p. 496). Since an eternal cannot be said to be now or not to be now, it is inconceivable, and hence it is not.

Although it is doubtful that Lovejoy would, in later phases of his career, have put much stock in such purely dialectical arguments based, in part, upon idealistic assumptions, his adherence to temporalism remained constant. The constructive factors in this temporalism can be discerned in Lovejoy's treatment of what he called "the temporal shadow of eternity." By this he meant the quantitative and qualitative constancy of the universe as postulated by cosmologies grounded upon classical physics. Not dialectical argument, but reflection upon the import of an empirical theory, spurred Lovejoy to reject this alleged constancy and to embrace temporalism. The empirical theory is, of course, evolution. For, according to Lovejoy, evolution demands that "the sum total of the universe cannot remain constant, but must be subject to augmentation" (13, p. 488).

The Nature of Temporalism

The dismissal of eternity and of the temporal shadow of eternity was, then, a prelude to a positive recommendation: "the practice of viewing things *sub specie temporis*" (13, p. 479). Lovejoy, indeed, restricted the philosophers' option to "only two types of philosophy that quite thoroughly know what they are about—Oriental illusionism and thorough-going temporalism,—Shankara and, if you please, Bergson. And between these alternatives I do not find it possible to hesitate" (13, p. 501). What, then, is temporalism? It is both a method and a metaphysics.

Temporalism as a Method. As a method, temporalism consists "in an attempt to identify with definiteness the particular moment of existence, the relative temporal *locus*, of each entity or process or relation referred to by any proposition" (14). The temporalistic method was a useful analytic instrument for Lovejoy in his treatment of the varieties of neorealism and pragmatism and his advocacy of critical realism. On these topics more will be said below.

Temporalism as a Metaphysics. As a metaphysics temporalism involves four propositions. First, "time is not 'ideal'" (12, p. 11). It is not unreal, or illusory, or an appearance of something nontemporal. Second, "temporal succession and duration constitute a qualitatively unique mode of reality, which can not, without falsification, either be reduced to any other type of serial ordering or be conceived as forming part of any whole which, as a whole, is nonsuccessive or changeless" (12, p. 11). Third, "since the experience of temporal succession involves an essential distinction between the givenness of past content of experience and the unrealized character of the future, the reality of the time-experience proves that reality as a whole can at no moment be truly called complete, self-contained, or organic unity" (12, p. 11). Fourth, "the reality of the time-experience likewise shows that the total sum of given reality receives from moment to moment an increase in *some* sort of content, and that, therefore, the notion of becoming or process is fundamental in the description of the general nature of reality" (12, p. 11). From these four propositions it follows, in summary, that "temporalism is the metaphysical theory which maintains the reality and the irreducibility of time (or at the least, of the successiveness of conscious experience), the essentially transitive and unfinished and self-augmentative character of reality known to us through experience and the pertinency and primacy of the time-concept and of temporal distinctions in the treatment of most, if not all, philosophical problems" (12, p. 11).

By virtue of its emphasis upon "the essentially transitive and unfinished and self-augmentative character of reality," temporalism is an evolutionism. Lovejoy's address to the Sixth International Congress of Philosophy contains his clearest statement of his position on evolution, a position which advocates a form of emergent evolution. Lovejoy defined emergence as "any augmentative or transmutative event, any process in which there appear effects that, in some one or more of several ways yet to be specified, fail to conform to the maxim that 'there cannot be in the consequent anything more than, or different in nature from, that which was in the antecedent' " (15). He then distinguished general from specific emergence. General emergence is predicable of the whole universe, but not necessarily of every part; whether it exists is incapable of proof or disproof. Specific emergence is predicable of some part or parts of the universe, but not necessarily of the whole. The thesis of specific emergence is "the assertion on empirical grounds of the occurrence, among the phenomena investigable by science, of events which are not mere rearrangements of preexistent natural entities in accordance with laws identical for all arrangements of those entities" (15, p. 25). This thesis is compatible with either causal determinism or causal indeterminism, and Lovejoy tended to favor the former. He distinguished two main modes of specific emergence: functional and existential. Functional emergence maintains that there come to be at later moments in the history of the universe types of change and physical laws applicable thereto which are neither predictable nor describable by physical laws that held in the past. Existential emergence holds either (1) that new qualities or classes of qualities, or (2) new entities, or (3) new events, or (4) increases in quantity come into being and cannot be accounted for in terms of earlier stages of the universe. Now Lovejoy was persuaded that the thesis of specific, existential emergence, at least with respect to new entities and events, was justified by empirical evidence. In particular he accepted the generative theory of sensa and chose to call his theory of evolution a theory of "transphysical emergence." As he remarked in conclusion, "we have . . . abundant reason to believe that in the history of our planet there have occurred genuine new births of time, a sheer increase and diversification and enrichment of the sum of things here" (15, p. 32).

The Historical Context of Lovejoy's Temporalism

Additional insights into Lovejoy's temporalism may be gained by a consideration of its context in relation to both past thought and contemporary thought. Characteristically Lovejoy himself presented his temporalism through historical and critical studies of the writings of others on the topic of time.

In Relation to Past Thought. Several of Lovejoy's contributions to the history of ideas deal with topics that are relevant to his temporalism. Only the major ones will be cited here.

The opening chapter of A *Documentary History of Primitivism and Related Ideas* is, as prolegomena to the rest of the volume, an analysis and classification of types of primitivism. However, since the first type of primitivism as chronological has to do with "the temporal distribution of good, or value, in the history of mankind, or, more generally, in the entire history of the world," the discussion offers a classification of theories of history and, consequently, of time (6, p. 1). In view of Lovejoy's conception of temporalism as emergent evolutionism, it might be expected that his theory would involve a theory of progress. The theory of progress, without being "a general and necessary law," would mean "that the course of things . . . in spite of possible minor deviations and the occasional occurrence of backwaters in the stream of history—has been characterized by a gradual progressive increase, or a wider diffusion, of goodness, or happiness, or enlightenment, or of all of these" (6, p. 3). Of course Lovejoy was cautious not to identify his temporalism with the idea of progress, since the process of evolution need not be in the service of values and since human nature has acted as a kind of constant in history. Nevertheless, his temporalism lent cosmological support to the idea of progress—as a hope if not as a law.

The relation of temporalism to past thought is underscored most sharply in the concluding chapter of *The Great Chain of Being.* Lovejoy's motive for the investigations which led to that book was the desire of the historian to understand the concept of the great chain of being, initially encountered in the writings of seventeenth- and eighteenth-century authors (16). This desire prompted him to retrace the history of the idea, now analyzed into its components of gradation, plenitude, and continuity, back to Plato. What he uncovered was the amazing yet concealed history of Western metaphysics. As an afterthought, in the last chapter, he tested this history, as a philosopher would, by means of the kind of philosophy he deemed to be warranted by logical principles and empirical evidence. Although he regarded the idea of the great chain of being to be "one of the most grandiose enterprises of the human intellect," he judged its history to be "the history of a failure; more precisely and more justly, it is the record of an experiment in thought carried on for many great and lesser minds, which can now be seen to have had an instructive negative outcome" (3, p. 329). For, in the first place, the idea of "the great chain of being" is contradicted by "one immense fact . . . in the natural order—the fact that existence as we experience it is temporal. A world of time and change—this, at least, our history has shown—is a world which can neither be deduced from nor reconciled with the postulate that existence is the expression and consequence of a system of 'eternal' and 'necessary' truths inherent in the very logic of being. . . . Any change whereby nature at one time contains other things or more things than it contains at another time is fatal to the principle of sufficient reason" (3, p. 329).

In the second place, the idea of the great chain of being fosters a "rationality [which], when conceived as complete, as excluding all arbitrariness, becomes itself a kind of irrationality. For, since it means the complete realization of all the possibles, in so far as they are compossible, it excludes any limiting and selective principle" (3, p. 331). The realm of possibles being infinite, and all possibles being realized, the world becomes a whirl of contradictions.

Lovejoy's reflection on the negative experiment had a positive terminus. He wrote: "The world of concrete existence, then, is no impartial transcript of the realm of essence; and it is no translation of pure logic into temporal terms—such terms being themselves, indeed, the negation of pure logic. It has the character and the range of content and of diversity which it happens to have. No rational ground predetermined from all eternity of what sort it should be or how much of the world of possibility should be included in it. It *is*, in short, a contingent world; its magnitude, its pattern, its habits, which we call laws, have something arbitrary and idiosyncratic about them. But if this were not the case, it would be a world without a character, without power of preference or choice among the infinity of possibles" (3, p. 332).

In Relation to Contemporary Thought. Lovejoy considered contemporary thought, insofar as it discarded eternalistic idealism and recognized the import of evolution, to be inherently temporalistic. However, there are varieties of temporalism. According to Lovejoy Bergsonism, pragmatism, new realism, and contemporary science, despite their temporalistic character, do not provide individually or collectively a tenable temporalism, although one does emerge from his critical discussions of these alternative contemporary theories.

1. Pragmatism. In an article published in the *Journal of Philosophy* in 1908, Lovejoy examined pragmatism and, instead of a single theory, found thirteen. One of the thirteen pragmatisms he distinguished is a form of metaphysical temporalism. "Temporal becoming is a fundamental character of reality; in this becoming the processes of consciousness have their essential and creative part. The future is strictly nonreal and its character is partly indeterminate, dependent upon movements of consciousness the nature and direction of which can be wholly known only at the moments in which they become real in experience" (10, p. 28). This ontological theory of pragmatism, he added, is sometimes confused with pragmatism as an epistemologically functionless theory concerning the "nature" of truth. According to the epistemological theory, "(t)he truth of a judgment 'consists in' the complete realization of the experience

(or series of experiences) to which the judgment had antecedently pointed: propositions *are* not, but only *become*, true" (10, p. 26). Although Lovejoy perhaps avoided this particular confusion of pragmatism, he nonetheless spoke and wrote—as John Dewey was quick to note (17)—as though he believed there was an essential or "true" pragmatism with special affinities to temporalism.

Lovejoy placed William James, whose psychology emphasized "the creative efficacy of the passing phases in each flowing stream of consciousness" (10, p. 99), in the mainstream of French temporalist philosophy after Renouvier and next to Bergson. The pragmatism of William James, Lovejoy dilated, "was primarily epistemological temporalism. It proposed to define 'meaning' and 'truth' in terms of intertemporal relations between successive phases of experience. . . . A judgment made by a human being . . . is always and essentially an act of a creature standing at a specific moment in the time-flow, facing the future, preparing in some way for that future by means of the activity of judging, and himself moving forward into the future even while he judges" (10, p. 108).

The "true" pragmatic method, therefore, is a form of the temporalist method. Regarding knowledge as a factor which acts upon and is interactive with the physical and social environment, pragmatism should sharpen and make precise the time distinctions pertinent to the situation in which inquiry arises. Pragmatism considers all judgment to be practical, and practical judgment looks backward and forward. The judgment made in the present relies on retrospective knowledge of the past, while it also points to and strives to affect or prepare for a future that will be. Practical judgment presupposes the reality of externally related moments of time.

However, the temporalism essential to pragmatism is subverted by another principle—the principle of radical empiricism (10, p. 187). According to Lovejoy, "false" pragmatism results from the radical empiricist reduction of all temporal distinctions to the concrete experience of the present moment or of some future moment which becomes present. Although William James was susceptible to the radical empiricist collapse of temporal distinctions and, consequently, to "false" pragmatism, Lovejoy concentrated particularly on John Dewey's doctrine concerning the past. Dewey was inclined to argue from the fact that judgments of past events are verified in present experience or by means of evidence sought for in the future, to the quite different theory that past events exist wholly, have their entire reality, in vestiges of them in the present or the future. Lovejoy summed up the absurdity of this theory concerning the past in the subtitle of one of his articles in reply to Dewey, "The Alleged Futurity of Yesterday" (18). Lovejoy maintained that in knowledge of past events the knower transcends the empirical present and refers to entities that are real yet do not exist in the present. When the pragmatist says that judgments of yesterday mean events in the future, he is uttering an absurd paradox. When, on the other hand, he simply holds that judgments of yesterday are verified in the present, he is asserting a platitude (19).

2. Bergsonism. Lovejoy's high regard for Bergson was evident in his remark in 1909 restricting the philosophers' option to Oriental illusionism or Bergsonian temporalism. Yet in early papers and in his recently published *The Reason, The Understanding and Time*, Lovejoy has effectively whittled away some of Bergson's stature as an original thinker. In fact, not only antecedent French thought, but the entire movement of German romantic philosophy from Jacobi to Schelling and Schopenhauer is revealed in these studies to be the source of Bergsonian conceptions. In addition to showing that Bergsonian temporalism is derivative rather than original Lovejoy spent many pages marking off the

defects of Bergson's philosophy and delineating his own temporalism by contrast.

Lovejoy rejected Bergsonism not only because it unnecessarily linked temporalism with anti-intellectualism, but also because its fundamental concept, duration, is self-contradictory. Bergson held that duration involves both indivisible contemporaneity and succession, and that, further, there is a direct perception or intuition of duration. Lovejoy underscored the paradox of Bergson's contentions and insisted that the conception of duration as indivisible contemporaneity and succession is inconsistent.

Succession consists of the before-and-after relation, the terms temporally excluding each other, whereas intuition of succession requires that both terms be present together. Thus Lovejoy argued that there can be no direct perception or intuition of succession, but that the idea of succession is derived from "the contrast within each present moment, of the fresh and vivid perceptual datum with the remembered and the anticipated, the 'no longer' and the 'not yet'" (12, p. 536). Every moment of time-consciousness, he amplified in a later work, is made up of three components: "first, some especially vivid content, usually sensory or affective, which *feels* 'new,' and thus serves to identify the moment as 'now'; second, imagery, vague or clear, or fading sense-content, which is *not* felt as simply 'new'; and, third—implicit in this very notion of 'newness'—a conceived pattern or *schema* of relations of before-and-after, in which all the other elements of content, including the 'now' itself, are thought as having relative positions, or dates of existence —*i.e.*, beforeness or afterness or togetherness with respect to one another" (7, p. 195).

The consciousness of succession requires that the moments, past and present, be externally related particulars with distinctive contents. Just as there can be no immediate perception or intuition of succession in experience, there is no need to suppose, as Bergson supposed, that change cannot be equated with the separable states but must consist in an actually experienced *transit* distinct from the states discriminable within it. For, as Lovejoy contended, psychologically no direct perception of such pure transits ever occurs; furthermore, duration itself consists of a series of concrete moments, each of which is indivisible, although the series itself is a divisible succession. Distinguishing the categories of "continuity" and "discreteness," which Bergson tended to coalesce, Lovejoy also added a third category, "unbroken sequence of distinct units." As he said: "It is the third—a mode of existence having in it something of continuity as well as of discreteness—which is attributable to time, according to our view" (12, pp. 536-537).

Because Bergson conceived duration as an indivisible succession perceptible immediately in experience, he suggested that the temporal flux could be concentrated in a kind of eternity, a concrete intuition of all time as an indivisible duration. Lovejoy explicitly criticized this association of the philosophy of creative process with the doctrine of eternity. "If the concept of eternity is to find any place in this philosophy, it can be applied *only* to the completed past; to the living present, which is living because it is moving into a future still to be created, that concept can have no relevance" (7, p. 202).

3. Relativity Physics. Though slow to be discerned, the impact of the special and the general theories of relativity upon temporalism has been disruptive. The relativity of simultaneity, advocated by the special theory, undermines the universality of a creative advance running through the entire universe during an absolute present, while the geometry of the space-time continuum assimilates time to space and deprives time of its creativity. Lovejoy, along with Whitehead, Bergson, and Mead, apprehended the clash between evolutionary temporalism and relativity physics as formulated and in-

terpreted by Einstein and his followers. Now generally forgotten, Lovejoy's discussions of relativity constitute a remarkable episode in the unwritten history of recent philosophy under the influence of Einstein.

Focusing on the ambiguities of "relativity," Lovejoy marked off three senses of the term: *conditionality, perspectivity*, and *respectivity*. Conditionality means "the dependence of the existence of a character, or set of characters, actually given in experience, upon the existence or occurrence of something else" (2, p. 111). Perspectivity means "besides the general idea of conditionality, the further notions of the existence or appearance of the character exclusively from the standpoint of the percipient, and of the necessary diversity of the characters experienced by percipients having different standpoints" (2, p. 113). Respectivity holds of a character "when the term designating it has no meaning, as a possible predicate of a subject of discourse, unless, besides that term and the subject, some definite third term is implicitly or explicitly specified" (2, p. 113). Objective relativism, a major philosophical tendency manifest in the writings of several prominent thinkers of diverse philosophical persuasions, had sprung up and capitalized upon the ambiguities of "relativity," until, of course, Lovejoy applied his critical intelligence to the position. He therefore advised nothing less than "the discontinuance of the use of this ambiguous word"—relativity (2, p. 175).

In addition to attacking some philosophical interpretations of relativity theory, Lovejoy criticized the scientific theories, too. He noted that the relativity of simultaneity, advanced by the special theory, was essentially a case of respectivity, and he attributed the paradoxes this theory held for common sense to equivocations in Einstein's presentation. He even sought to designate an admissible common sense conception of absolute simultaneity within Einstein's theory and to reserve this conception under the term "simultaneity," employing other terms to designate the paradoxical concepts in the theory (20).

Furthermore, he agreed with Bergson (21) that the time of relativity physics is not real time. And, like Bergson, he seized upon the paradox of the twins, allegedly deduced from the theorems of the special theory. According to this paradox, if one of the twins travels out into space, he finds, when he returns to earth years later, that the other is older than himself. After critically examining the treatments of this paradox by the physicists, Lovejoy concluded that the temporal retardations and contractions resultant from relative motion are not real physical effects on either moving system but rather reciprocal quasi-perspective distortions of objects in the one system as these objects are perceived by observers in the other system. Since there has been no actual retardation of clocks nor delay of senescence, the twins "will both, other circumstances remaining the same, have lived the same number of days, eaten the same number of breakfasts, had the same number of heartbeats, and so on. They will, in short, find reason to conclude that there is, in Bergson's words, 'an indefinite multiplicity of fictitious times' but 'only one real Time.' And the physicists are quite right in feeling that [contrary to Bergson's sentiment] this does *not* leave the theory of relativity 'intact' " (22).

REALISM AS DUALISM

Lovejoy's acknowledged position in the history of recent American philosophy is due not so much to his temporalism as to his critical realism. Having criticized the neorealists for their epistemological monism (23) even before they had aired their views in the co-operative volume, *The New Realism* (1912), Lovejoy arrived at the dualistic epistemology of critical realism long before the critical realist movement had formed. His early paper, "Realism Versus Epistemological Monism" (24), sought to save realism by separating it from the epistemological monism which was based on the new realist conception of consciousness as an external relation, and expressed ideas which were to be influential in the formation of the movement of critical realism. In 1920 Lovejoy was one of a septet of prominent American philosophers, including Durant Drake, James Bissell Pratt, Arthur K. Rogers, George Santayana, Roy Wood Sellars, and C. A. Strong, who published the cooperative volume, *Essays in Critical Realism*.

From Temporalism to Critical Realism.

"My approach to realism was through a criticism of the idealistic philosophies prevalent when my reflection on these matters began" Lovejoy has written (11, pp. 98-99). The regnant idealism, as previously noted, was challenged by temporalism, for the temporalistic method insisted upon temporal distinctions which by no dialectical argument could plausibly be transubstantiated into or embraced within the eternal. The upshot was what Lovejoy called "lengthwise pluralism"—the externality of the past, present, and future moments of time.

This same temporalism is the logical motive of Lovejoy's realism. He rejected new realism because its epistemological monism, which equated the idea (the object in consciousness) with the object external to consciousness, could not account for errors and illusions nor—and here his argument was unique—for cognitions of past objects and events. As a temporalist, he held retrospection, or remembrance, to be "the primary mode of knowing," and he considered retrospection to be intrinsically dualistic, since "to remember *is* to be aware of a contrast between the image presented and the event recalled" (2, p. 381).

Hence Lovejoy's realism is a critical realism and as

such is dualistic. It is an intermediate position between idealism, which upheld the reality of ideas at the cost of the reality of external objects, and new realism, which equated ideas with external objects or aspects thereof. For critical realism offered "a conception of knowledge as indirect and substitutional; it involved, in short, a theory of representative ideas" (11, p. 99). Representative ideas are indispensable in cognition of past objects or events, since past objects or events do not now exist and must be known through substitutes. By generalization Lovejoy inferred that all knowledge is representative. It consists in the making present, that is, the presentation, of objects that are absent. This is tantamount to representation, not in the sense of presentation again, but in the sense of effective substitution (10, p. 253). The paradox of knowledge—of making present what is absent—is resolved by means of thoughts or ideas. "A given moment of thought may consist in a representation of a whole world of objects in relations of many kinds—temporal, spatial, logical—in which it is itself, *as represented,* a mere fragment. Thus it is that a given thought, e.g., a memory, can, and does, cognitively or representatively transcend itself, without any existential self-transcendence" (10, p. 281).

Dualism

In *The Revolt Against Dualism* Lovejoy examined critically the main strands of the revolt in the first quarter of the twentieth century: new realism, objective relativism, Whiteheadian epistemology, and Russell's various endeavors to unify mind and matter. The treatment accorded these various theories is detailed and technical, establishing through minute analysis their untenability. A tedious review of Lovejoy's critiques is unnecessary here. Suffice it to observe that his procedure illustrates superbly his conception of proper philosophical method. "The true procedure of philosophy as a science

—as distinct from the philosophic idiosyncrasies of individuals—is thus that of a Platonic dialogue on a grand scale, in which the theses, proposed proofs, objections, rejoinders, of numerous interlocutors are focused upon a given question, and the argument gradually shapes itself, through its own immanent dialectic, to a conclusion" (2, pp. ix-x).

Although on ultimate issues philosophy may not come to a single conclusion, but rather allows each philosopher his own option, "in accordance with the particular mental constitution with which Nature has endowed [him]" (2, p. 320), nevertheless philosophy does demand the exercise of logical circumspection, which requires that every philosophical belief asserted be examined in relation to its implications and its relations with other asserted or implicit philosophical beliefs. When subjected to the rigors of logical circumspection, the different positions in the revolt against dualism collapse. As Lovejoy said: "The logical elements which so many philosophers, since our century began, have been trying to synthesize into a coherent body of doctrine, refuse to combine. Where they are not directly at variance with one another, they are at variance with empirical facts, or with inferences from empirical facts which realistic philosophers who believe that natural science gives us some probable information about an external world, cannot consistently deny. Neither knowledge nor nature seems to be quite so simple, unitary, and transparent a thing, nor the phenomenon of knowing so much all-of-a-piece with the rest of nature, as it would, in many respects, be agreeable and convenient to believe" (2, p. 324). Thus the entire movement in revolt against dualism is interpreted as an experiment in thought which reached a negative result.

The effectiveness of Lovejoy's argument may be measured by the reaction it produced. A. E. Murphy, who had coined the phrase "objective relativism," charged

Lovejoy with the dogmatic dualism of common sense, but went on to argue that there are seventeen dualisms mingled in Lovejoy's thought (25). Lovejoy immediately replied, with a distinction between good and bad dualism, and with the judgment that objective relativism is an instance of bad dualism. In regard to Murphy's discrimination of seventeen dualisms, Lovejoy retorted, "I can only hope that he has underestimated the number" (26). A. N. Whitehead's response to Lovejoy's critique of his thought was more positive. In *Adventures of Ideas* Whitehead paused to register his "high appreciation [of] Professor Lovejoy's brilliant book in criticism of this revolt" and to add that, in one sense, his own position is dualistic. "The universe," said Whitehead, "is dual because each final actuality is both physical and mental" (27).

Lovejoy distinguished two main types of dualism: epistemological and psychophysical. Epistemological dualism consists primarily in the theory of representative perception, whereas psychophysical dualism "conceives empirical reality to fall asunder into a world of mind and a world of matter exclusive and utterly antithetic" (2, p. 3). It is possible, Lovejoy noted, to be an epistemological dualist without being a psychophysical dualist, although it is natural for the two dualisms to be joined in a comprehensive philosophy.

Epistemological Dualism. According to Lovejoy, "the natural and spontaneous epistemological creed of mankind" is realistic (2, p. 18). It supposes that there are things-to-be-known (*cognoscenda*) which lie beyond the bounds of the knower but which the knower reaches through knowledge. Concerning these *cognoscenda* there are five common assumptions: (1) that they exist in places external to the body of the knower; (2) that they include things that are not, i.e., bygone things or things yet to be; (3) that they are entities "as they *would be if unknown*, existences not relative to the cognitive situation—in short, . . . things as they literally are in themselves"; (4) that they include the experiences of others of the knower's kind; and (5) that they are "potentially, if not actually knowable by these other knowers; they must be things capable of verification in experiences other than the one experience in which, at a given moment, they are in some sense before him" (2, pp. 16-18).

The natural realism of mankind is intrinsically dualistic. The data in the consciousness of the knower prove, upon reflection, to be existentially distinct from the objects to be known. This fact is brought home not only by the existence of errors and illusions, but also by the nature of intertemporal cognition. Such cognition, whether as remembrance or forecast, refers to entities and events which are not in existence now, and so are known mediately only through substitutes. Since, furthermore, there are temporal intervals between the existence of the occurrence of events and the perceptions thereof, since perspective distortions are universal, and since changes in the medium of perception or in the body of the percipient organism condition our percepts, it follows that the data which make possible the consciousness of objects differ existentially from these objects.

Psychophysical Dualism. Although epistemological dualism and psychophysical dualism are logically distinct, they have been fused historically. Psychophysical dualism grows naturally out of epistemological dualism when data are assigned to mind and *cognoscenda* to the physical world. But independently of this connection with epistemological dualism, psychophysical dualism arises out of a universal fact of human experience—"the actual disparateness of the properties and behavior of two great classes of objects" (2, p. 38).

There is, on the one hand, the world of physical objects, exhibiting an order qualified by five essential characteristics: (1) spatiality, manifest in the extensionality of objects; (2) continuity of existence during interperceptual intervals; (3) the operation of constant rates of change and causation; (4) the continuous operation of causation during interperceptual intervals; and (5) the presence of this order as "a common factor in or behind the experience of all percipients" (2, p. 34). In this description of the physical world Lovejoy's temporalism is evident, for this world is "conceived as filling for thought the temporal gaps between actual perceptions, as keeping the business of nature going while you or all men are heedless or asleep" (2, p. 34). As he contended, the very attribution of "independence" to physical things has "to do primarily with the *time* of their existence" (2, p. 332). He continued: "It is not the 'outerness' of the object perceived, *when* it is perceived, but the *persistence of something which is in some manner connected with what is perceived, during the interperceptual intervals*, that is the primary natural postulate out of which the belief in an external world, in objects which exist though they are not given in experience, arises" (2, p. 333).

There are, on the other hand, entities which do not conform to the rules of membership in the physical order. Such entities, failing perhaps to conform to anticipated causal relations, are "wild data," disrupting the tidiness and good order of the physical world, unless they can be assigned elsewhere. As Lovejoy observed: "The world of 'mental' entities served as an isolation-camp for all the 'wild data,' the refractory and anomalous facts" (2, p. 36). In this fundamental way, psychophysical dualism "has in fact served throughout history as the safeguard of developing physical science, as the means whereby men have been enabled increasingly to conceive that 'the public world' is one of 'orderly happenings'" (2, p. 38).

Belief in a physical world, an order of objects causally, spatially, and temporally related, has as its complement belief in a world of mental entities, including wild data, sensa, and ideas. Such a physical world, moreover, can be known only mediately through ideas and sensa. Hence Lovejoy concluded that realism in philosophy must be dualistic, both epistemologically and psychophysically.

HISTORY OF IDEAS

Lovejoy's general method of the history of ideas is the logical complement of his temporalistic realism. This is not to say that Lovejoy's work as an intellectual historian is an application or an entailment of his temporalistic realism. Nor does it mean that his temporalistic realism is an implication of his work in the history of ideas. On the contrary, Lovejoy's contributions to the history of ideas are coeval with his formation of the philosophy of temporalistic realism, and the developments of his thought in both fields were parallel. The logical complementarity of Lovejoy's temporalistic realism and his conception of intellectual history signifies first, that his temporalistic realism would provide the philosophical rationale of his conception of intellectual history if a philosophical rationale were sought, and second, that his conception of intellectual history is conformable to his temporalistic realism.

Since Lovejoy's temporalistic realism has already been explored, it is necessary here to examine his conception of the history of ideas. At the outset, it should be clear that, as Lovejoy confessed in the Preface to *Essays in the History of Ideas*, the general conception of the history of ideas "grew out of rather than preceded most of the inquiries into special topics." These inquiries "are not examples of a deliberate effort to impose a predetermined 'method' upon refractory material," but upon reflection, it is found that they "express some underlying common assumptions and procedures" (4, p. xi). These "common assumptions and procedures," making up Lovejoy's theory of intellectual history, are dispersed throughout his works, but they receive focal formulation in two places: the opening chapter of *The Great Chain of Being* and his article, "The Historiography of Ideas," first published in *American Philosophical Society Proceedings* (1938), and reprinted in *Essays in the History of Ideas*.

What, then, is Lovejoy's conception of intellectual history?

In the first place, the history of ideas is distinguished by the basic units with which it deals. Lovejoy was especially discontented with the manner in which the history of philosophy is usually set forth. Too often the historian of philosophy is concerned with the recital of major systems and movements, and as a consequence he overlooks the logically dynamic elements of which systems and movements are at best, organizations and at worst, confusions. As Lovejoy sharply commented: "The history of philosophy and of all phases of man's reflection *is*, in great part, a history of confusions of ideas" (3, p. 22).

The historian of ideas, therefore, probes behind the major systems and movements to discover the primary, persistent, and recurrent dynamic units of thought. These units of thought comprise a heterogeneous class with several principal types. There are, first, "implicit or incompletely explicit *assumptions*, or more or less unconscious mental *habits*, operating in the thought of an individual or a generation" (3, p. 7). Second, these endemic assumptions become "dialectical motives" when, vague and general as they are, they "influence the course of man's reflections on almost any subject" (3, p. 10). Third are "susceptibilities to diverse kinds of metaphysical pathos" (3, p. 11). By "metaphysical pathos" Lovejoy meant "any description of the nature of things, and characterization of the world to which one belongs, in terms which, like the words of a poem, awaken through their associations, and through a sort of empathy which they engender, a congenial mood or tone of feeling on the part of the philosopher or his readers" (3, p. 11). Closely related to "metaphysical pathos" are, fourth, the sacred words or phrases of a period or a movement, which, though ambiguous, mold fashions of thinking. Finally, there are the "ideas" proper. More definite and explicit than the other basic units, and consequently easier to isolate and clarify, an idea "consists in a single specific proposition or 'principle' . . . , together with some further propositions which are, or have been supposed to be, its corollaries" (3, p. 14). Needless to mention, Lovejoy's most successful and ambitious undertaking in the history of ideas, *The Great Chain of Being*, concentrated on the idea proper.

In the second place, the history of ideas traces the unit-ideas "through more than one—ultimately, indeed, through all—of the provinces of history in which it figures in any important degree, whether those provinces are called philosophy, science, literature, art, religion, or politics" (3, p. 15). At present, according to Lovejoy, the "historiography of ideas" is pursued under at least twelve different labels: (1) history of philosophy, (2) history of science, (3) folklore and ethnography, (4) parts of the history of language, especially semantics, (5) history of religions and theology, (6) history of literatures, (7) comparative literature, (8) history of art, (9) history of economic development and theory, (10) history of education, (11) political and social history, and (12) historical sociology (4, pp. 1-2). The dispersion of studies on the same topic over these separate fields obstructs a synoptic and penetrating comprehension of this topic. By traversing the conventional boundaries of these twelve disciplines, the history of ideas has a greater opportunity to discover the entire background and the full import of its subject.

Appropriately the history of ideas is, in the third place, much like comparative literature, since it engages in studies which cut across the conventional divisions of literary and other historical studies by nationalities or languages.

In the fourth place, the history of ideas is "especially concerned with the manifestations of specific unit-ideas in the collective thought of large groups of persons, not merely in the doctrines or opinions of a small number of profound thinkers or eminent writers" (3, p. 19). Too often the history of thought salutes the same thinkers, neglecting to observe that the originality imputed to them is not their due. Moreover, the complex ramifications of an idea are worked out in a great number of works by various thinkers, many of whom are deservedly obscure. However, the investigator who wants to understand the idea and its implications should exhume these writings of neglected men and extract from them the pertinent materials. The intellectual historian is led to perceive the history of thought as a co-operative and cumulative enterprise, drawing upon the offerings of countless, generally forgotten men.

In the fifth place, "it is a part of the eventual task of the history of ideas to apply its own distinctive analytic method in the attempt to understand how *new* beliefs and intellectual fashions are introduced and diffused, to help to elucidate the psychological character of the processes by which changes in the vogue and influence of ideas have come about; to make clear, if possible, how conceptions dominant, or extensively prevalent, in one generation lose their hold upon men's minds and give place to others" (3, p. 20). Lovejoy's two major works, *The Revolt Against Dualism* and *The Great Chain of Being*, critically examine major intellectual movements, contemporary and classical, as experiments in thought with instructive but negative results. As Lovejoy stated: "An idea, in short, is after all not only a potent but a stubborn thing; it commonly has its own 'particular go'; and the history of thought is a bilateral affair—the story of the traffic and interaction between human nature, amid the exigencies and vicissitudes of physical experience, on the one hand, and on the other, the specific natures and pressures of the ideas which men have, from very various promptings, admitted to their minds" (28).

In the sixth place, the history of ideas must be a co-operative enterprise if it is to succeed. "Trustworthy historical synthesis is not a one-man job. If the pieces that are to be put together—even for the understanding of one part of one subject—are to be sound pieces, they must be provided, or at least be critically inspected, by those having special training and up-to-date technical knowledge in the fields to which the pieces primarily belong" (4, p. 10). Just as the thought of the past is the product of many minds, it can be recovered only through the co-operative efforts of many other minds.

What the history of ideas seeks to accomplish is nothing less than the recovery of past thought. It assumes what temporalistic realism maintains—that there was a real past external to the present moment. Accordingly, Lovejoy emphatically repudiated the view that the historian's selection of materials from the past is tantamount to a recreation of that past from the standpoint of the present and in response to problems that exist only in the present (16, pp. 477-489). Although Lovejoy conceded that the historian of ideas investigates only what interests him, his interest is attuned, insofar as he is historian, to the desire to recover all that men have thought on the topic under investigation, whether or not what has been thought is pertinent to current issues. On the other hand, Lovejoy admitted, a philosopher may center his investigations on ideas only when they are "considerations" which support lines of thought pertinent to contemporary philosophical problems. Whereas *The Revolt Against Dualism* exemplifies the treatment accorded the thoughts of others from the standpoint of the philosopher, *The Great Chain of Being* illustrates an inquiry conducted according to standards of historical investigation.

Historical knowledge, to which Lovejoy devoted so much of his thought, relates the knower, enclosed in the present, to vast regions of reality which lie beyond, behind in the past.

At the conclusion of his Carus lectures Lovejoy retold the story of Plato's *Timaeus*. Of course he changed the story to fit his evolutionary conception of life as proceeding from lower to higher forms of organisms and also to enforce his realist epistemology of representative knowledge. His version of the myth, therefore, accentuates the imperfection of the universe of living creatures, bound by Space as the home of all created beings and by Time as a passage of externally related moments. Each creature is restricted in his own region of space, separated from the others; and each is locked up in his own moments of time, moments successively lost in the Past. The externality of things to one another and their transiency betray a radical imperfection in the world. But, he interjected, "a world in which all that comes into being not only perishes but leaves no rumor of itself behind, and in which every part of the Whole is blind to all the other parts, is surely more imperfect than even a world of mortal creatures need be" (2, p. 400).

Knowledge, Lovejoy noted, is the remedy for this imperfection. For knowledge enables a creature, imprisoned in a particular region of Space and moment of Time, to transcend these limits and to be related through representative ideas with other regions of Space and Time. More than this, knowledge enables the knowing animal, man, "to frame some general image of the Whole—not, indeed, of all things which are parts of the Whole, for that is not a gift possible to mortals—but of the nature of a Whole having many parts, of which the animal itself, with the time and place in which it exists and perceives any qualities, is seen by it as but one part and that a small one, having fixed bounds, beyond which lie the other parts. By means of such an image this animal will be able to ascribe qualities which it at any time beholds to regions of the Whole lying outside the bounds within which, when beheld, they exist; it will have the power of imputing otherness and beyondness to what it perceives, and thus need not be blind to the rest of the universe" (2, p. 401).

NOTES TO CHAPTER 8

1. A. O. Lovejoy, "On Some Conditions for Progress in Philosophical Inquiry," *Philosophical Review*, XXVI (1917), 148.
2. A. O. Lovejoy, *The Revolt Against Dualism: An Inquiry Concerning the Existence of Ideas* (La Salle, Ill.: Open Court Publishing Company, 1930; 2d ed., papercover, 1960). All citations are to the second edition.
3. A. O. Lovejoy, *The Great Chain of Being: A Study of the History of an Idea* (Cambridge: Harvard University Press, 1936; New York: Harper Torchbook, 1960). All citations are to the Harper Torchbook edition.
4. A. O. Lovejoy, *Essays in the History of Ideas* (Baltimore: Johns Hopkins Press, 1948; New York: George Braziller, Inc., 1955). All citations are to the 1955 publication.
5. "Arthur O. Lovejoy at Seventy-Five," with articles by George Boas, Maurice Mandelbaum, William Pepperell Montague, Marjorie Nicolson, and Theodore Spencer, *Journal of the History of Ideas*, IX (1948), 403-446. A symposium in memory of A. O. Lovejoy, with articles by John Herman Randall Jr., Philip P. Wiener, Lewis S. Feuer, V. J. McGill, and Charles A. Baylis, appeared in *Philosophy and Phenomenological Research*, XXIII (1963), 475-537.
6. A. O. Lovejoy and G. Boas, *Primitivism and Related Ideas in Antiquity: A Documentary History of Primitivism and Related Ideas*, Vol. I (Baltimore: The Johns Hopkins University Press, 1935).
7. A. O. Lovejoy, *The Reason, The Understanding and Time* (Baltimore: The Johns Hopkins Press, 1961).
8. A. O. Lovejoy, *Reflections on Human Nature* (Baltimore: The Johns Hopkins Press, 1961).
9. W. H. Werkmeister, *A History of Philosophical Ideas in America* (New York: The Ronald Press Company, 1949).
10. A. O. Lovejoy, *The Thirteen Pragmatisms and Other Essays* (Baltimore: The Johns Hopkins Press, 1963).

11. A. O. Lovejoy, "A Temporalistic Realism," *Contemporary American Philosophy*, G. P. Adams and W. P. Montague, eds. (New York: The Macmillan Company, 1930; reprinted by Russell & Russell Inc., 1962), II, pp. 85-104.

12. A. O. Lovejoy, "The Problem of Time in Recent French Philosophy," *Philosophical Review*, XXI (1912), 11-31, 322-343, 527-45.

13. A. O. Lovejoy, "The Obsolescence of the Eternal," *Philosophical Review*, XVIII (1909).

14. A. O. Lovejoy, "Reflections of a Temporalist on the New Realism," *Journal of Philosophy, Psychology and Scientific Methods*, VIII (1911), 599, n. 2.

15. A. O. Lovejoy, "The Meanings of 'Emergence' and its Modes," *Proceedings of the Sixth International Congress of Philosophy* (New York: Longmans, Green & Co., 1927), p. 22.

16. A. O. Lovejoy, "Present Standpoints and Past History," *Journal of Philosophy*, XXXVI (1939), 481.

17. See John Dewey, "Realism without Monism or Dualism," *Journal of Philosophy*, XIX (1922), 309-317, 351-361.

18. A. O. Lovejoy, "Time, Meaning and Transcendence," *Journal of Philosophy*, XIX (1922), 505.

19. A. O. Lovejoy, "Pastness and Transcendence," *Journal of Philosophy*, XXI (1924), 601-611.

20. A. O. Lovejoy, "The Dialectical Argument Against Absolute Simultaneity," *Journal of Philosophy*, XXVII (1930), 617-32; 645-654.

21. See Henri Bergson, *Durée et Simultanéité*, 3d ed. (Paris: F. Alcan, 1926).

22. A. O. Lovejoy, "The Paradox of the Time-Retarding Journey," *Philosophical Review*, XL (1931), 167.

23. A. O. Lovejoy, "Reflections of a Temporalist on the New Realism," *Journal of Philosophy*, VIII (1911), 589-600.

24. A. O. Lovejoy, "Realism Versus Epistemological Monism," *Journal of Philosophy*, X (1913), 561-572.

25. A. E. Murphy, "Mr. Lovejoy's Counter-Revolution," *Journal of Philosophy*, XXVIII (1931), 29-42, 57-71.

26. A. O. Lovejoy, "Dualisms Good and Bad," *Journal of Philosophy*, XXIX (1932), 380.

27. A. N. Whitehead, *Adventures of Ideas* (New York: The Macmillan Co., 1933), pp. 244-245.

28. A. O. Lovejoy, "Reflections on the History of Ideas," *Journal of the History of Ideas*, I (1940), 23.

Chapter 9

THE CORPORATISM
OF ELIJAH JORDAN

SOCIAL CONTEXT OF PHILOSOPHY

Of Elijah Jordan (1875-1953), Max Fisch has said: "He was one of the few non-Marxist philosophers who took seriously the rise of Standard Oil, General Motors, the C.I.O. and the T.V.A. Philosophy, he thought, was not ready to take them in; it had to extend itself, and it was hard put" (1, p. xiv). One of the most original social and legal philosophers in the history of American thought, Jordan spent his life in the Midwest, near the rural setting from which he came. He received his Ph.D. from the University of Chicago in 1911. After a couple of years as instructor of philosophy at Cornell University, he accepted a professorship at Butler College in Indianapolis, where he served from his appointment in 1913 until his retirement 31 years later. Jordan wrote a half dozen volumes that are a unique contribution to American philosophy, the full significance of which has still to be measured: *The Life of Mind* (2), *Forms of Individuality* (3), *Theory of Legislation* (4), *The Aesthetic Object* (5), *The Good Life* (6), *Essays in Criticism* (7), and on the eve of his death he was at work on his *Meta-physics* (1). Generally neglected in his lifetime, Jordan's work has in recent years begun to win increasing consideration from philosophers and social thinkers (8). It may well be that in the next few decades Jordan will be acclaimed America's leading social philosopher. It is the purpose of this chapter to explore his philosophy insofar as it bears upon the topic of law and social order.

The neglect of Jordan's philosophy has been imputed in part to the difficulties of his style, which was always obscure and sometimes vituperative. The obscurity stems not only from the complexity of thought, but also from his aesthetic conception of how communication should constitute its objects; the vituperation was the result of his moral passion. Further, neglect of Jordan must also be ascribed to the discordance between his philosophical outlook and the modes of philosophy and social thought that prevailed in America during the first half of the twentieth century. Although Max Fisch has suggested that Jordan's philosophy was intimately related to and colored by its rural Midwestern setting (1, p. xiv), Jordan's intellectual adventure was pursued in almost total isolation, unaffiliated with the prevailing currents of opinion. Perhaps no American thinker can match Jordan in the penetrating dissection and bitter condemnation of contradictions which inhere in democracy. Yet Jordan remained unquestionably hostile to the totalitarianisms of Fascism and Marxist Communism which swept over much of the world during his lifetime. And though Jordan explicitly rejected the socialist creed, his attitude toward a civilization built upon private business is summed up in the title of one of his books: *Business Be Damned* (9).

Jordan also repudiated the behavioral sciences for the kind of thinking about man and society they fostered. Their positivist methodology, restricted to gathering and classifying facts, the investigation of origins, causal explanations, analysis into simples, cannot, Jordan believed, adequately or profoundly illuminate the nature of social relations and the constitution of public order. Only metaphysical speculation, in touch with the concrete complexity of facts but sensitive to objective tendencies within the systems of fact and capable of conceiving the ideals in which these tendencies end, can serve to advance an accurate general theory of nature, man, institutions and culture. Therefore, Jordan undertook a critique of modern civilization in its ostensible forms as well as in its implicit metaphysical postulates and offered positive speculative metaphysical suggestions to provide more stable foundations for culture and to expedite its improvement and development. Jordan's enterprise was spurred by his remarkable sensitivity to the dilemma which must inevitably strike any man who thinks on the present practical situation: "Either . . . there must be something wrong with the conceptions . . . upon which civilization appears to have rested, or the principles and agencies which dominate the practical life are metaphysically evil. Either those influences that lead to universal war and strife are wrong and false or else war and strife and hatred are right" (4, p. 170).

Modern civilization, Jordan maintained, is based upon the subjectivist metaphysics of individualism, with the doctrine of interest as its practical corollary. Defining mind as individualized consciousness and reducing individuality to the isolated, atomistic individual, this subjectivist philosophy arose when Christianity superseded the Greek conception of personality. The Greeks had appreciated the unity of human mind, nature, and culture, and had understood the human person to be "the obligatory tie which bound him to his objective self in the 'nature' which embodied his purposes in final harmony" (3, p. 93). But with the collapse of classical civilization ensued the religious concentration on individual spiritual salvation, and individuality came "to mean a mass of inner, private, exclusive feelings centered around their own intensity" (3, p. 95). Unlike Christian medieval thought which, despite its retreat into subjectivity, still bears the mark of Greek objectivism since it links interest with the prerogative of a special class as materialized in the objective relation between property and class action, modern individualism has come to look upon interest as private and exclusive, stripped of all spiritual significance. The Christian identification of individuality with "a self-inclosed, self-sufficing, qualitatively homogeneous, isolated unity" (3, p. 101) has consequently degenerated into what Jordan has called "the subjectivism of the organism," namely, the contemporary secular equation of the individual with "the psychobiological human being with his matter-of-fact and common-place interests in making a living and raising a family and winning a place of respectability in the local group where his lot happened to be cast" (3, p. 106). Hence the Greek "world of overt objects" has given way to the modern "world of invert objects, or subjects" (3, p. 3).

In human relations the subjectivity of modern individualism has entailed the doctrine of interest, apparent in the several branches of practical philosophy in different guises. In legal and political philosophy interest means "exclusiveness, privacy and the divisive concept of the power to compel" (3, p. 6). In economics it denotes "the hypothetical causal unit of production or consumption of goods and . . . the theoretical locus of the subjective phenomena of want, need, desire" (3, pp. 6-7). In ethics, it operates as "the subjective principle which distinguishes and disperses humanity and the realm of values, as the ground of right and good, into isolated persons and their distinctive appurtenances of specific goods or properties" (3, p. 7). In brief, interest is "the expression of the subjective attitude in which the realities of life are estimated with respect to inner aspects of personality" (3, p. 14). Even right "is justified, explained, and blessed, in the mere fact that an individual *claims* it, finds it with an accidental status within his mental processes" (3, p. 17).

For Jordan the extreme subjectivism of modern civilization, expressed in the doctrine of interest, contaminates all moral and practical concepts and relations, undermining the principles upon which a sound and just social order must rest: "(*I*)*nterest is incompetent as principle.* The doctrine that the state is a harmony of interests, that law is the instrument of effecting and maintaining the harmony, that the purpose of morality is to find and define the characters of interest that make a harmony possible, that religion should look upon conflicting interest and call it good; all this neglects the simple fact that *no organization of subjective phenomena is possible,* that subjective facts do not submit to order, that the order of mind is not the superficial juxtaposition of mental states" (3, p. 20).

The reduction of practical values and relations to private psychological facts has fostered a variety of serious misconceptions and malpractices. It has wrongly equated man with the abstract "economic man" of classical economics, aiding and abetting a business civilization so amoral, massive, and monstrous that it pollutes all cultural values, tramples down all personal concerns, and victimizes all men—including businessmen. It has worked as "the peculiar nemesis of ethics," since isolated individuals can be bound by no obligations which would integrate them into a community of men. It has adversely affected legal theory and practice, wrongly construing contractual relations in which individual interests are primary as the substance of legal order, viewing property as the exclusive possession of individuals despite its public function, and justifying the law by the sheer, amoral power that enforces it.

The upshot is cyclical collapses of the economic world, blatant political corruption, flagrant prostitution of public institutions to private interests, and periodic wars between states. All these evil features of modern civilization testify to the incompetence of interest as principle of order, and the aesthetic category most applicable to modern civilization is the grotesque (5, p. 266). As Jordan remarked: "Modern civilization, in fact, built its house upon interest; for a time it prospered, as long, that is, as interest met with appropriate opportunity in the exploitation of nature. But the winds blow and the rains fall" (3, pp. 19-20). And in a later work he said: "Nothing will work in the world but the right and the true, and this bears no relation to interest" (4, p. 384).

Since interest proved to be the principle of chaos rather than order, Jordan deemed it necessary to seek a different principle of order. But since the doctrine of interest stems from an extreme subjectivism, he sought nothing less than the elimination of subjectivism and the establishment of a new objectivity which embraces both "overt objects" and "invert objects, or subjects." "The modern *practical* problem is therefore how, and upon what principles, can the two modes of objectivity get integrated into a higher unity—that is, how can we find an effectual unity of the natural and the mental in the new objectivity?" (3, p. 27). Jordan's philosophy aims to overcome the modern bifurcation of nature and culture into a spatiotemporal, causally determined world of atomistic, simply located objects, on the one hand, and a shattered society of dispersed, monadic, particular subjects whose psychological states comprise the only values in the world, on the other. At the level of the formal categories of metaphysics Jordan was intent on establishing "the unity of value and existence." This intention took the form of "deducing" two forms of categories, one for value and another for existence (5,

Chaps. IV and V) and of correlating them through what he has called "the principle of analogical identity" (1, pp. xi-xiii).

The solution of the modern practical problem, as Jordan expressed it in his book, *The Forms of Individuality*, consists in "the discovery of the corporate character of cultural objects, the theory of corporation being the logical formulation of the new objectivity" (3, p. 3). Moreover, inasmuch as "(t)he essence of individuality is corporeity" (3, p. 187), the solution to the modern practical problem includes a conception of individuality different from individualism, a conception which Glenn Negley has aptly called "corporatism" (10). Hence the logical formulation of the new objectivity involves a speculative metaphysics of mind and individuality and a novel practical philosophy of corporate institutions.

PHILOSOPHY OF MIND

Jordan's quest for the principle of social order centers on the philosophy of mind because, just as the subjectivist type of mind underlies the contemporary social disorder, so other distinguishable types of mind are associated with different social conditions. An understanding of social order therefore requires an understanding of mind. Further, Jordan's thinking had been profoundly influenced by Kant (11) and Kant's famous contribution to philosophy, it should be recalled, was his Copernican revolution. The universal forms of reality as experienced, the necessary laws of nature, Kant taught, spring not from reality and nature, but rather from the human mind. World order resides in the structure of mind. For Jordan, following Kant, social order is interlocked with types of mind.

Jordan gave Kant's doctrine one startling twist and in this respect he was closer to classical Greek philosophy and the post-Kantian idealists. Whereas for Kant nature

and its laws are the product of mind, all objectivity being
the result of subjectivity, for Jordan mind is objective:
Mind incorporates fact. "The 'Copernican revolution,' "
he wrote, "insists then, as the condition of a valid practical philosophy, upon turning away from subjective
naturalistic-religious individualism and sociological op-
portunism and pragmatism, into which practical thought
has fallen, and in approaching all problems from the
viewpoint of corporate mind as the ultimate practical
postulate" (4, p. xvii).

At the outset, of course, it should be clear that, although Jordan taught psychology as well as philosophy
at Butler College, his theory of mind is emphatically
metaphysical, having little to do with empirical experimental psychology. *The Life of Mind*, published hastily
as a textbook in psychology and just as hastily withdrawn
from distribution, vehemently attacks empirical psychology for interpreting human nature as "a function of
physical nature," charging that, since it does not deal
with mind, it is *"not psychology at all"* (2, p. 7). Indeed
Jordan dismissed empirical psychology as "physiosophy,"
meaning thereby a science which, though correctly treating "human nature" as "a mediating nexus between nature on the one hand and culture on the other," erro-
neously tries to reduce all judgments about "human
nature" to judgments about "raw nature" (2, p. 8). He
reserved the term "psychology" for the philosophy of
mind, defining mind "as the medium and substance of
human culture" (2, p. iv).

Jordan distinguished three major types of mind: individualized mind, socialized mind, and institutionalized
mind. While at present modern civilization, in view of
the extent to which individualism and interest prevail,
is dominated by mind as individualized, factors in social
science indicate the socialization of mind, and other factors, e.g., in legal prodecures and institutional life, signify the presence of mind as institutionalized. Of the

three types of mind, Jordan held, mind as institutionalized is mind in the fullest sense, and its highest form
is corporate mind—institutionalized mind moralized.

Mind: Individualized and Socialized

Mind as individualized is mind dispersed to absolute
and multiple particularity. Divided against itself in a
pluralism of particular minds, each bent on the satisfaction of its own private, exclusive interest, mind as individualized is self-contradictory and inevitably fails to
be an adequate principle of order. Mind can serve as
principle of order only if it can become objective, be
embodied or congealed in objects, i.e., be incorporated
—but this excludes its being individualized.

For Jordan, socialized mind serves no better than individualized mind. It is the "artificial if useful methodological abstraction" of social science, yet "is a mind in
no practically real sense of the term at all" (3, p. 88). As
the type of mind with which social science deals, mind
as socialized is impugned by the fallacious methods employed by these sciences. Modelled after the natural
sciences, the social sciences, Jordan contended, gather
facts without grasping their meaning, i.e., their reference
to ends. Aping the atomism of natural science, social
science postulates simple individual men, analyzable into
further simple individual units of instinct and habit, related only by means of mechanical causation. Mind as
socialized therefore is not real mind; it is mind conditioned by the antecedent causes of custom and precedent
rather than directed toward the realization of ends. Or
it is mind manipulated and abused by advertising, propaganda, and the mechanical routines of industry. Socialized
mind is regimented mind, mind deprived of its creativity
and standardized for the performance of routine movements. It is mind, locked perhaps in the interstices of
institutions, but not yet institutionalized, since it is ig-

norant of or even alienated from, instead of being realized in, the ends incorporated in the institutions.

Mind and Objectivity

If follows therefore that neither mind as individualized nor mind as socialized is mind in the fullest sense, since neither satisfies the conditions of the objectivity of mind. Now the term "objectivity," with its cognates "object" and "objective," covers in Jordan's writings three distinct, yet intertwined ideas: (1) an external material *object*, (2) a Kantian categorial activity which universally and necessarily orders facts, and (3) an independent ideal or end which functions in Platonic fashion as the *objective* of willed action. Mind is intimately linked with objectivity in these three senses; indeed, one might well say that for Jordan mind is precisely the objective linkage of the three types of objectivity—of using objects to attain objectives, of transforming objectives into objects, of constituting wholes of objects and objectives through universal laws.

Jordan enunciated the three basic principles of his philosophy of mind in *The Life of Mind* (12): "(1) Mind always acts through its body, and is known only in and through its action. (2) (M)ind always acts as a whole or as a unity, and is known only as such, . . . [so that mind] . . . can be defined as the active unity which manifests itself in and comprehends the organization of objects in our world. (3) (M)ind . . . completes itself in the objects of our external or practical world, and is controlled only through the manipulation of the things of the practical world" (2, pp. 4-5).

Jordan's theory of mind includes an elaborate reinterpretation of the traditional faculties of knowing, willing and feeling in terms of their objectivity or objectification, especially since Jordan's insistence on the unity of mind rules out the compartmentalization of internal

faculties. These faculties are equated with distinguishable but interlaced facets of systems of objective fact.
In *The Life of Mind*, knowing, regarded as subjective
mind, consists in *"forms of attention,* the various ways
by which our minds take hold of objects which make up
our environment and condition our lives" (2, p. 18).

In *The Aesthetic Object*, Jordan's most poetic work,
feeling is held to be more basic than cognition: "The
cognitive state comes out like a star from the illimitable
solid substantiality of the firmamental blue of feeling"
(5, p. 47). Nonetheless, feeling is not the subjective content of isolated consciousnesses. Rather, feeling is the
primordium, the affective continuum, from which all
distinctive sensations and isolated emotions are inferred.
Feeling therefore is a metaphysical principle, "the *Ur-
stoff* of all value . . . the substantial stuff from which
the world of values is created" (5, p. 55). "Feeling is the
material basis of values and culture, as existence is the
material basis of nature" (5, p. 56). Further, in *The
Aesthetic Object* and later in his *Metaphysics* Jordan
sought to establish for feeling a set of objective categories
on the analogy of the Kantian deduction of universal
categories for understanding. As Kant proved that Space
and Time are *a priori* forms for sensible intuition and
scientific understanding, so Jordan attempted to deduce
Color and Tone as *a priori* forms for feeling.

Will, too, is objective. Despite the commonplace supposition that human individuals have wills in the ordinary sense, actually their wills are so hemmed in by external circumstance that they prove to be feeble forces,
their effectiveness restricted to self-preservation and reproduction. In a deeper sense, however, there exists "a
general will which expresses itself through natural persons in the unity of the state considered as the instrument and as the harmony of natural wills" (3, p. 240),
so that the freedom of the individual human wills "is
the positive and constructive urge which an individual

will gives to the propulsiveness of the general will by the assent of the former to the larger purposes defined by the latter" (3, p. 242). Will is the objective propulsiveness upon which the realization of ends and execution of purposes depend, and is therefore fundamental to the practical life. As Jordan wrote: "Will is . . . merely the propulsive tendency to order fact, or the fact that fact can exist only as ordered, and it is a character of perhaps all facts whether regarded as 'mental' or not" (3, p. 237).

Institutionalized Mind

Both individualized mind and socialized mind are condemned by their subjectivity as incomplete types of mind. Both types of mind take the natural individual to be basic, and this is a serious mistake. What remains, therefore, as the highest type of mind is mind as institutionalized. Accordingly, mind is *ordered fact* taking "its practical character from the dominant quality of the sum of detail of fact" (3, p. 113). The identification of mind with the objective quality of its circumstance entails a revision of the prevalent conceptions of what one's self really is. "I, as individuality, am the tangled clot of existent valued elements which are, as spatially and temporally ordered, the facts of nature" (3, p. 159). Mind is the active synthesis of these external circumstances. Jordan asserted: "I am what my pencil, my pipe, my hoe, my pocket-knife, my books, my wife, my god, my associates and friends, the public instruments I want to use or have to use, make me. Not of course in the crude causative sense, but in the sense that the sum of enumerable means which I use indifferently (publicly) constitute me; I concentrate them and thus individuate them as the stuff of my personality; I am *their* personality; but they, concentrated about another reference point, become the stuff of another personality in which I am a detail—an important one, to be sure, since I am individuated by the same principle as he" (3, p. 161).

Mind is objectified in institutions, or, conversely, an institution may be defined as objectified mind. This does not mean that institutions are conscious; on the contrary, consciousness is the particular form mind assumes for psychobiological individuals, although to the extent that institutions include men, they include consciousness. Fusing corporeal objects and human individuals into organizations embodying will as evident in systematic tendencies to persist and to grow, institutions, when moralized, provide men with the avenue to self-fulfillment, simultaneously subordinating men to their institutional roles and consuming human lives in the institutional life. By maintaining that the foundation of social order and the subject matter of social theory is mind objectified in institutions, Jordan was calling for an institutional sociology, and by insisting that institutions are embodied in corporate objects, he was among the first to call attention to the central importance of the artefact in the analysis of society. From the vantage point of an institutional social theory, moreover, new light is cast on the seeming conflicts of interests between human individuals, for upon examination they are detected to be conflicts between the institutions in which these individuals are absorbed (3, p. 167). The quest for a new objectivity, therefore, finds its end in the institution, since the institution embraces object and subject in the higher synthesis of corporate mind.

CORPORATE THEORY OF INDIVIDUALITY

Jordan's theory of the objectification of mind in institutions is in accord with his thesis that institutions are higher forms of individuality. Types of mind denote degrees of reality, and to be real, for Jordan, is to be individual. Jordan's metaphysics of mind and individuality owes much to British Hegelian idealism—particularly to Green, Bradley, and Bosanquet. As he wrote: "The

'idealistic' doctrines that what is real is always individual (but not for that reason 'specific'), and that individuality is real as a system of qualitatively determinable
degrees, are taken for granted, and the proof for them is
indicated in the development of philosophic thought
from Plato to Hegel and on to our own day" (3, p. 186).
The principle of individuality, or individuation, must
not be confused with the process of individualization.
Individuation means order and synthesis, whereas individualization isolates and particularizes (4, p. 197). Jordan's conception of individuality is quite close to the
Hegelian doctrine, which holds that the Individual is
the concrete universal, or the Whole. The Whole is Individual because its parts form a unity through their
mutuality. This mutuality of parts within the Whole,
furthermore, is equivalent to self-reference, the distinctive
essence of Subjectivity, so that the Whole is Subjective.
But its Subjectivity is tantamount to Objectivity, since
the structure of self-reference of objective parts is objective and since the parts are objects. In the Hegelian Individual subject and object are synthesized. This Hegelian principle of individuality is the key to the new
objectivity Jordan sought, the principle which threads
together the different individuals in nature and culture
(13). "The outstanding stages in the compendious whole
of individuality are," Jordan observed, "man, the incorporate institution, and the state" (3, p. 302).

The Biological Organism

Jordan's metaphysics of social order is not a simple
organic theory of society, for what Jordan sought was
"a consideration of social relations as *logical* in character, and of the social body not as an organism, but as
an *organon*" (4, p. 321). The root metaphor of Jordan's
theory is not the biological organism, but corporeity
viewed as a logical whole. As Jordan contended: "The
organism is not a full individual" (3, p. 199). Biological

organism, governed by causality, merely maintains itself in self-repetition or reproduces itself in another individual of the same form; it never succeeds in growing into a corporeal entity with its end fulfilled in its own body. Nevertheless, the biological organism does foreshadow the principle of individuality; it is "a corporate individuation of biological functions" (3, p. 188). And although the particular organism conspicuously falls short of individuality the species, as the law of organisms, makes an approach to individuality in that the species is a concrete universal which not only imparts unity to the particular organism but also establishes its unity with its environment and its continuity within the species. In this sense "(t)he organism is an imperfectly realized form of individuality; or better, it is a distinguishable impulse toward the realization of Individuality" (3, p. 213).

The Human Person

Higher in the scale of individuality than a mere biological organism, the human person is the juncture between nature and culture. The continuity of nature and culture through the natural human person has been distorted or neglected by modern individualism which has misconceived man either as an isolated consciousness or a particular psychobiological organism dominated by exclusive interest. Jordan therefore demanded a re-interpretation of human nature: "(E)very period of advance in culture," he remarked, "has had its inception in a thorough-going analysis of human nature, and the reconstruction of the institutions of life which such analysis implies" (3, p. 55). Jordan's analysis of human nature stresses the continuity of nature and culture through man, while scoring the breakdown of modern practical relations because of the prevalent individualism. Human desires and purposes, embodied in objects, crystallize in institutions, defined as systems of "such objects organized with reference to the working out of a larger purpose in the mutual activity of persons" (3, p. 168). The larger purpose of an institution is "a plupurpose" which, transcending the sum of individual purposes, combines the capacity to conceive an ideal end with the capacity to realize it and accepts life and nature as parts of a corporate whole. Just as institutions originate in nature, with natural individuals and external circumstance contributing to their ground, so also human persons draw their substance from institutions. Jordan maintained: "The logical ground of the individual person is the system of institutions with reference to which as universal he is determined as particular" (3, p. 80). Human personality is a function, then, not only of natural individuals but of corporate institutions, of the state as the whole of such institutions, and of law.

The Corporation

Jordan advanced his argument into the field of law, but he did so without claiming expertness in legal matters and technicalities. Considerations of legal matters, he held, underscore the inadequacy of modern individualism and the need for the principle of corporate individuality. The practice of law, regardless of its preconceptions, must accommodate itself to the facts of practical life. Seeking this accommodation it resorts to subterfuges which are so transparent that through them a more basic legality, yet to be articulated, may be discerned. Legal substance is the precipitate of legal procedures, but there is a lag during which contradictions abound. Although, for example, law defines the legal person as the subject of rights and duties, then construes this individual along the lines of individualist doctrine as an entity with inalienable rights and as the exclusive seat of responsibility, law must contravene these basic assumptions and acknowledge "the transfer of rights" and "liability without fault." Since for law, moreover, the individual is "the entity which can sue and be sued, be hailed into court, be compelled to act or refrain, and do all things necessary to the constitution of the end" (3, p. 129), legal individuals are not always identifiable as human individuals, but often are corporations, associations, or unions. To adhere to individualist conceptions in spite of their incorrigible shortcomings, law resorts to the doctrine of fictions, of which Jordan has asserted: "The most monstrous fiction of the law is the theory of legal fictions" (3, p. 309). The vicious consequences of individualism in practical relations are most conspicuous in property and contract.

Contract. So long as contract is construed, in consonance with the assumptions of individualism, to signify the convergence of absolutely self-enclosed wills for the realization of exclusive interests, each will serving another to the extent of its own gain, contract fails to be the principle of social order, despite individualism's claim to make it so. As Jordan observed: "The central fallacy of individualism from the practical point of view is the assumption that interests and ends and purposes are necessarily and in the nature of things incompatible with each other" (3, pp. 442-443). Each contractor will seek to defraud the other, and all will conspire to defraud the public. "The principle of contract has become the tool," Jordan observed, "by which unsocial forces slacken the pace of civilization and arrest progress until private greed is satisfied" (3, p. 415). But Jordan also recognized that the principle of contract has a significance distinct from that imposed upon it by individualism. More than merely a reciprocal agreement between individuals for the satisfaction of exclusive interests and enforceable by external authority, contract in the proper sense derives its validity from the mutuality of ends that engage and embrace in common action all the men comprising a social whole, and in this sense, contract underlies all social order and public law. "Contract is the principle through which personalities objectify in a common end, the law by which the synthesis of persons is effected in the Person" (3, p. 422).

Property. As revolutionary as Jordan's treatment of contract is his metaphysics of property (14). Jordan claimed that property is *"the essence of the person"* (3, p. 351). However, by "property" Jordan meant not the indispensable objects consumed in the processes of living, but those more endurable objects such as land, industrial plant, and art objects. Thus the person of whom property is the essence cannot be the natural human individual. The human individual does not possess but is possessed by property: "The 'mine' really is that which esthetically or morally possesses me, and it is a commentary on the quality of my sensibility if its object is crude" (3, p. 268). Not only is individualism wrong concerning property, Jordan concluded, but the same error infects socialism, since the socialist theory in proposing the distribution of property also assumes the human individual to be the owner of property. Such distribution is plainly not feasible with capital goods, since it would undermine the industrial bases of modern civilization. Nevertheless, the shortcomings of socialism did not, for Jordan, vindicate capitalism. The existence of durable property does not demand private "owners" whose interest in profits leads to capital investments. On the contrary, insofar as profit reverts to the private owner to purchase consumable objects, the store of capital is reduced. Further, exclusive ownership of property is, Jordan insisted, practically unintelligible and evil since the property exists in its public function. The system of property objects on its own generates further objects, and the private "owner" is at best superfluous and at worst an obstacle to its function and growth. But then the question remains: If property belongs to persons, and property in the proper sense cannot belong to human individuals, to what sort of person does it belong?

Institutions and Morality

In addition to legal relations pertaining to property and contract, other specifically moral relations, Jordan contended, are unintelligible unless they refer beyond human individuals. *The Good Life* is Jordan's contribution to ethical theory. It is marked by the theme that he pursued throughout his career: Subjectivism must be overcome. Jordan's theory focuses on action as the translation of the mind into objects, and logically comes to center on institutions. Without the suitable ordering of institutions with respect to the men they subsume, with respect to each other, and with respect to a system of ends upon which, when moralized, they converge, the virtues which are attributable peculiarly to the individual human person, the "subjective or partial virtues" of sympathy, generosity, friendship, and integrity, are ineffectual, in no way dependably issuing in the good life for man. Jordan defined the good life in his formula of the law of morality: "The good life posits a person or actor endowed by nature and by culture with all the capacities that are possible to him, with these capacities developed to their fullest possible degree; the person living in a world so organized and ordered as to guarantee to the person full and free access to all the means and instruments necessary to the adequate and appropriate expression of his capacities and to the realization of his acts in satisfying objects" (6, p. 59). The good life is unattainable by an individualized subjective consciousness or by a robotistic organization man, since neither is intimately, creatively, or freely related to nature and culture. Besides exemplifying the subjective virtues, the good man is obliged, if he seeks the good life with expectation of finding it, to develop the objective virtues of wisdom, courage, temperance, and justice, but since these virtues reside not in human individuals primarily but in institutions, the moral man must enact himself into institutions. As isolated subjects or "socialized" ciphers, human individuals are poor candidates for the important role of moral persons. And nothing could be practically more futile, Jordan repeatedly emphasized, than the commonplace moral sentiment that a change of heart or mind alters the good and evil in the world. No moral advance is possible unless the objective institutional world in which human individuals are contained is acted upon. Furthermore, such action can be carried on only through and within institutions.

Practical relations in law and morality make sense neither in themselves nor as holding between merely human individuals. Very early in his career Jordan had concluded: "(T)here must be *another person* hidden somewhere which we have not seen. . . . (T)here is a superpersonal person involved in *every* practical relation, whether that relation be selling a carrot or saluting a saint" (2, p. 275). Such a superpersonal person, incorporating the virtues of wisdom, justice, temperance, courage in overt form, is precisely what an institution is when it is moralized. Property is the body of the corporate institution; institutions are the persons to whom property belongs. And when property, as the instruments with which men attain their ends and as the stable physical basis of culture, is perceived to serve public functions with which exclusive private interests interfere, it logically follows that property belongs to the institution that comprehends all institutions, the Whole, the State. But at present it suffices to recognize that institutions, containing men and objects in a self-referent organization exhibiting will, and directed toward common ends, are persons. "The body of property and the will that is instrumented in it, once it has become institutionalized and incorporated in human affairs, is, then, the active agent or person, the person that is the ground of all interpersonal or 'social' relations. It is the ultimate moral person" (6, p. 145).

Moreover, institutions are natural persons, just as human individuals are, but are devoid of the characteristic weaknesses of human individuals although susceptible to other blindnesses. As Jordan wrote: "Institutions grow; they are natural; they reproduce themselves continuously by the reappropriation of themselves as orders of objects to human functions. As such, institutions are persons" (3, p. 308).

Modern individualism has blinded men to the naturalness of institutions and the corporate, public function of property. So blinded, law had adopted the contradictory notion of the private corporation, and by ignoring the internal dynamism of corporations as they propulsively move and grow without consideration of men, it has dubbed the corporation a fiction. Herein resides the root of the self-destructive forces that menace contemporary civilization, Jordan argued. Business, the activity of the so-called "private corporation," has invaded all the higher institutions of the family, art, science, religion, education, the state, and has subverted all the professions from their ideal roles to service in behalf of business. The inherent self-contradictoriness of private business corporations is evident in the fact that they tend to destroy, devour, or merge with each other. Practically what is required is the elimination of business through a rational reorganization of institutions (15). The initial steps in the direction of the ideal order of practical relations depend upon the recognition that corporate institutions with public functions are objective moral persons, not fictions in the interests of a few men. And this is tantamount to acknowledging the validity of the principle of individuality which has operated in philosophy from Plato to Hegel. The metaphysical foundation of social order, if that order is to be improved by the general acceptation of correct practical concepts, must be shifted from individualism to individuality. In this fundamental way metaphysics functions as the ultimate *Practica* (16).

LEGAL PHILOSOPHY

The reorganization of the corporate institutions in modern civilization, in particular the rationalization of industry, is for Jordan the problem of politics and the task of the state. But by politics Jordan did not mean what commonly goes by that name. Nor did he equate the state with the government, since government at its best is the organ of the state and at its worst is a tool of private interests hostile to the public good. Representative government as practiced in the constitutional democracies attracted his criticism. Representative government, he claimed, is self-contradictory; it assumes that political capacity and responsibility may be delegated. Then, as if aware that the assumption is wrong, it resorts to devices, such as checks and balances, by which to restrain its representatives. Further, representative democracy, an offshoot of individualism, is hedged by formal constitutions which presume the state to be artificial rather than natural.

Theory of the State

Harking back to the Greek political theorists, and sustained by the idealist metaphysics of individuality, Jordan contended that the state is natural. At the same time he resuscitated the classical conception of politics as a speculative science supported by metaphysical foundations, yet fundamentally practical in that it secures "the rational ordering of the objective institutions of human life" (3, p. 37). Politics is institutionalized in the state. "(T)he concept which the state at present most clearly represents is that of a system of autonomous institutions which operate as the instruments through the use of which public will achieves its specific purposes. It is characteristically that of a *working* system of machines, or more properly organs, co-ordinated into a whole by the ends which intelligence sets up in the system of policy. This system of ends as a whole implements itself in an Idea whose autonomy does not require an instrument in overt form, since its *act* is ideal—the formulation of policy. Consequently, the State has always been and will always remain, an idea. And theory of the State is speculative philosophy" (4, pp. 406-407).

Paradoxically the concept of the state, for Jordan, connotes what is both natural and ideal. As man is the juncture of nature and culture, and as cultural institutions are higher forms of individuality which grow from nature, so the state is a natural individuality which constitutes the whole of cultural institutions and men, but constitutes the whole through its function as an Idea harmonizing the ends which are pursued by institutions and are embodied in corporate property. The state exists through the medium of law, whereby the Idea is articulated.

Law and Life

Jordan elaborated his philosophy of law in *Theory of Legislation*. Like *Forms of Individuality, Theory of Legislation* is a metaphysical treatise, "written as a sort of footnote to the *Forms of Individuality*" (4, p. 7). The differences in approach of the two works are evident in two words in the subtitles: the term "grounds" in the earlier book, "dynamics" in the later. Jordan's metaphysics in *Forms of Individuality* is motivated by the logical quest for the ground of social relations, and the result of the quest, formulated in the principle of individuality, is the discovery of a series of individuals comprising the social order and the consideration of them primarily as entities for logical analysis. Supplementing the somewhat static approach of *Forms of Individuality* is *Theory of Legislation*. In the later book Jordan examined the dynamics of the entities discussed earlier, and the result is a philosophy of law, since the dynamics of public mind is explicit in legislation.

According to Jordan, who painstakingly sought to show what many thinkers had suggested—the roots of law in life, the *"legality of life,"* as he put it (4, p. 96)— law, like corporate institutions and the state, is natural. "(L)aw of whatever sort is made . . . out of the automaticity of life as embodied and embedded in the institutionalized relations of experience. . . . Laws come, for the most part, out of the life-processes which are indigenous to the relations among institutions; and they are laws rather than scientific principles merely classificatory of fact—they are norms precisely in their tendencies to stabilize these processes and relations into orderly forms" (4, p. 38). Jordan therefore sided with the natural law theory of Aristotle against the legal rationalism of Plato. Unlike the legal rationalist, who posits objective ideal norms which law promulgates and externally imposes upon life processes, Jordan located the source of law in life. Consequently, he repudiated the theory that law is artificially, externally enforced regulation of life, and emphatically argued for the continuity of life, will, and law. Life itself is continuous with fact; it is a definite kind of organization of fact which evinces the tendency to maintain itself, to assimilate external circumstance, and to reproduce itself. This growth-change of fact which characterizes organic individuals involves in rudimentary fashion the distinction between means and ends, though at this level the distinction pertains solely to spatiotemporal natural objects, mutually determining each other's natures. Nevertheless, organic activity, displaying direction toward ends relevant to means, is inherently legislative, despite the restricted application of the term "legislation" to "the determination within public life of means and ends with respect to purposes" (4, p. 57). Will is the link between life and law; and the philosophy of law consequently depends upon the metaphysics of the will. Whereas life, at the purely organic level, dynamically moves toward existing objects that contribute to its preservation and reproduction, will attains a higher degree of objectivity. A "plupurpose" which absorbs and transcends individual human purpose, will is embodied in the corporate person, dynamically moving toward a universal objective, or end. As will is objective to organic purposes, so law is objective to will. As the act of the political state, legislation embraces and transcends all ends in the End, established as the Idea of the state.

Jordan's deduction of law from life through will, a bold and novel reinterpretation of natural law doctrine, yet supports the normative, directive function of law by the acknowledgment of the reference to ends. Law "as a practical concept" exhibits a flexibility "which law as a technical or natural category for science does not have" because there is always possibility of interpreting the facts in a different way and of choosing to formulate a different principle in legal experience. Thus while law as a natural category is recognized because "it expresses a necessity," law as a practical concept, though deduced from life, is "to be observed, because it exemplifies an obligation" (4, pp. 452-453).

Law, then, as normative, refers to ends which obligate but do not compel. The ends, however, are in consistent fashion intimately linked to the dynamics of life and will embodied in objective fact. An end is neither an abstract logical ideal nor a subjective psychological phenomenon. It is not the former because such Platonism is incompatible with the naturalness of law, and it is not the latter because such subjectivism is repudiated by Jordan's entire philosophy. Although an end "is the substance in which action *ends*," an end is more than a consequent, it is also a ground directing action (4, p. 160). And end is the identity of ground and consequent. "End is therefore ground, considered as logical form, converted into content or experience-stuff by action" (4, p. 162). The attainment of ends, furthermore, does not restrict action to specific means. On the contrary, the agent makes contact with ends through an organ which is not an instrument, not a natural condition or cause, not a specific detail of fact, but rather a universal, a law (4, p. 175). Through law the agent *enacts* himself and the end consists in the incorporation of the agent and his circumstance in a higher form of individuality. Hence "order principled by law is the End" (4, p. 183).

Thus politics introduces no new content but posits through the medium of law the formal harmony of all ends, the order of all institutions. All the basic components of life, will, and law, manifest in objective fact, comprise a continuity from life through will to law, within which the phases of legislation, administration, and adjudication are discernible. As Jordan stated: "Life, will and law are therefore aspects of the same fact-body; and law is effective and has power for the same reason that life idealizes ends in image and will realizes them in action. The ultimate legislator is therefore life, and its representative or agent is will, and the ultimate issue of that agent's act upon the material which life supplies is law as the harmony of the whole. The stages in the act of legislation are, therefore, the definition of ends in idea or the act of policy; the exemplification of policy in fact, or the try-out of administration; and the demonstration in order, or judicial legalization, of the disparate forces of life. In experience terms the same thing is said in the statement that legislation begins with the urgency of the will, passes into agency with intelligence, and issues in substantiated order through reflection" (4, p. 113).

Political Methodology

Despite his emphasis on the continuity of life, will, and law with the threefold dynamics of policy-making, administration, and judicial process, Jordan nevertheless conceived the problem of legislation as flowing from a fissure at the center of the practical life.

Jordan was unusually sensitive to the tragedy which haunts all private lives. "The object within which tragedy creates itself," he wrote in *The Aesthetic Object,* "is . . . the truth of life" (5, p. 246). "The essence of tragedy lies in the fact that its object is a demonstration . . . of the utter impossibility of any complete unity of value with existence *in life*" (5, p. 245). Jordan's language erupted with unusual passion as he continued: "At its best, at its nearest approach to beauty, life remains sordid, vulgar, brutal, and obscene. For the benefit of those optimists who in the fatuous shallowness of their muddled vacuity remonstrate, I point to the fact—the reality of the world wallowing in the mire of its own filth and prolonging for the moment its futile existence in fevered draughts of its own dripping blood. This is the eternal truth of the Christ: the blood is shed." And he added that "the categories of life are all tragic concepts. . . . Culture itself is carrion vestured in cloth of gold" (5, p. 246).

The Problem of Legislative Control. Human tragedy in practical relations stems from the radical division between the capacity to know and the capacity to do. "(M)an, as individual, can *see* more than he can *do*" (4, p. 212). Except in artistic creation, individual men cannot effectively do what they can envision and propose. As Jordan put it: "The individual will . . . *sees* more than it can *reach*; *knows* more than it can *do*; it can *only* speculate upon ends; which are effected, if at all, by other agencies than itself; *or* devise means which, of themselves, have no end. Its function is therefore to speculate and to create in idea the ends that are to be realized by life as a whole, and to devise the abstract means which may, if intelligence suffice and if power present itself, order those ends into the End" (4, p. 228).

The executive impotence of individual men within the public world necessitates that, if the ends men envision are to be realized, other nonhuman agencies must effectuate them. Thus men turn to corporate institutions as higher forms of individuality with effective will. But Jordan observed: "The corporate will is . . . *blind*; all its effectiveness, which is the totality of direct effectiveness in human affairs, since all human ends can be attained only through its agency, is directed toward maintaining the status quo of its own structure. It has no 'soul' of purposed objectivity of ends beyond itself. It can *do*, but it cannot *see*; whereas the human individual can *see* but cannot *do*" (4, p. 244).

Hence the problem of legislation and control arises. As Jordan summarized it: "Life as effective will in the human being, either individually or collectively, is essentially speculative by nature and its function is to see—to foresee—to envisage and idealize ends. But it is powerless to attain any of these ends in objective form. Life as effective will in the corporate individuality of institutions attains its ends in immediate form, but it does this blindly, and the ends attained are raw concreteness without meaning. The one can see but cannot attain; the other attains but attains nothing of objective and ultimate form. It is this situation as present in the facts of life which sets for practical philosophy the problem of legislation and control" (4, pp. 248-249).

The problem of legislative control falls within the province of political methodology for solution, because politics, alone among all sciences, undertakes to comprehend the practical life as a whole and therefore overcome, if not absolutely mend, the rift between the capacity of individual men to think ideals but not to be able to enact them and the capacity of corporate institutions to act but not to think ideals. Political methodology as legislative process, according to Jordan, involves three distinct, but interrelated phases: (1) legislation as speculation, (2) legislation as experimental administration, and (3) legislation as judicial process.

Legislation. Legislation as speculation is the first phase of the political methodology of legislation. The speculative act "comprehends in one view not only the total of given factual means as embodied in the natural and social environments, but also . . . it comprehends the world as fact within the same unity with the world regarded as ideal plan. . . . (I)n thus comprehending the compossibility of the world of nature and culture as means with the world of plan and ideal as end, the legislative fiat, as speculation, provides both the structure and organization of the practical world and the plan and functional purpose of that world" (4, p. 312). Legislation as speculation is "experimentation under logical conditions" (4, p. 315). Although legislation in its first motive draws upon all the descriptive sciences to know about the structure of the actual world of culture and nature, yet it is essentially metaphysical speculation, since its role "is one of speculatively determining, in advance of the experiencing or living through them, the ends and principles which, when experienced or lived through, will be felt intermediately as the fulfillment of human nature in the substance of the relations which incorporate the human with the natural into a world" (4, p. 144).

Critical of the validity of political democracy with its false assumptions that the "people" can think speculatively or delegate this capacity to others, Jordan rejected democracy as the political framework in which legislation as speculation can be performed, and adopted the Platonic proposal of the philosopher-kings, legislation by an intellectual élite. "There must be maintained within the social or political body," he asserted, "a corporate class of free intellects whose speculative imagination is allowed to wander at will in the construction of the schema of ideas; and whose hand is free and absolutely unhindered in the process of experimental verification of those ideas within the laboratory of social life until they can be reduced to law" (4, p. 345). This "aristocracy of mind," however, does not primarily depend, as Plato thought, upon the selection of a special group of superior individual men; it is drawn rather from the system of cultural institutions. Legislative bodies secure the opportunities of expression for the aristocracy of mind, whose function is to talk. Through the medium of discussion ideas undergo experimentation under logical conditions as provided by the parliamentary body serving as a kind of laboratory (4, p. 346).

Briefly, the work of legislation in its first phase is to propose laws as ideals to direct action, not to enforce it. Thus the laws would be general, sketching in large the ends toward which the society ought to move in the light of its actual situation, and creating in idea the organization of objects, the institutions, requisite to the effectuation of the End.

Administration. Legislation as administration, the second phase of the political methodology, has as its work the actualization of ends and objects within a system of order. In contrast with the first phase, where speculative thinking is primary, in administration action is primary. Carried on in institutions, administration is wedded to the actual facts and objects, adding specific maxims for action and acting to implement and realize the general policies proposed by legislative speculation. Flexibility is of paramount importance for effective administration; and its method is the tryout of experimentation. Whereas the clear definition of ends in speculation is immune to stumbling and falling upon brute, recalcitrant facts, administration is susceptible to error, though upon it hinges control. Jordan wrote: "Control by intelligence over the legislative process is . . . always and necessarily indirect, and is mediated through the ideal capacity of the objects which are formulated as ends in policy and the *actual* capacity of objects, which are realized in administration. Control is effected in the same way that direction is maintained by a man riding a bicycle; he must keep his eye upon the distant objects which draw the line of his direction, and risk the rest to the inherent and spontaneous power of those objects *somehow* to control the movements of his hands and feet. . . . The discovery and rough-hewing of the things and objects which can be made into objectives depend upon the experimental or administrative act of life where mistakes can be made and corrected" (4, pp. 437-438).

Adjudication. The judicial process is the final phase in the political methodology of legislation, and its method is deliberate reflection. "(T)he judicial process is the process of testing the principles of policy as worked out by the speculative motive in legislation, in their relations to maxims of action as established experimentally in administration" (4, p. 441). An implicate of the practical life, just as legislative speculation and administrative experimentation are, the judicial process is institutionalized in the established judiciary. Here is found the activity of interweaving law and fact, the application of general principles to specific cases, and the investigation and re-investigation of cases to detect the details of fact which suggest the appropriate principles. The judicial process, moreover, is oriented to the end of harmonizing ends and objects, facts and values, speculative legislative hypotheses and practical maxims of action. It is the process which, regardless of what facts are given to it (provided, of course, that it works effectively and with the proper laws), will render those facts legal, i.e., locate them in the harmony of value and existence imaged in the State. A fact is illegal if it does not fit in with the total organization of facts and ends. But such illegality evinces a failure in the organization, i.e. its exclusion of this fact, and necessitates the legislative processes for the development of law with which to constitute the fact and its circumstances in a superior organization, a more inclusive whole.

CONCLUDING REMARKS

Jordan's philosophy of law has been criticized on the grounds that it is remote from what the lawyers know and mean by law—that, in other words, it has little to do with legal experience as it occurs in the passing of statutes, the routines of administration, and the litigations in court (17). This is a curious criticism, for Jordan did not mean to demonstrate superior knowledge in the technicalities of law, but to show how law stems from the practical life and how phases in these practical life processes are or should be institutionalized in the organs of the State. If what is regarded as law does not have some similar or analogous relation to the practical life as Jordan indicated, then it is not law, but the rule of force. Law enforcement, Jordan held, is self-contradictory. The application of force to human relations testifies to the absence of legality in the facts as they exist. "Law rests upon will, not upon force" (4, p. 362).

What Jordan offered, therefore, is a kind of ideal theory of legislation by which to judge actual legislative processes. And what he sought to demonstrate was that this ideal political methodology is natural, since it is rooted in the dynamic practical life. The existing practices, fostered by the fallacious subjectivism and individualism of modern civilization, are far less natural, and the upshot is the contemporary crisis in practical affairs at every level. While the first steps in the solution of this crisis involve, according to Jordan, the recognition of the metaphysics of corporate institutions and the cultural devastation that ensues from their subversion to private interests, the completion of the task of rationalizing the public life demands the legislative act of the State. For "the state . . . is the generalized instrument of morality, the instrument or tool through which the larger aims of morality are accomplished. It is also the final object or end of morality, both in the sense of the ultimate goal to be reached and in the sense of the perfect body or organ through which moral action is most effectively embodied" (6, pp. 338-339). Upon the State, then, falls the task of moralizing the world and of guaranteeing the good life.

Jordan was not optimistic that the State would be realized; but since optimism and pessimism are both subjective occurrences, he would not have regarded them as germane to the problem of practical control. Acknowledgment that existing agencies operate against the realization of the good life in no way minimizes the correctness of recognizing what in practical relations and institutions may be conducive to it. And though all the avenues to action seem closed there still remains for the individual man his primary obligation, namely, the obligation to know. As Jordan put it: "As a practical capacity . . . *the individual's obligation is the obligation to think; to prepare in idea and anticipation the intent of the whole of experience which as objective agency may become active in the execution of a plan*" (4, p. 228). As critic and metaphysician of modern civilization, Jordan lived up to this obligation in fullest measure.

NOTES TO CHAPTER 9

1. Elijah Jordan, *Metaphysics; An Unfinished Essay* edited with "Preface" and "Bibliography" by Max Fisch (Evanston, Ill.: Principia Press of Illinois, 1956).

2. Elijah Jordan, *The Life of Mind* (Indianapolis: Charles W. Laut & Co., 1925).

3. Elijah Jordan, *Forms of Individuality; An Inquiry into the Grounds of Order in Human Relations* (Indianapolis: Charles W. Laut Co., 1927).

4. Elijah Jordan, *Theory of Legislation; An Essay on the Dynamics of Public Mind* (Indianapolis: Progress Publishing Co., 1930); second edition with a new preface (Chicago: University of Chicago Press, 1952). Except for the prefaces,

the contents and pagination of the two editions are the same.

5. Elijah Jordan, *The Aesthetic Object: An Introduction to the Philosophy of Value* (Bloomington, Ind.: Principia Press, 1937).

6. Elijah Jordan, *The Good Life* (Chicago: University of Chicago Press, 1949).

7. Elijah Jordan, *Essays in Criticism, with an Introduction and Synopses*, Robert D. Mack, ed. (Chicago: University of Chicago Press, 1952).

8. See George Barnett and Jack Otis, *Corporate Society and Education, The Philosophy of Elijah Jordan* (Ann Arbor: University of Michigan Press, 1962).

9. Elijah Jordan, *Business Be Damned* (New York: Henry Schuman, 1952).

10. Glenn Negley, *The Organization of Knowledge*, (Englewood Cliffs, N. J.: Prentice-Hall, 1942), Appendix II, pp. 301-326.

11. Jordan wrote his doctoral dissertation on Kant, of which an abridged version was published. See Elijah Jordan, *The Constitutive and Regulative Principles in Kant* (Chicago: University of Chicago Press, 1912).

12. These same three principles are repeated in italics and with minor verbal changes in *The Good Life*, pp. 308-309.

13. Jordan, however, viewed his theory of individuality in which mutuality of positive content is stressed, to be a correction of the Hegelian theory of individuality, which he interpreted to signify primarily a negation of specific content in order to emphasize universality. See Elijah Jordan, "The Definition of Individuality," *Philosophical Review*, XXX (1921), 566-584. The question of the direct relation of Jordan's philosophy to Hegel's is an interesting one. Commenting on the critical opinion that his thinking was a variety of Hegelian idealism, Jordan admitted: "I regret that I have never read the work of Hegel consistently, most of it not at all" (*Theory of Legislation*, p. 7). Max Fisch has pointed that if Jordan's philosophy "be Hegelianism, it is Hegelianism without the dialectic and without optimism" (*Metaphysics*, p. xiv). It is of course sometimes unenlightening to assign philosophical labels to thinking as complex and original as Jordan's. For example, Jordan's book, *The Good Life*, was hailed by Charner M. Perry in *Philosophical Review*, LIX (1950), 514-527, as naturalism and by H. W. Schneider, *Journal of Philosophy*, XLVII (1950), 387-393, as idealism.

14. See Elijah Jordan, "Possession and Individuality," *Philosophical Review*, XXXI (1922), 369-387.

15. Of course Jordan sharply distinguished between business and industry. "Business and industry . . . are vastly different things." Business is defined "as the system of mechanics for

the control of industry." Industry is the "production, exchange, distribution and appropriation of goods to use" (*Business Be Damned*, p. 2). Industry demands "intelligent work"; the methods of business are "force and fraud."

16. Jordan was firmly convinced that philosophy has a paramount social duty to perform and that its evasion of this duty by devotion to narrow epistemological topics has contributed to the catastrophes of war and economic breakdown suffered in the present century. In his undelivered presidential address to the Western Division of the American Philosophical Association, written in the middle of World War II, he stated strongly: "(T)he responsibility for the situation is philosophy's." Elijah Jordan, "Concerning Philosophy," *Philosophical Review*, LII (1943), 114.

17. See, for example, Max Radin's review of *Theory of Legislation* in *Harvard Law Review*, XLIV (1931), 877-878.

Chapter 10

THE
PERSONALISM OF
EDGAR SHEFFIELD BRIGHTMAN

PERSONALISTIC CONCEPTION OF PHILOSOPHY

"Of the idealistic systems," Werkmeister has said, "personalism seems to be most widely accepted today" (1). European in origin, personalism has flourished on American soil. In 1789 Schleiermacher introduced the German term for "personalism" into German thought and in 1865 John Grote used the English word. Walt Whitman in 1868 was the first American to employ the term. Adumbrated in the philosophies of Lotze in Germany and Renouvier in France, personalism found vigorous expression in the thought of Borden Parker Bowne at Boston University and George Holmes Howison at the University of California, Berkeley. Assigning supreme value and reality to total personality, personalism has spread to several continents and is represented in a multiplicity of literary and philosophical statements. Through all the variations of personalism the essential thesis is that "the whole universe is a society of intercommunicating selves or persons, of which God is the creative center" (2, p. 293). "Personalism . . . is the hypothesis that all being . . . is either a personal experient (a complex unity of consciousness) or some phase or aspect of one or more such experients" (3, p. 135).

Since World War I the most prominent personalistic philosophers in the United States have been Ralph Tyler Flewelling, founder and longtime editor of the journal, *The Personalist*, and head of the School of Idealistic Philosophy at the University of Southern California; A. C. Knudson, professor of theology and dean of the Divinity School at Boston University; and Edgar Sheffield Brightman, Borden Parker Bowne Professor of Philosophy at Boston University. While Flewelling's version of personalism is primarily that of the popularizer, editor, and teacher, and Knudson's contribution is that of the historian and theologian, Brightman's role has been that of the creative thinker who has imparted to personalism systematic coherence, empirical inclusiveness, and conceptual originality of the first order.

Born in 1884, Brightman studied at Brown University, where he received his B.A. and M.A. in 1906 and 1908. He entered the Divinity School of Boston University, where he earned his S.T.B. in 1910. After a year of study at Marburg and Berlin, he returned to Boston University to receive his Ph.D. in 1912. After several years as professor of ethics and religion at Wesleyan University, he became professor of philosophy at Boston University in 1919, serving there until his death in 1953. Brightman's earliest interests were in religion; his first book was a contribution to the field of Biblical scholarship (4). In philosophy he showed from the beginning a scholarly and constructive concern for German idealism (5). His first book in philosophy, an introductory textbook, stated the themes that were to preoccupy him throughout his prolific authorship—values, persons, and God (2).

William Ernest Hocking, in his sensitive contribution

to the memorial issue of *The Personalist,* rightly captured the spirit of Brightman's thought when he singled out the two distinctive qualities of existential concreteness and impetus toward system (6). Brightman defined philosophy *"as thinking which aims at maximum concreteness, or thinking which seeks to discover connected truth about all available experience"* (2, p. 5). Here the Hegelian conception of the concrete as the whole, as the interconnection of the parts within the system, dominates. For Brightman, "synopsis is the characteristic method of philosophy" (2, p. 39). Any object whatever is viewed as a whole or part of a whole, and viewed preferably not as a separate fact but from the standpoint of the whole and its connection with the whole. Concreteness consists in just this relatedness within the whole; abstractness, in separation from the whole. The movement toward existential concreteness and the impetus toward system meet. Because of this impetus toward system it is natural that Brightman, though writing most extensively in the area of the philosophy of religion, sought to elaborate a system of metaphysics. And because of his insistence upon concreteness, upon the relevance of all experience to the establishment of philosophical concepts, it is natural that his metaphysics (which he never completed during his life but which fortunately fell to the editorship of Peter Bertocci) is empirical and experiential. In Brightman's words: "the goal of metaphysics is to think as concretely as possible about experience" (3, p. 13).

Brightman defined metaphysics as "the mind's effort to view experience as a living whole and thus [his conception] is close to Hegel's basic intent, however far it may be removed from his conclusions" (3, p. 18). Ruling out the purely abstract, Brightman called for empirical adequacy and systematic coherence in philosophy. Empirical coherence as the proper philosophical method signified a personalistic method. As Brightman said: "Personalistic method is an empiricism which recognizes the demands of reason and of experiential fact; of descriptive fact and of value; of part and of whole. It is both descriptive and inductive, both rational and empirical" (3, p. 33). Ever ready to regard the most abstruse theological and metaphysical topics empirically, including the question of the existence and nature of God, Brightman nonetheless cautioned against reducing the experiential method of testing metaphysical and theistic hypotheses to the experimental method of the laboratory sciences: "(T)he experiment of testing the reality of God by trying to find him through every avenue of our being . . . is very different in many respects from a strictly scientific experiment under precisely controlled physical conditions. . . . (I)f a person believes that the only approach to truth is the approach of the laboratory, he will never be able to find a spiritual God. God is a property of the universe as a whole, and not of its observable parts. He is not a sense object.

"The Kingdom of Heaven cometh not by observation. It comes by the appreciation of the signs of the presence and power of God in our inner experience" (7, pp. 29, 30, 31).

The experience from which philosophy starts, therefore, is not mere sensory experience, but rather the metaphysician's own present, varied, many-faceted personal experience. The "shining present" is Brightman's term for this starting point (3, p. 36). It is, as he put it elsewhere, "the situation-experienced" (8, pp. 347-349). It comprises "all presently observable consciousness—all sensations, images, reasoning, loves, hates, fears and hopes of Now, all conations, strivings and efforts, desires, aversions" (3, p. 36). Despite the fact that the shining present exhibits a certain constant structure (3, pp. 47-53), it requires an explanation which reaches beyond itself, as the explanation of what is experienced consists in beliefs about states of affairs beyond the reach of the immediate experience, i.e., "the situation-believed-in." In this manner the most coherent hypothesis possible can be framed to organize and clarify what is given in experience. Hence, "the being of the present involves and requires the being of the absent if the present is to be understood" (3, p. 36). The set of conditions which explain the shining present Brightman has called "the illuminating absent" (3, p. 67).

Whereas "being" embraces "(a)ll shining presents plus all (more or less) illuminating absents" (3, p. 75), the classification of being into shining present and illuminating absent, though helpful for understanding the structure and method of metaphysical knowledge, is not a proper ontological classification. Brightman's philosophical system, while attentive to the methodological considerations that go into the discrimination of shining present and illuminating absent, does not halt with methodology, but contains a theory of realms of beings and a doctrine of categories. This metaphysics of personalistic idealism is contrasted often and explicitly with the naturalistic materialism of Santayana.

For Brightman a category is "a principle the denial of which would make the entire universe of discourse to which it applies either impossible or fundamentally incoherent" (3, p. 98). Here Brightman utilized a form of argument common among idealistic metaphysicians of his generation and already particularly noted in the work of W. M. Urban, namely, that the existence or validity of an entity or a concept is justified dialectically by the demonstration that its denial is absurd or self-contradictory. Categories are more than dialectical principles, however, for, like realms, they are rooted in experience. Whereas many categories, such as space, are restricted to specific realms, others, e.g., time and substance, hold of all possible realms of being, when by "possible" is meant "experienceable, thinkable, or imaginable in view of experience" (3, p. 103). Brightman saluted time as "the most pervasive category of experience" and "the most fundamental category of all possible being" (3, p. 103). Thus personalism becomes a temporalism: "All being is temporal and therefore all being is personal" (3, p. 135). As time is the most pervasive category, substance is the most perplexing one (3, p. 177). The coherence it imparts to experience, the empirical function it serves, is the correlation of permanence and change, both indispensable aspects of experience (3, p. 178). The model of explanation and analysis is person *as experienced*. "The personalistic theory of substance may be summarized in the words 'substance is person' " (3, p. 199). Emphatically, of course, substance is not a nonexperiential support or substrate. As Brightman declared: "All substance is a complex unity of consciousness, energizing as will" (3, p. 193). The doctrine that substance is empirical and personal is the "central thesis" of Brightman's metaphysics (3, p. 113), because in the person are found unity, continuity, endurance, and complexity.

Distinct from categories, realms are, according to Brightman, arbitrary classifications of beings made by philosophers in consonance with their theoretical interests for synoptic and coherent explanation. No realm of being is totally arbitrary, since the impetus toward system favors only those classifications which can be coherently related, and since existential concreteness demands that every classification have an empirical foundation. "A realm," wrote Brightman, "is an order of experience and of illuminating absents related to experience" (3, p. 219). Beings, moreover, are divided into four realms: essence, nature, values, and persons. The theory of these realms, established by the philosopher's decision, though subordinate to the demand for empirical coherence, Brightman offered as a tentative hypothesis. Never did he promise absolute proof for his philosophy: "Only the Absolute is absolute. . . . Each metaphysican must embark on his own voyage of exploration" (3, p. 88).

REALM OF ESSENCES

Nowhere perhaps is the contrast between Brightman's personalism and Santayana's materialism sharper than in the conception of the realm of essence. Brightman defined essence "as meaning any *quale*, or experienced content or quality, whether simple or complex (that is, whether atomistic or *Gestalt*-like), considered apart from its relations to the rest of experience and apart from activity of any kind. It is both immediate and abstract" (3, p. 220). Essences comprise the Given, both rational and nonrational, the principles of ideal logic as well as sensory and emotional qualities. Further, the realm of essence is precategorial, although categories may be detected in it. So far essences for Brightman are like essences for Santayana. Pure, self-identical, passive, qualitative, or logical, like a shade of redness or a figure of squareness, essences simply are—indubitable elements enmeshed in the Given. But whereas Santayana could conceive essences as objects independent of any experience, Brightman denied such independence. Located in experience, essences are rather contents as experienced (3, p. 224).

Nor for Brightman are essences universals. Being precategorial, they are also preuniversal and preparticular. They assume the characteristics of universality or particularity according to the manner in which they are regarded by persons with particular purposes in mind. In effect, the metaphysical separation of universals from particulars as usually viewed, since it would shatter the possibility of a coherently understandable unified cosmos, is ruled out. The distinction between them, then, is teleological; it is "a distinction of the purpose of thought to universalize or to particularize" (3, p. 237). Only the concrete universal, the most conspicuous type of which is personal consciousness (3, p. 236), is metaphysically

real, and it especially makes possible the distinction between universal and particular. Thus personal consciousness is "a universalizing particular; that is, mind is a concrete individual, one function of which is to grasp the
meaning of universals; and universals are the purpose of
mind to think in universal terms" (2, p. 136).

Do essences exist? To deny existence to essences, as
Santayana did, signifies for Brightman the personal decision to "forget, omit, and suspend for the time being all
ideas of relation or cause or context" (3, p. 233). That
essences are found in experiences testifies to their existence—at least, to their psychological existence—in that
they must occur in order to be experienced. Hence essences "are discovered by an analysis of existence as we
know it. So far as we know, they are inseparable from
an experiential context and integral to the very being of
existence" (3, p. 225).

Important by virtue of their presence "in the unity of
the shining present, which is the evidential basis of all
metaphysics" (3, p. 225), essences must not be hypostatized. What is necessary according to Brightman is merely
"to postulate such illuminating absents as will provide a
context and a coherent setting in substance for otherwise ghostly and nonexistent essences" (3, p. 226). The
personalistic hypothesis is particularly suited to solve this
metaphysical problem. "For personalism, essences of all
sorts are experiences of persons. They belong to the unity
of consciousness and have no other existence or function
of any sort, except as indicating that selves are interrelated with each other" (3, p. 226). Like Whitehead's
eternal objects, Brightman's essences define "the possibilities of further actuality and the limits of all actuality.
They constitute the Given which all activity must use
and control" (3, pp. 226-227). Moreover, since essences
exist only in shining presents, it follows that, if they are
eternal, as there is every reason to believe, "they presuppose an eternal shining present of which they are con-

tent. Thus essences involve the existence of an eternal Person—an efficient and final cause, an Experient of unbegun and unending duration, whose use and control of the essences is evinced in the explicitly and implicitly rational structure of experience" (3, p. 227).

REALM OF NATURE

Over against "the lifeless, timeless, ghostly realm of essence" is "the living, ordered, temporal, concrete realm of Nature" (3, p. 239). To the contemporary naturalistic tendency of equating reality with nature and of relying exclusively upon the scientific method for knowledge Brightman imputed much of the difficulty, theoretical and practical, that bedevils modern thinkers. He distinguished the metaphysical conception from the positivistic conception of science. The former maintains that "the sciences reveal to us the true nature of reality as it is independent of experience," whereas the latter is concerned "wholly with the facts of experience, but not with their source in the nature of reality nor with the ultimate origin of experience itself" (9, p. 43). Of the two conceptions of science Brightman rejected the metaphysical view, since it posits a real nature existing apart from personal experience; he accepted the positivistic view "as much more probable than the metaphysical" (9, p. 52). "On this view . . . physical nature is the resultant ideal construction in conscious experience when mind is stimulated in a certain way by the creative powers of the universe" (9, p. 47).

In particular Brightman inveighed against the dominant naturalistic outlook which divides human reality into two worlds: a natural world of matter and energy in a spatiotemporal, causally interlocked cosmos that excludes values, and a human world of values and ideals that are devoid of objective reality. Indeed, he addressed an entire volume, *Nature and Values*, just to the question: "Is man's world broken into two worlds?" (10, p. 27). His answer was a personalistic philosophy of life stated in three principles: respect for personality (10, p. 159); "nature as a revelation of Divine Personality" (10, p. 160); and spiritual liberty (10, p. 163). "All the energies of nature," Brightman taught, "are activities of a cosmic mind—the mind that our value experiences reveal to be the eternal God. Every law of nature is a law of God, every energy of nature a deed of God" (10, p. 120).

It might appear simple to infer from the personalistic conception of Nature that it is Divine Order to be appreciated mystically and poetically, as romantics and pantheists have done, without employment of objective scientific methods. However, for Brightman nature, as a realm of being, is defined as "an illuminating absent, that is, an objective order of some sort which gives evidence of its objectivity in and to the observing and thinking mind" (3, p. 239). The concept of nature, then, is based on immediate empirical evidence but implies a set of conditions which stand behind the immediately experienced as its explanation. As a distinguishable realm, nature consists of phenomena organized in space and time and described by laws discovered by scientific methods. The realm of nature, approached scientifically, indicates other realms of being, especially since contemporary physics tends to equate the basic natural substance with energy, force, or activity—and to Brightman this suggests "the energizing of a will other than human" (3, p. 247).

What is the relation of nature to its energizing will, God? In answering this question, Brightman was unusually sensitive to the imperfections of nature, to manifest cruelty and suffering. God, he believed, could not have created nature *ex nihilo*. Nature in one sense originally stood over against God as a chaotic irrational Given. God created the order within nature, and so in another sense nature is now within God. God creates nature as the artist creates—on a material given to him. "Insofar as Nature is within God, it is a creation of new order and meaning, analogous to the creation that occurs in the mind of a poet, a musician, a novelist, or a scientist" (3, p. 248). Literally, then, for Brightman the relation of Nature to God is properly construed as "the immanence of Nature in God" (3, p. 249). "Nature is one area of Divine experience, exhibiting God in action, God controlling the Given, and God communicating and interacting with other persons or selves" (3, p. 250).

REALM OF VALUES

In contrast with the realm of nature is the realm of values. Modern philosophy has converted this contrast into a dualism in which one pole, nature, is favored at the expense of the other. Against this demotion of values recent idealism has protested assiduously, stressing that the ideal is the more real. Almost from the beginning Brightman's personalistic idealism has taken up the case for values so persistently that it may be labeled, after the title of one of his books, "A Philosophy of Ideals." Brightman's study of religion originates in large measure from the desire to defend and promote values. Indeed, religion is defined as a concern for experiences of supreme value and as devotion to the agent or agencies which conserve and create value (8, p. 17). But he never intended to repudiate the contrast between nature and values. Acknowledging that there are conflicts between these realms, he also recognized that personality is the medium in which these conflicts exist and may be resolved. He wrote: "Personality is the arena in which all this conflict appears" (10, p. 66). And he argued: "Without personality, no other values exist. Unless personality is value, all else is devalued" (11, p. 18).

In defense of values Brightman clarified and ex-

pounded in precise fashion the concept and structure of
the realm of values. Thus, he differentiated values, ideals,
and norms (12), and attempted to state their relation
to existence (3, pp. 286 ff.).

A value, or value claim, is an immediate experience of
some experient. It is an actual state of consciousness.
Citing Ralph Barton Perry, Brightman has defined *value*
as "whatever is actually liked, prized, esteemed, desired,
approved, or enjoyed by anyone at any time. It is the
actual experience of enjoying a desired object or activity.
Hence, value is an existing realization of desire" (8,
p. 88). Value theory demands the empirical observation
and description of these immediate value experiences
as prerequisite to the conceptualization which classifies
them according to common characteristics. Not an immediately experienced value, or value claim, each con-
ceptualized class of values provides the definition of a
value.

Ideals

"Ideal" is Brightman's word for this concept of a class
of values, i.e., true value. As he expatiated: "*Ideals* constitute a special class of instrumental values. An ideal is a
general concept of a type of experience which we value.
. . . The value of an ideal is purely instrumental in that
it may serve as cause of or means to the actual intrinsic
value" (8, p. 90). A *Philosophy of Ideals* is almost wholly
focused on the nature and function of ideals. In that
book Brightman wrote: "The complete normative definition, the definition of true ideals which ought to be
acknowledged and realized, would run as follows: *An
ideal is a general concept of a type of experience which
we approve in relation to a complete view of all our experience, including all our approvals, and which we acknowledge that we ought to realize*" (9, p. 86).

In this definition several component ideas deserve
mention and clarification. First, as a generalized concept,

an ideal is not a perceptible item in sense experience, but a perfect possibility of desired experience which only thought can grasp (9, pp. 69-70). Second, an ideal implies an hypothesis about future experience. "If and when we have experience of the type described, the ideal asserts that we shall then approve it" (9, p. 70). Third, an ideal "unifies our experiences in relation to our approvals," and these approvals in relation to the whole of our experiences; thus it is "a principle of unity" (9, p. 70). Fourth, "an ideal is a principle of control and selection," since it directs our attention to the possibilities that ought to be realized, and since, in unifying our experience, it exerts control over it (9, p. 71). Fifth, an ideal is "a plan of action" (9, p. 71), particularly in that it prescribes an end or goal toward which action moves and at which it stops (9, p. 72). Sixth, an ideal is a social principle. Every mind, Brightman held, "stands in social relations, and its ideals are formed in those social relations" (9, p. 73). Finally, an ideal is "a principle of love. . . . In every ideal there is at least a dim love of power, of unity, of truth, or of other persons" (9, p. 74).

Moral Laws

Brightman perceived that only some ideals ought to be realized. The valid, or coherent ideals, he called *norms* (3, p. 288), or *moral laws* (13). Though derived from actual experiences of values, norms are moral laws which impose demands upon experience in the form of obligations felt by experient persons and establish standards for performance and criticism; they also cohere to constitute a system of moral laws. Brightman's ethical theory, presented in *Moral Laws*, was written "with the conviction that ethics is truly a science; not, indeed, a natural science or a merely descriptive one, but a normative science of ideal principles" (13, p. 9), so that the task of ethics is "to construct, out of the data of experience, a coherent system of laws" (13, p. 82). These moral laws are "universal principle(s) to which the will ought to conform in its choices" (13, p. 45). The main purpose of *Moral Laws* is to establish the system of ethical principles; eleven laws—formal, axiological, and personalistic—are defined and stated (13, pp. 89-91). Without entering into a detailed discussion of the norms, true ideals, or moral laws (14), it suffices to observe that Brightman formulated a coherent system of laws which organize the obligations and values of the experient person, and which project ideals to guide and evaluate life and action.

For Brightman the study of all values is inseparably joined with the philosophy of religion. "The longing for spiritual values is the essence of religion" (15, p. 25). "The search for God is a search for the purpose of life and for an unfailing source of eternal value" (16, p. 23). Nonetheless, he defended the autonomy of moral value from the invasion of theology. Indeed, he declared that "moral law is more fundamental than religion" (13 p. 265). And in one sense his theology is dependent upon his theory of morality, since he offered the theistic hypothesis that God exists as the most adequate and coherent interpretation of moral experience. Now the situation of obligation, which consists not merely in the experience of externally imposed duty but also in the internal motivation, is the crux of morality. " 'I ought' means 'I approve the principle by which all rational beings everywhere ought always to act when placed under circumstances similar to mine' " (17, p. 47). Although this Kantian formula of obligation is autonomous, the moral man is led to acknowledge a realm of persons other than himself and beyond this the existence of a personal God. "A moral God, eternally active, eternally creative, eternally reasonable, is indeed a God who will forever and changelessly be loyal to the same fundamental principles of obligation and value" (17, p. 68).

Reflection upon the source and authority of norms,

or moral laws, leads inescapably to acknowledgment of a realm of persons and of God. As Brightman said: "Personality . . . is the final seat of authority, the source of all sources. The ultimate ideal is 'for, of, or in a person' " (9, p. 128). Besides positing a community of selves that have moral experiences in social relations with each other and their environment (13, p. 97), morality, in positing the objectivity of normative ideals, postulates the existence of "the cosmic Mind [which] knows them to be norms, or better, purposes that human beings should achieve coherent value-realization only through living in accordance with them" (3, p. 292). Hence true ideals, or norms, are considered to be "purposes of the Cosmic Spirit, God, the Holy Spirit" (18, p. 124). Not only does the cosmic Mind guarantee the objectivity and rationality of imperative ideals, but also a special dimension of personality—which Brightman has termed "Spirit," with due respect to the Third Person of the Blessed Trinity—effectuates their realization. Through this power of personality ideals are not simply noble aspirations but attainable realities. As Brightman has said: "One ideal made real in personal life is worth all the unrealized ideals in the Platonic heaven, unless those ideals are what Whitehead takes the eternal objects to be —potentials for actual occasions. If there is an impotent spirit that can father no persons as its children, that spirit is no norm for real persons. Unless what ought to be really ought *to be* and to some extent *can be*, its ought is as empty a gesture as was ever made by a marionette" (18, p. 55).

REALM OF PERSONS

The key metaphysical principle of personalism is, of course, the person. How, then, is the concept of the person to be defined? Here Brightman has been quite clear that experimental psychology, restricted to scientific methods of observation and causal explanation, cannot grasp the essence of personality; he has agreed with Hocking that what it studies is not mind but near-mind (10, p. 43). Scientific method itself presupposes, among other metaphysical principles, the existence of an experimenter, or personal self, who possesses a self-identifying unity through the course of the experiment (3, p. 258; 8, p. 345; 19). If the concept of the person is to be defined, scientific psychology of the experimental type must be replaced by what has been called "self-psychology," and self-psychology must be supplemented by metaphysics. The definition of the person begins from the datum-self, i.e., the immediate experience of the shining present. As Brightman put it: "I—the experient, the person, the Situation Experienced—am not to be identified with what sustains my being. I am not my nervous system, the sun, or God. I am what I experience myself as being—a conscious self" (8, p. 349). Nevertheless, personality cannot be defined merely by attending to the given; for the valid metaphysics of personality must transcend immediate experience to grasp the meaning and being of the person.

Definition of Person

A first approximation to the definition of the person occurs with the distinction between the concept *self* and the concept *person*, despite a widespread tendency among personalists, including Brightman, to employ the terms interchangeably (3, p. 261). Accordingly, he proposed "the word *self* . . . for any and every conciousness, however simple or complex it may be," and conceived a *person* to be "a self that is potentially self-conscious, rational, and ideal. That is to say, when a self is able at times to reflect on itself as a self, to reason, and to acknowledge ideal goals by which it can judge its achievements, then we call it a person" (8, p. 350). Hence, as he put it succinctly: "A self is given; a personality is achieved" (8, p. 362). Simple consciousness, or the minimum self, exhibits a structure marked by eight characteristics: (1) self-experience; (2) qualities, sensory and emotional; (3) time and space consciousness and experience; (4) transcendence of time and space; (5) process and conation; (6) awareness of meaning; (7) response to environment; and (8) privacy (8, pp. 351-352). A person, he added, has "each of the eight characteristics . . . developed to a higher level" (8, p. 352). Because personality is a development of selfhood, which is deemed to be more elementary and perhaps more universal, the metaphysics of personalism, strictly speaking, is stated in terms of the self: "Nothing exists except in, of, and for a self" (20, p. 41).

At last a definition of the concept of the person is forthcoming: "*A person is a unity of complex conscious changes, including all its experiences—its memories, its purposes, its values, its powers, its activities, and its experienced interactions with its environment*" (10, p. 56). The personal self, therefore, is monadic, mentalistic, activistic and organic (21). Explicitly rejecting the epiphenomenalist, the analytic and the substantialist theories of the personal self, Brightman has labeled his theory the *organic* theory. According to the organic theory, the personal self is "a living whole of conscious experience, whose parts have no existence in isolation from the whole and whose nature is to be conscious as a whole" (8, p. 357). "This view," he added, "recognizes the interaction of the unitary personality with the bodily organism and thus finds a partial truth in epiphenomenalism; it insists on the need of analysis for understanding but supplements analysis by synopsis; it grants that substantialism is right in seeking for unity, but holds it to be wrong in the unempirical unity asserted" (8, p. 357). Perhaps it is germane to note that Brightman, because of his opposition to the substantialist conception of the person, had to concede the metaphysics of multiple personality, admitting that "there are or may be other streams of consciousness than that of the normal self, connected with one organism" (2, p. 210).

Self-Transcendence

The most noteworthy feature of personality is its transcendence of the self, of immediate experience. Although the personal self is given immediately in its complex-unitary experiences of sense, feeling, willing, and thinking, permeated with temporal and spatial consciousness, it is engaged in activities of self-transcending. It transcends the present moment in its memories of the past and its anticipations of the future (22, p. 295). It transcends space by reference to a possible aspatial mode of existence as well as by reference to absent and imaginary spaces (22, pp. 295-296). Transcendence is implicated directly in sensation which, besides existing within some self as part of its private consciousness, "is a sign to a self that something not his will is acting on him and in him" (22, p. 296). Similarly, feeling, such as liking, disliking, approving, disapproving, is not merely self-centered but essentially other-centered (22, p. 296). What is true of feeling is equally true of willing and thinking, since willing has as its object the realization of ideals that subsist beyond the present experience and thinking aims at knowledge and rational control instead of the immediately existent opinion and random desire (22, p. 297). The fundamental conception of the personal self as "a union of change and identity" involves self-identification that threads together past, present, and future moments of experience in a continuing process which creates novelty without impugning the permanence of the continuant person (22, pp. 296-297).

Just as personality transcends the self as a higher development of immediate consciousness, so personality rises to an even higher level of existence. This dimension of personality, consisting in the realization of the highest personal ideals through the exertion of personal power, Brightman has called *spirit*. Spirit is defined as "conscious, powerful, noble, rich, courageous, free, rational, personal experience" (18, p. 37). "Spirit refers to the ideal aspects of personality, and especially to the actual realization of a person's potential values" (18, p. 52). In one sense, then, spirit is a quality of experience which persons achieve. In another sense, it is the potentiality of persons, this potentiality being interpreted "as a field of choice made available to man by the purpose of God" (18, p. 62).

The self-transcendence of personality testifies to a world beyond the personal self and its immediate experience. Personal self-transcendence implicates the datum self of immediate experience in a real personal self which contains its present moment as a focal appearance. It implicates the self in a realm of Nature and a realm of Values, as well as in a community of persons like himself; and beyond nature, values, and persons, it relates the self to the Divine Person, God (22, pp. 300-301).

The Divine Person is the creator of the persons for whom His purposes are imperative norms to be realized in a field of freedom. God as Holy Spirit is a kind of "field of choice . . . regarded as an assemblage of potentials, that is, of intentions on the part of divine will to respond to any point where human will makes a selection" (18, p. 62). Even Nature is immanent in God. It might seem that Brightman's conception of God is a total panentheism, in which all being is contained in God. However, despite the location of nature within God, since the "creation" of nature resides in the imposition of a form or meaning upon an internal Given, human persons, created *ex nihilo*, exist independently of God (8, pp. 332-333). "The personalistic hypothesis is that persons other than the cosmic Person cannot be literally parts of the eternal Person without contradiction" (3, p. 248). Paradoxically, the body of a man is part of nature and hence part of God, while his personal self is independent of God. Associated with the body, which is part of God, the human person may communicate with God through the human body, for the body is "a point of interaction between the supreme Mind and the human mind" (2, p. 219).

THE DOCTRINE OF GOD

Brightman's originality as a philosopher is perhaps most obvious in his conception of God. Though he agreed with traditional personalism, with its emphasis on religion and on the conception of God as personal, he tied cosmological to axiological considerations. Simultaneously he stressed the test of empirical coherence for his doctrine of God. Further, sensitive to the presence of evil in the world not attributable to human responsibility, he concluded, in departure from a large body of fellow personalists (23), that God is finite.

Approach to God

Brightman's approach to God is both experiential and axiological. The ways of finding God are several. First, the acceptance of a particular historical conception of God as provided by revelation is a way to find God, but, observed Brightman, it is "not the *only way* to that God. The God of all would not confine his working to one stream of tradition" (16, p. 41). Revelation does not therefore exclude reason as a way to God. "Carried far enough and honestly enough, reason is one of the ways that leads man into the very presence of God" (16, p. 72). Similarly, moral experience, as already noted, is a way to God; so is religious experience, especially since the latter is "(a)ny consciousness of the presence of God" (16, p. 94).

But these approaches to God tend to support the view that God is finite. Moral loyalty to God, as required by moral experience of obligation, can persist in the face of evil only if God is finite; otherwise God's goodness is impugned by the evils that exist (16, pp. 91-92). Furthermore, religious experience leads to the conception of a finite God, since "(n)o possible experience would reveal unlimited and absolute power" (16, p. 115).

God as Finite

The theistic doctrine of God as Personal yet Finite is, for Brightman, an hypothesis which affords the most coherent interpretation of experience. But the experience from which Brightman inferred the existence and nature of God is not this or that particular experience, but rather experience as a whole, although paramount consideration was accorded the experience of values and, in particular, of the values constituting the moral situation. Brightman's original exposition of God as a Finite Person is found in his remarkable book, *The Problem of God* (24). Here he defined God as "a Person supremely conscious, supremely valuable, and supremely creative, yet limited by both the free choices of other persons and by restrictions within his own nature" (24, p. 113).

Whereas there has been a conventional problem of limiting God vis-à-vis the freedom of human persons, Brightman underscored other limitations, involving even the very nature of God. Indeed, he marshaled evidence for the finiteness of God from several sources. Here of course the problem of evil crops up. Unless God is finite, the existence of evils beyond human origination, such as natural calamities, would be imputed to God, an aspersion on His perfect goodness. Instead of jeopardizing the goodness of God, Brightman proposed to conceive God as "a power which aims at ends and achieves them, and also . . . is working under great difficulties" (24, p. 125).

Evolution joins moral and religious experience to support the doctrine of a finite God. Though purposive, evolution is conspicuously more wasteful and destructive with the abundant species through which it works than it is coherent with the omnipotent God concept. That God creates through evolution, then, indicates either that he is partly malevolent or that he is finite. Further, since evolution involves time to reach its ends, God is implicated in time insofar as he works through evolution. Such a God is "a God into whose very being time enters . . ." (24, p. 129). Thus the God of evolution is not now perfect. "(H) is perfection and the perfection of his world consist in their perfectibility" (24, p. 130).

Consciousness also suggests the finiteness of God. Just as human consciousness in its free choices operates within the context of a given situation, so God acts with reference to the Given. "With all the creative power of God there may be something Given in his nature as subject matter for his choice" (24, p. 132). Every conscious being that acts is limited by the laws of reason and its own nature, and God, being a conscious person, is likewise limited. Nowhere in experience do we actually find the kind of absoluteness the idea of God as Absolute and Infinite involves. Rather, almost everywhere is found a duality which betrays limitations. The duality of active and passive elements, universal for consciousness, is predicated of God, with the passive element construed as an obstacle internal to his nature. As Brightman said: "We must acknowledge a duality of nature at the very eternal heart of things, in which the active is indeed in control, but maintains its control with struggle and pain" (24, pp. 134-135). Here he borrowed a page from Hegel on the dialectical character of experience. The divine life is composed "essentially of struggle and victory over opposition, a victory for which a price has always to be paid even by God himself" (24, p. 136).

Although the duality in God's nature might suggest a dualism, Brightman emphatically rejected dualism as regards God and the Given. Granted the Given assumes the functions of primordial matter, the devil, the irrational, "(y)et there . . . [is] no dualism either of stuff or of ultimate principle in the universe; there would be only a dualism of process within the Supreme Person" (24, p. 185). Thus the Given is internal to God. "In addition to his reason and his active creative will, [the Given is] a passive element which enters into every one of his conscious states, as sensation, instinct, and impulse enter into ours, and constitutes a problem for him. . . . The evils of life and the delays in the attainment of value, in so far as they come from God and not from human freedom, are thus due to his nature, yet not wholly to his deliberate choice. His will and reason acting on the Given produce the world and achieve value in it" (24, p. 113).

Perhaps the clearest statement of the nature of the Given is to be found in *The Finding of God*, the sequel to *The Problem of God*. Brightman held that "The Given . . . is the name which describes the total complex of eternal factors in the divine nature which he [God] did not create and with which he always has to deal in the eternal activity of his perfectly good will" (16, p. 174). The Given divides into two types: the rational and the irrational. In *The Problem of God* Brightman had failed to grasp the Given as rational, but in *The Finding of God* he furnished an account which discriminates five prominent aspects of the Given. First, "it is the conscious experience of God" (16, p. 174). Second, it is complex, standing for "the entire uncreated and eternal nature of God" (16, p. 175). Containing moral and rational laws, "it also includes . . . an empirical factor, an eternal subject-matter . . . which eternal divine thought and goodness have to reckon with in all their dealings" (16, p. 175). Third, "it is eternal" (16, pp. 175-176). It was not created, nor can it be eliminated. Fourth, as previously stated, "The Given is internal to God" (16, p. 176). And finally, "The Given is controlled.

Control implies subjection and guidance, but not creation. . . . Divine control does not mean the divine willing of all the evils of life; but it does mean a possible divine future beyond every frustration and pain" (16, p. 177).

The material perfection of God is not, therefore, a static attainment prior to creation. Rather it is a growing perfection, realized through effort and developing in time. God creates in a twofold sense. He creates Nature by imposing order and significance on the Given, while Nature is immanent in God. He creates other persons, but these persons stand outside God, although they communicate with each other and with Him, and they comprise a cooperative community of persons in quest of common ideals. That goodness has the power to survive and prevail in the universe is possible only if God is eternal, perfectly good, and sufficiently powerful and wise, for He must struggle with "a problematic resisting force that produces a tension and a drag within the divine nature" (16, p. 186).

The Finite God defines himself: "Not by might, nor by power, but by my spirit" (16, p. 189). Such a God is wholly personal, a being who struggles and suffers, yet wins victories in behalf of the highest ideals of personality. Such a God, findable without special revelation or commitment to Jesus Christ, is superbly represented in Christianity. As Brightman said: "Jesus reveals a God who bears an eternal cross; and it is this cross which I have called The Given.

"Jesus does not reveal a God who creates a cross because suffering is beautiful, but rather one who bears a cross because it is only by cross-bearing that the purposes of love can be achieved (7, p. 80).

"Humanity cannot profit by the Beatitudes unless it also learns the lesson of the Woes" (7, p. 83).

NOTES TO CHAPTER 10

1. W. H. Werkmeister, A *History of Philosophical Ideas in America* (New York: Ronald Press, 1949), pp. 576-577.
2. Edgar Sheffield Brightman, An *Introduction to Philosophy*, rev. ed. (New York: Henry Holt and Co., 1951). The first edition of this textbook appeared in 1925. Unless otherwise indicated, all references will be made to the 1951 revised edition of this work.
3. Edgar Sheffield Brightman, *Person and Reality: An Introduction to Metaphysics*, edited by P. A. Bertocci in collaboration with J. E. Newhall and R. S. Brightman (New York: Ronald Press, 1958).
4. Edgar Sheffield Brightman, *The Sources of the Hexateuch* (New York: Abingdon Press, 1918).
5. Edgar Sheffield Brightman, *Immortality in Post-Kantian Idealism* (Cambridge: Harvard University Press, 1925).
6. William Ernest Hocking, "Brightman: Colleague and Friend," *The Personalist*, XXXIV (Autumn 1953), 363-364. Excellent discussions of Brightman's philosophy are also to be found in the pages of *Philosophical Forum*, an annual journal published by Boston University Department of Philosophy.
7. Edgar Sheffield Brightman, *Is God a Person?* (New York: Association Press, 1932).
8. Edgar Sheffield Brightman, *A Philosophy of Religion* (Englewood Cliffs, N. J.: Prentice-Hall, Inc., 1940).
9. Edgar Sheffield Brightman, *A Philosophy of Ideals* (New York: Henry Holt and Co., Inc., 1928).
10. Edgar Sheffield Brightman, *Nature and Values* (New York: Abingdon Press, 1945).
11. Edgar Sheffield Brightman, *Persons and Values* (Boston: Boston University Press, 1952).
12. See Edgar Sheffield Brightman, "Values, Ideals, Norms, and Existence," *Philosophy and Phenomenological Research*, IV (1943), 219-224.
13. Edgar Sheffield Brightman, *Moral Laws* (New York: Abingdon Press, 1933).
14. For an up-to-date restatement of Brightman's *Moral Laws*, see Peter A. Bertocci and Richard M. Millard, *Personality and the Good* (New York: David McKay Co., Inc., 1963), Part IV.
15. Edgar Sheffield Brightman, *Personality and Religion* (New York: Abingdon Press, 1934).
16. Edgar Sheffield Brightman, *The Finding of God* (New York: Abingdon Press, 1931).

17. Edgar Sheffield Brightman, *Religious Values* (New York: Abingdon Press, 1925).
18. Edgar Sheffield Brightman, *The Spiritual Life* (Nashville: Abingdon Press, 1942).
19. See Edgar Sheffield Brightman, "The Presupposition of Experiment," *The Personalist*, XIX (1938), 137-143.
20. Edgar Sheffield Brightman, "Personality as a Metaphysicial Principle," *Personalism in Theology: A Symposium in Honor of Albert Cornelius Knudson* (Boston: Boston University Press, 1943), p. 41.
21. Edgar Sheffield Brightman, "The Finite Self," *Contemporary Idealism in America*, Clifford Barrett, ed. (New York: The Macmillan Company, 1932), pp. 169-196.
22. Edgar Sheffield Brightman, "Personalistic Metaphysics of the Self: Its Distinctive Features," *Radhakrishnan, Comparative Studies in Philosophy Presented in Honour of His Sixtieth Birthday* (New York: Harper & Brothers, 1951).
23. See, for example, the remark by Dean Knudson: "Some of his [Brightman's] students have, in my opinion, overemphasized its [the doctrine of the finite God] importance. Brightman's greatness, I think, lay not in his departure from classical theism, but in his kinship with it," in "Brightman: A Personal Word," *The Personalist* XXXIV (1953), 366. See also Herbert C. Sanborn, "Hegelian Influences in Brightman," *The Personalist*, XXXIV (1953), 371.
24. Edgar Sheffield Brightman, *The Problem of God* (New York: Abingdon Press, 1930).

INDEX

ABOUT THE AUTHOR

Associate Professor of Philosophy at Tulane University, Andrew J. Reck was born in New Orleans in 1927. He received his B.A. and M.A. from Tulane University, where he was an Honor Scholar and was elected to Phi Beta Kappa. As a Fulbright Scholar he was a research student at the University of St. Andrews, Scotland. He received his Ph.D. from Yale University. He served in the United States Army in Berlin, Germany. He has also studied at the University of Paris. Before joining the Tulane University faculty, he taught English at the University of Connecticut (Storrs) and philosophy at Yale University. In 1961 he was a grantee of the American Council of Learned Societies, and in 1962-63 he was a Fellow of the Howard Foundation, affiliated with Brown University. A contributor to *Experience, Existence and the Good: Essays in Honor of Paul Weiss* (1961) and to *Philosophic Interrogations* (1963), he is the editor of George Herbert Mead's *Selected Works* (1964) and the author of over thirty articles and twenty reviews which have appeared in the *Journal of Philosophy, The Review of Metaphysics, Ethics, New Scholasticism,* and numerous other periodicals in the United States and abroad.